How
Confidence
Works

www.penguin.co.uk

How Confidence Works

The new science of self-belief,
why some people learn it
and others don't

IAN ROBERTSON

BANTAM PRESS

TRANSWORLD PUBLISHERS

Penguin Random House, One Embassy Gardens,
8 Viaduct Gardens, London SW11 7BW
www.penguin.co.uk

Transworld is part of the Penguin Random House group of companies
whose addresses can be found at global.penguinrandomhouse.com

First published in Great Britain in 2021 by Bantam Press
an imprint of Transworld Publishers

A CIP catalogue record for this book
is available from the British Library.

ISBNs 9781787633711 (cased)
9781787633728 (tpb)

Typeset in 11.75/15.5 pt Caslon 540 LT Std by Jouve (UK), Milton Keynes
Printed and bound in Great Britain by Clays Ltd, Elcograf S.p.A.

The authorized representative in the EEA is Penguin Random House Ireland,
Morrison Chambers, 32 Nassau Street, Dublin D02 YH68.

Penguin Random House is committed to a sustainable
future for our business, our readers and our planet. This book
is made from Forest Stewardship Council® certified paper.

For Fiona – who taught me about the mind – with love and thanks

Contents

Introduction

:>

S UPPOSE WE WERE to discover something that could make us wealthier, healthier, longer-living, smarter, kinder, happier, more motivated, more innovative. Ridiculous, you might say, but, in fact, we already have.

What is this elixir? Confidence. And it is to human endeavour what food is to the body – without either we would wither and die. If you have it, it can empower you to reach heights you never thought possible, but if you don't, it can have a devastating effect on your prospects, despite your objective achievements.

When tennis legend Venus Williams was asked, aged fourteen, on ABC News how confident she was about beating her opponent in a tough upcoming match, she responded by saying, 'I'm very confident.' The reporter replied, a little surprised, 'You say it so easily. Why?' 'Because I believe it,' the future champion replied matter-of-factly.

Interviewed nearly twenty-five years later, in 2018, by the *New York Times*, she said, 'I feel that I owe my own success to my belief in myself, and have found that confidence can be learned and developed. In fact, my own self-confidence is something I work on every day, just like going to the gym or training on the court.' This book will probe the science and neuroscience behind the idea that confidence can be learned, or whether it is necessarily something you inherit.

Optimism, hope and self-esteem are all concepts that are easily confused with confidence but, as I will show, they differ in one fundamental way – confidence *empowers action*. You can be an optimist who is hopeful that things will work out OK in the end without ever believing that you can play a part in that outcome, or, indeed, having any realistic grounds for that optimism. And you can have high self-esteem and feel good about yourself without feeling confident that you can achieve a particular goal.

The future is uncertain. Confidence is a mental stance towards the future that defies this uncertainty by betting on success. Self-belief is a calculated wager on oneself that often wins because it is a bet based on past performance. Confidence creates the future because it is grounded in action. And, as Venus Williams said, it can be learned.

Confidence is made up of two parts. The first is the bet you make with yourself that you can do something. This is the *can do* element. The second is a belief that if you do that thing, then the world will change a little. This is the *can happen* part.

Maybe you believe that you can take more exercise (*can do*), but you doubt that it will make you lose weight (*can't happen*). Or say you accept that if everyone were to cut down their fossil fuel use, we could reduce global warming (*can happen*), but you don't think you can do this yourself (*can't do*). For confidence to work its full-blooded magic, it requires a potent combination of *can do* about the inner world and *can happen* about the external world.

Confidence, therefore, lies at the core of what makes things happen. It is a bridge to the future. It is that uniquely human capacity to visualize something that does not yet exist and work towards achieving it. For millennia it has been the driver of all of humanity's advances, from the medical breakthroughs that have lengthened our lives, to the sending of NASA's *Voyager 1* spacecraft out into the Milky Way.

On 25 May 1961, US president John F. Kennedy announced to a special joint session of the US Congress that his country would land a man on the moon before the end of the decade. He had no idea how this would be achieved – the rockets, the technology and the know-how didn't exist when he made that speech. But, spurred on by the Soviet Union's recent dramatic successes in space travel, he was able to envisage that imaginary future event and expressed the confidence that it would happen. And it did – on 20 July 1969.

This achievement did not rest on the personal confidence of one man – Kennedy was galvanizing and expressing the faith of an entire country in their common goal. So I am not just talking about individuals here. Confidence, or the lack of it, can be collective. In news bulletins, we hear phrases such as 'consumer confidence', 'market confidence', 'business confidence', and even 'national confidence'. So how does personal confidence relate to these broader economic and political concepts?

Economics and politics can bleed into the self-belief of millions of individual people – and vice versa. For example, studies have shown that eighteen- to twenty-five-year-olds who live through an economic recession believe less strongly that they can get ahead by their hard work.

This was starkly illustrated during the economic turmoil caused by the Covid-19 pandemic of 2020. In a UK study of two thousand sixteen- to twenty-five-year-olds, 41 per cent said that their future goals seemed 'impossible to achieve', and 38 per cent felt they would now 'never succeed in life'.

Such a dramatic drop in the confidence levels of almost half a generation will reverberate for decades in the social, economic and political fabric of the UK and elsewhere. Economic good times make it easier for young people to have the confidence to aspire and achieve. But individual confidence is so central to national development that it will be much harder for countries that have experienced a haemorrhage of confidence among their youthful population to return to those economic good times.

Confidence also matters because self-confident people live longer, happier and healthier lives. For example, studies have shown that you will live longer after heart failure if your partner feels confident about your condition. And confidence is contagious. Families, communities and whole countries can rise and fall depending on how confidence – or the loss of it – spreads. The gradual decline of 'Rust Belt' communities in the US from the 1980s was caused not only by industrial closures but also by a viral contagion of low confidence that sapped people's morale and drove away the ambitious problem-solvers. And as with individual confidence, collective confidence can also be learned, as we will see later in the book.

Research shows how such contagion can also spread through families, sports, businesses, neighbourhoods and whole countries. As confidence waxes and wanes, we see profound changes in the physiology of the brain and the rest of the body. For example, feeling confident about being able to face up to something you are frightened of actually boosts your immune system, despite the fear you feel. The confidence makes it much more likely that you will face up to your anxiety. The opposite is also true – if you lack confidence in your ability to cope with what scares you, you will be less likely to deal with it successfully.

So what *is* it, this thing we call 'confidence'? We think we know it when we see it, but we can only really understand it by delving into the remarkable scientific research that has emerged in recent decades. How does confidence play out in our minds, our brains – and, indeed, our bodies? Where does it come from, and how does it spread? Is it universal, or does it play out differently according to your culture, sex or class? Can we have too much of it and, if so, what are the consequences? Equally, if we lack it, how can we learn to be more confident? And most importantly of all, how can we – as individuals, families, communities, companies and whole countries – use our newfound understanding of confidence to harness it for the benefit of all?

CHAPTER 1

What Is Confidence?

:3

A T 4.35 P.M. on 19 November 2018, the tyres of a private Gulf-
stream jet – call sign N155AN, and one of the fastest and
longest-range corporate jets in the world – squealed on to the run-
way at Tokyo's Haneda airport against the backdrop of a pale winter
sun sliding below the city's vast horizon.

As the boarding steps unfurled, the plane's sole passenger looked
up absently from his tablet and glanced out of the oval window. A
jolt of alarm surged through his body at the sight of a white van pulling up alongside the aircraft. He watched as a column of men in
dark suits from the Tokyo District Public Prosecutors Office rushed
up the steps to arrest him.

Carlos Ghosn, the first non-Japanese head of a Japanese car manu-
facturer, and the architect of an unprecedented global alliance of
Renault, Nissan and Mitsubishi, had engineered dramatic turn-
arounds in each of these three struggling companies. When he
arrived at Nissan as chief operating officer in 1999, the company had
$22.9 billion of debt. By the time he had served three years as CEO,
eight years later, it was showing a $7 billion profit.

Ghosn tore up the corporate and cultural rule books by first rescuing and then welding together three enormous corporations on opposite sides of the globe. He went on to become the leading advocate for a revolution in personal transport as he pushed forward the world's biggest-selling electric car – the Nissan Leaf.

In 2004, Andy Grove, legendary CEO of tech giant Intel, told Ghosn that car companies would not be the ones to manufacture electric cars. And in an influential 2011 documentary, *Revenge of the Electric Car*, Dan Neil of the *Wall Street Journal* said to Ghosn, 'You are putting your career and Nissan's future on the line by going for the electric car and the Leaf.'

But Ghosn went ahead with his vision. He listened to another voice – his own – and more specifically, to the voice of confidence. Here is how he reasoned:

> We have an analysis as a corporation that zero-emission cars are part of the future, no matter what. We can discuss about when and how much, but nobody today can seriously say there is no place for zero-emission mobility in the panorama of the car industry. So all of this led to an obvious decision, that if we have the technology and we can produce an affordable car that will have good performance, well, we're going to need to launch a product. Within the next 10 years, 10 percent of the marketplace will be made by electric cars.

Ghosn went on to reflect on his thinking and motivation:

> Because at a certain point in time, when the necessary technology is ready, and you make your own analysis, and you know that you need to move into this direction, someone's going to have to say, 'OK, we're going to bite the bullet, and we're going to move forward.' In every technology,

somebody's going to have to move first. It's us, and we're proud of moving first because we think it's going to bring a lot of benefit.

The Nissan Leaf was named the 2011 World Car of the Year and, as of 2020, had been the world's bestselling electric car for almost a decade. Ghosn's audacious 10 per cent prediction has been long exceeded in one country – in 2018, 45 per cent of all new cars in Norway were electric.

What gave Ghosn the confidence to risk the future of his company in this way? He had decided to invest half of his company's $5 billion 2007 research budget on electric-vehicle development – against the warnings of experts worldwide. What was the source of this self-belief?

A week after his arrest, a bewildered Carlos Ghosn stared at the single barred window in the door of his 4.8-square-metre cell in the Tokyo Detention House. The downtown prison houses three thousand inmates and a very recently deployed gallows where Shoko Asahara, mastermind of the 1995 Tokyo subway sarin-gas attack, was hanged.

Ghosn was allowed thirty minutes of exercise per day and three bland, near-identical meals. In winter, many Japanese public buildings – including schools – are unheated. The Tokyo Detention House is no exception. He was cold, and not allowed to sleep during the day. How could it have come to this for one of the most famous, most successful executives in the world? And what, if anything, does this outcome tell us about confidence – not just its positives, but its negatives?

Nadia Murad was nineteen when, on 15 August 2014, the black flags of ISIS appeared out of an ominous plume of desert dust. They streamed out behind the Toyota Land Cruisers that roared into her Yazidi village of Kocho in northern Iraq. Within hours, her mother and six brothers had been slaughtered, and Daesh's hollow-eyed warriors carried her off as a sex slave.

They transported Murad to Mosul, where she was raped and beaten. She was bought and sold like an animal, and passed from hand to tainted hand for three months before she managed to escape through a door left unlocked by her then 'owner'.

The shame of sexual victimhood in Yazidi culture led to most of Murad's fellow captives hiding away once they were free again, but not Nadia. She held her head high and spoke the truth with a determination and confidence summoned from somewhere deep inside. Fuelled by this intangible but potent energy, she became the voice of the Yazidi and other female victims of theologically sanctioned slavery and rape. She spearheaded an unprecedented change of attitude within this profoundly conservative culture, which previously would have shunned any young female with the taint of unsanctioned sexual activity upon her. Now, thanks to Murad, they are much more likely to be accepted back into society.

In the split second after Denis Mukwege pushed open the front door of his home on 25 October 2012, he saw the gun at his daughter's head. An instant later, his guard – house watchmen are a common feature of middle-class African life – fell dead in front of him, and the bullets meant for Mukwege hissed over his head as he dived to the ground.

Mukwege had devoted his career as a surgeon to treating the sexual injuries inflicted upon tens of thousands of women during the Congo's ghastly wars. Even though his family survived this attack by the perpetrators of such violence, Mukwege could stand it no more, and left his suffering country for the safety of Belgium. The staff of his beloved Panzi Hospital, which had cared for nearly one hundred thousand scarred and violated women, were left devastated by his departure.

But three months later, unable to relinquish his vision of providing first-class care to his scarred and traumatized patients, Mukwege returned. Waiting for him on his arrival, to welcome him back to Panzi, was a twenty-mile cordon of people lining the road from Kavumu airport. His patients and supporters had raised funds to pay for his return ticket by selling pineapples and onions.

Nadia Murad and Denis Mukwege shared the Nobel Peace Prize in 2018 in recognition of their courage and commitment to preventing sexual violence as an instrument of war. Courage means overcoming fear to take action, and it can flourish in the freeze-frame confusion of immediate danger. But in the cold light of day, sustained bravery over days, months and years needs another ingredient that was implicit in these two Nobel Prize winners' citations – confidence. Despite the seemingly insuperable odds stacked against them, they believed that they could achieve their goals.

As for Carlos Ghosn, we'll return to the end of his story in the last chapter of the book, but confidence-inspired action doesn't have to lead to Nobel Prizes or international business acclaim to be meaningful.

Cathy Engelbert was five months pregnant and had just resigned from a high-paying job in New York City at the international accounting firm Deloitte. Years later, she told a reporter from *Forbes* magazine that she lacked confidence. She was about to take another less demanding job when two senior colleagues approached her. They told her that she had real potential and asked why she would give it up, explaining that men have to play a role in helping women to achieve their potential.

In March 2015, Engelbert was elected the first female CEO of Deloitte and, indeed, of any of the Big Four professional services companies in the US. As CEO, she pushed through a controversial family leave scheme, guaranteeing sixteen weeks' paid leave after the birth of a child or for family illness – a major advance for a US company. The *Forbes* journalist who interviewed her saw this as requiring 'a dose of bravery'.

That same year, on this side of the Atlantic, another woman broke through a CEO glass ceiling. Within months of Cathy Engelbert taking over at Deloitte, Sacha Romanovitch became the first woman to be appointed to run a big City of London accountancy firm – Grant Thornton.

An adopted child of south London parents, Romanovitch – like Carlos Ghosn and Cathy Engelbert – had the confidence to do things that were unprecedented in her industry. First, in a step that bewildered other City executives, she capped her salary at twenty times her company's average wage. Then she introduced profit-sharing among all the employees, not just the partners. And, most controversially, she repositioned her organization's strategy to focus on 'profits with purpose', meaning that she turned down less ethical clients.

Then, one day, some of her colleagues issued a memo criticizing her. They released her confidential annual appraisal and alleged that she was pursuing a 'socialist agenda' (the average partner salary fell to £365,000 per annum under her leadership). She told a reporter from the *Financial Times* that some of her colleagues did not like the short-term reduction in profits caused by her policies. She believed that if profits were properly aligned to values and purpose, they would rise in the long term, and that if they were not, this would rebound on the company's profitability.

On 15 October 2018, Romanovitch stood down as CEO, but not before she had tweeted a link to Serena Williams's rendition of Maya Angelou's anthem to self-belief, 'Still I Rise'.

So what *is* this mysterious energizer of Ghosn, Murad, Mukwege, Engelbert and Romanovitch that we call confidence? Is it something we are born with, or can we learn it? What are its origins, and how does it work?

Each of these five people time-travelled across a bridge into an uncertain future. Doing so meant conceiving of things that didn't yet exist: Ghosn imagined his electric cars, Engelbert her family-friendly company, Romanovitch her more egalitarian consultancy, and Mukwege his healing hospital. Murad's vision was to change the norms of a highly traditional society so that abused young women were accepted back into the fold.

We all build and cross bridges every day – more commonplace and less heroic than those above, but confidence bridges nevertheless. Take something as mundane as deciding you want to lose weight. How confident are you that you can take the first small step by eating a healthier lunch than usual – say, a salad? One of the two main strands of confidence entails a belief such as *If I eat less, I will lose weight*. In cognitive psychology, this is known as an *outcome expectation*, and is a belief about the external world – a view that if x happens, then y will follow. Such beliefs are about the world external to your mind – for instance, *If I stop smoking, I'll live longer*.

But not everyone believes such things about the outside world. *It doesn't matter how much I eat, I still put on weight* is something I've heard many overweight people say. *My dad smoked till he was eighty and was fit as a fiddle, so stopping smoking isn't going to do me any good* is another example of a faulty assumption about the world.

The second element of confidence concerns beliefs about what we can do, rather than what may or may not happen. Let's suppose, for example, that you do accept that eating less will make you lose weight. Great, but doubts begin to creep in – *Will I be able to stick with just a salad?* In your mind's future-simulator, you start to anticipate pre-lunch hunger pangs and the post-lunch emptiness. Your forecast about your future self is not good – you imagine yourself staring into the fridge, thinking, *Oh God, not the salad!*

So it doesn't matter if you're convinced that your decision would have consequences if you made the right one. If you don't think that you can do it, you won't. The cognitive psychology term for this type of prediction is *efficacy expectation*. If you neither believe that you *can do* it nor that the result *can happen*, confidence dies before it is born.

So, let's call outcome expectations *can happen* beliefs, and effi-cacy expectations *can do* beliefs. That yields four different types of confidence, each with a different thought, emotion and brain activ-ity pattern: *can't do/can't happen*; *can do/can't happen*; *can't do/can happen*; and *can do/can happen.*

Can't do/can't happen

This first state of mind leads to a chasm of paralysis. Let's say your doctor tells you that you need to exercise because your blood tests reveal you're pre-diabetic. As your mind wanders to images of tak-ing exercise, it fogs over with thoughts of discomfort and effort that make you think, *No, I just can't.* Then you remember that your mother had diabetes and you think, *What's the point of taking exer-cise? It won't stop the disease.* As your mind skids away from the doctor's words, *can't happen* is the conclusion it reaches.

In this state, your mind disengages and your body slumps in resignation. There is little to be anxious or depressed about because *there is nothing to be done.* What's left in your brain is apathy and a ramping-down of your motivation in a part of the cortex called the anterior cingulate, Oxford University researchers showed in 2015. There is no bridge across that chasm.

Can't do/can happen

In this scenario you believe the doctor's words. *Yep, she's right,* you think, only for your mind to swirl with self-doubt. It skips back to your desultory attempts at exercise in the past, when you gave up in sweaty discomfort after a few minutes. You recall all the times you planned to don a tracksuit and go jogging, only to slump back into the armchair at the last minute. *I can't,* you conclude bleakly.

You don't have the comfort of the fatalistic outlook that there is nothing to be done – you believe the doctor. But that means you feel *anxious.* Your shoulders hunch and shame washes over you because even though you know that exercise would work, you won't do it. You don't think you can. And so your mood sinks, taking with it your opinion of yourself. Your brain's self-appraisal system in the middle of the frontal lobes whirls with thoughts of failure and self-doubt, Stanford University researchers discovered in 2002. There is only half a bridge here – not enough to cross the chasm.

Can do/can't happen

Here, you're prepared to do the exercise and anything else the doctor recommends. All the same, you're hit by diabetes, and it will keep getting worse. It's not fair – you know you can do what she advises, but you just don't believe that it will work. The same thing happened at school – they told you that if you studied hard and passed your exams, you'd get a good job. You did what they said because you believed them, but the decent job never materialized. It left you with little trust in what experts tell you about the world.

In this half-bridge version of confidence, you feel frustrated, aggrieved, angry and anxious. In its primed-for-action state, your brain's reward network signals pain, New York University researchers showed in 2015. Despite believing that you could follow the doctor's advice about exercise, you just don't think it will help with the diabetes.

Can do/can happen

You get straight back home from the doctor, put your tracksuit on, and the exercise regime begins. You can do it for sure. You checked a reputable medical website and saw how important exercise is for managing diabetes, so you think, *Yep, that'll work.* In this state, your mind is engaged, your body is prepared, and there's an expectation of success. Your brain anticipates reward with a surge of dopamine activity, University of Michigan investigators showed in 2015. It lifts your mood and quells the anxiety you felt after hearing the doctor's bad news. There is a solid, two-strand bridge across the chasm, and you're crossing it.

That's the simple version, but of course, life's more complicated than that. Not least because sometimes we have to cross a bridge where the *can happen* span is obscured in mist. Every entrepreneur, sportsperson and would-be lover faces this, where there is no guarantee of *can happen*, no matter how much *can do* they have. Most businesses fail, most sportspeople never win a championship, and most would-be lovers don't find true love the first time around, and perhaps not at all.

We can suppose that Carlos Ghosn was in this *can do/can happen* state of confidence for most of his professional life. He was sure he could bring the corporate behemoths Renault and Nissan together (*can do*). Ghosn further predicted that it would financially benefit both companies (*can happen*). He also thought that he could create an electric car for the mass market (*can do*) and that it would be a commercial success (*can happen*).

Both Cathy Engelbert and Sacha Romanovitch believed they could become CEOs (*can do*) and could bring positive changes to their companies (*can happen*). For Engelbert, this was something she learned after that 'aha' conversation with her two senior colleagues. Nadia Murad had confidence that she could speak out (*can do*) and that doing so would benefit her and other women like her (*can happen*). Denis Mukwege believed that he could set up services for injured women (*can do*) and that it would benefit many (*can happen*).

But few things in life are as cut and dried as this neat summary suggests. Ghosn couldn't be sure that the merger would benefit all three partner companies. Nor could he be certain that the electric car would be a commercial success. Neither were Romanovitch and

Engelbert sure that their changes would work. Both eventually were ousted as CEOs because their colleagues didn't believe that the predicted benefits would transpire. And Mukwege couldn't be sure that the clinics he established would be able to function in war-torn Congo. For Murad, her actions might have been ineffective or, worse, harmful to the women she wanted to help.

These five game-changers weren't confident because they thought highly of themselves – that is, because of their self-esteem. Self-esteem is assessed by asking people how much they agree with statements such as *On the whole, I am satisfied with myself* or *I have high self-esteem*. The more you agree with them, the happier and more satisfied you are likely to be with your job – and also with your partner, among many other benefits.

While self-esteem looks back, confidence catapults you into the future, whether in work, finance, relationships, sports or education. Self-esteem doesn't do this; it is a running summary of how you value yourself, *not* a prediction about how well you will perform. Confidence *is* that prediction, and so it is not surprising that it can forecast how well a child does in school much more strongly than her level of self-esteem, a study of over two thousand teenagers by the University of Bergen showed in 2014.

Confidence also predicts how well you'll cope if your company goes through a reorganization, and presages how many interviews and job offers you'll receive on a job search. It also has many other benefits, including how quickly you'll return to work after a car crash causing orthopaedic injury, as well as your performance in sport.

Despite being different things, self-esteem and self-confidence tend to go hand in hand. However, while confidence grows your self-esteem, the opposite is not necessarily true. University of Basel researchers showed this in a fourteen-year study of over seven thousand fourteen- to thirty-year-olds in the US. Over time, a sense of mastery – closely linked to confidence – strongly predicted an individual's self-esteem. But self-esteem did *not* predict confidence as the years went on. In other words, liking yourself is fine if you just want to feel good. But if you're going to get things done, you need confidence.

One of the greatest sources of confidence is the sense of mastery that comes from overcoming challenges, as the stories of Ghosn, Engelbert, Romanovitch, Mukwege and Murad so vividly show. And, most importantly, because confidence can develop in this way, you can learn to be more confident, as we will see later on.

The mental energy it takes to protect self-esteem can, in fact, sidetrack people from the practical action that is central to building confidence. For example, a 2009 study at Northwestern University manipulated students' self-esteem about their morality by asking them to write stories about themselves. The students in one group were asked to use a set of neutral words such as *keys* or *house* in their stories. A second group were given morally negative words such as *disloyal, mean* or *greedy* to use. A third group's autobiographical anecdotes had to be written incorporating some morally positive words, such as *caring, generous, fair* and *kind*.

At the end of the study, the students were told that research participants usually donated a small amount of money to a charity of their choice, and they were invited to do so too. The group using the neutral words donated, on average, $2.71. Those who had written a story with morally negative words gave, on average, $5.30. What about those whose moral self-esteem had been uplifted by an autobiographical story full of generosity and kindness? They barely scraped a dollar at $1.07.

This phenomenon is called *moral licensing*, meaning that merely thinking morally well of yourself gives you an excuse to *behave* less well. It is a largely unconscious way of boosting self-esteem. Unlike confidence's focus on the external world, self-esteem protection pulls our attention inwards to chalk up mental brownie points by merely thinking about doing good.

Just the thought of worthy action in the future gives us a licence to act less well in the present. In other words, we bank moral credit for our self-esteem on the back of good intentions that go on to sabotage our actual behaviour.

In this respect, self-esteem can yield opposite effects to confidence by diverting people's energies from real action in the world to shoring up their self-admiration instead. Had Ghosn, Engelbert, Romanovitch, Mukwege and Murad been *primarily* motivated to prop up their self-esteem, they couldn't have achieved what they did in the real world.

I'll show in the next chapter that confidence works because it affects every emotion and thought in our mind, every neuron in our brain, every ounce of our motivation, and each action in our daily life. This is because the human mind is a prediction machine, orchestrating its activities according to what it expects to happen in the future.

Confidence, too, is an ingenious prediction device that humans evolved to survive and flourish. It is about predicting success – whether in sinking a putt in a game of golf, giving a public talk, or recalibrating one's life after an unhappy break-up. And above all, it can be learned. So let's now consider how confidence works in our minds and our brains.

CHAPTER 2

How Confidence Works

꞉꞉

I N July 2007, under the bulbous clouds of cold Carnoustie on Scotland's east coast, the Irish golfer Padraig Harrington won one of golf's most prestigious competitions – the British Open. The story of how he did this, one of the most remarkable finishes in golfing history, illustrates in a very tangible way how confidence works.

The Claret Jug – the Open's famous prize – was within Harrington's grasp as he teed off at the second last hole of the tournament. He had a one-shot lead on his arch-rival Sergio García. He was entirely in the zone, and later said, 'I was six under par and could have been more. Nothing could go wrong. I am literally the most confident person at that point in time.'

But then, something strange happened:

I got up on the tee-box, I was going to bust it down the middle . . . I had hit it dead straight all day – I had never felt better . . . and I got a tiny twinge of doubt at the top of the back swing.

At that moment, somewhere in his mind, a needle of doubt hovered over his bubble of confidence. Then he sliced the ball into the murky waters of the notorious Barry Burn, a stream that meanders across the golf course. As Harrington walked over the bridge to take his penalty shot, he crossed paths with Sergio García.

> Sergio smiled at me. I didn't want to look disappointed, I wanted to look resolute. He's back in it, he knows I've taken a penalty, he knows I'm still in trouble and should be feeling very bad – but I wasn't . . . I was still positive at this stage.

Harrington squared up at the eighteenth and final tee. The Claret Jug still shimmered before him. Disaster. He lashed the ball into the Barry Burn again. The needle finally burst through the membrane of his confidence.

> I've never experienced this reaction in my life . . . I've now lost the Open . . . I've never been on a golf course in my life when I wanted to throw the towel in. I wanted to give up – I was embarrassed, I had choked . . . It was my Open . . . I'm one ahead and I'm gonna win . . . and I had thrown it away.

The golfer's confidence dissolved. He barely remembers the first fifty yards as he trudged up the fairway of the final hole to take yet another penalty shot. Luckily, his caddy, Ronan Flood, was by his side. As they walked, Flood kept saying to Harrington that he was the best chipper and putter (the two strokes he needed to stay in the tournament) in the world. 'One shot at a time, you're the best chip and putter in the world, one shot at a time, you're the best chip and putter in the world.' Over and over, Flood repeated it.

> This is what he did . . . he kept at me . . . I'd say he took the club off me . . . I think I would have hit him with it . . .

I was gone . . . but he just kept at me . . . one shot at a time – they were only clichés . . .

Despite Harrington's clear distress and complete loss of confidence, Flood kept at it, repeating those words and not letting any other thoughts enter his mind. As they approached the ball for Harrington to take his second to last shot and attempt to salvage his tournament, Harrington's mindset had shifted. He took his position above the fateful ball.

I stood there, really excited about it, and I fired it in there, nice and low . . . I don't think I've ever been more in the zone than in that chip shot in my life. It's really easy to hit a great shot when you're feeling good . . . it's really difficult to hit a great shot when you're feeling bad. I should have been feeling the lowest ebb at this point.

His caddy's constant, almost mechanical repetition of his conviction that Harrington would do it had somehow reinflated the confidence bubble.

In the circumstances, to come back in the zone and hit the shot . . . I have to give all credit to Ronan . . . without him I wouldn't have done it . . . I'd forgotten about the mess I'd made . . . I'd forgotten nearly about the Open Championship at this moment . . . I've just got an opportunity, in front of twenty to thirty thousand people who are sitting in the stands here, of hitting a great shot and giving them something to cheer about.

Those two shots won Harrington a playoff with García. He triumphed to raise the Claret Jug in front of a roaring crowd that had just witnessed a remarkable manifestation of the ebb and flow of confidence in sport.

But according to a close acquaintance of Harrington, whom I spoke to in Dublin, that's not the end of the story. After the first delirious celebration on the green, the champion and his caddy parted for several hours of ceremony and press interviews. They were reunited at the end of the evening in the limousine that took them back to their hotel. Padraig looked over at his caddy and said, 'You know, Ronan, I thought I'd blown the Open – and so did everyone else in the world – except Ronan Flood.' Ronan started to laugh. 'What's so funny?' Harrington asked, puzzled. Flood replied, 'I thought you'd blown it too – I didn't think you had a chance!'

Just saying the words

Where exactly did Padraig Harrington's 'twinge of doubt' at the top of his back swing come from?

Stop what you are doing for a few moments and try to catch the thoughts flitting through your mind. Here's my attempt:

> Sensation of thighs pressing against chair . . . noise of keyboard as I type . . . what will I have for dinner . . . seagull just flew by my window . . . is this what I should be writing . . . wooden frame of window . . . iPhone is blank, no messages . . . notebook open . . . have to phone the airline . . . full up from lunch . . . should I do something about that stiffness in my leg . . . tree rustling in wind . . . I'd better get some exercise later . . . memory-image of beach at weekend . . . feeling of cold water when swimming in sea . . . will I ever get this book finished . . . another gull . . . amazing linearity of the horizon, sea mottled, grey clouds, bad summer . . . will it be warm at weekend . . .

I could catch only some of them, and many images and sensations that didn't have words linked to them darted by me. Try it again – see if you can catch your thoughts as they flash through your mind.

These are just our conscious thoughts. There are many more mental events in our minds, of which we are never aware. Sensations from the outside world – such as sounds or smells – trigger them, as does the constant churn of remembering and daydreaming. For example, you might find yourself lifting your empty cup for a drink without consciously realizing that you have been thirsty. Or you might wonder why you're feeling tense before realizing that yesterday's sarcastic comment by a colleague has been circling in the back of your mind.

Given the thousands of thoughts and images that pass through our minds, asking where Harrington's 'twinge of doubt' comes from is the wrong question. If you are holding a narrow lead in a world-class sporting event, how could it *not* occur to you that you might screw up?

Here is some more of what Harrington said about that feeling: 'I got a tiny twinge of doubt at the top of the back swing . . . and when you are not expecting it, that can manifest itself in a huge reaction.'

That one little thought – probably something like *I could mess this up* – did indeed trigger a reaction. It was the sudden prospect of a dizzying prize vaporizing on the brink of being seized. Anxiety would have flooded through Harrington's brain at this thought. To the brain, not getting a prize you expect is the same as being punished, and the prospect of punishment makes us fearful. With waves of such disruptive activity going through the golfer's brain, it is little wonder that he swiped the ball into the Barry Burn – not once, but twice. So, we return to the question of how does Harrington – or the rest of us thought-cluttered humans, for that matter – *not* continually fall victim to these twinges of doubt?

Our minds run on great daisy-chains of associations. So, if we are thinking about success, thoughts of failure inevitably follow.

Success and failure are like Siamese twins – locked together in language, and centuries-old myths and stories, so that rousing one will surely awaken the other.

So why aren't we all a jumble of self-doubt, conflicting impulses and abandoned projects? Well, some of us – too many of us – are exactly that. Habit, routine, familiar people and places help to regulate our thoughts and emotions. In this way, they keep us functioning well, undistracted by self-doubt and vacillation. It is this external scaffolding that keeps the surge and flow of our thoughts and images in tidy channels.

We usually aren't aware of the scaffolding until it falls away – if we are made redundant, for example, or a relationship breaks down. And being in the lead at a famous international sporting event has no scaffolding of habit to regulate the mind and keep in check any little twinges of doubt: the competition is so fierce and the difficulty of maintaining focus so great that few champions can last long in that elevated place (Tiger Woods being a famous exception to this rule). So how did Harrington manage it – especially after he felt humiliated by his two off-the-wall shots into the water? Let's go back to what he was thinking during this remarkable sporting interlude:

> . . . and by the time I got to my golf ball I was believing him. I stood there, really excited about it . . . I don't think I've ever been more in the zone than in that chip shot in my life . . . I have to give all credit to Ronan . . . without him I wouldn't have done it . . . I'd forgotten about the mess I'd made . . . I'd forgotten nearly about the Open Championship at this moment.

How did Harrington keep his thoughts of failure in check? *Attention*. He focused his mind on the next two shots only – to the point that he forgot about the wider competition. His brain's attention system ordered his thoughts and mental images into just those relevant to this immediate task – performing these two shots that he had done so many times before. Banished were thoughts of winning the Claret Jug, and with them, images of failure disappeared also.

Attention cleared the way for his shots like a gate that opens and closes to control what was in his mind at any given moment. And what is in the mind shapes what emotions we feel.

Look at how Harrington's emotions surged and plunged – entirely at the whim of what thoughts attention allowed into his consciousness. One minute he was seizing the Claret Jug, and the next he wanted to run away and hide. Nothing had changed between the seventeenth and eighteenth holes – except his thoughts.

At both holes, he hit the ball wide. At the first, however, he felt secure and resolute, while after the second, he was emotionally ravaged. *Only his thoughts changed, nothing else.* His attention was the gate that opened on the positive thoughts for the seventeenth hole and on the negative ones for the eighteenth.

In his mind – and also in his caddy's – after the debacle of those shots he was finished. But Ronan Flood knew a thing or two about attention – and therefore about confidence. It didn't matter that Flood didn't believe his own words. He was controlling Harrington's attention because his boss had lost control of it himself. He was a farmer letting sheep through the narrow gate, one by one, into the dipping pen, but in this case, the caddy's sheep were Harrington's thoughts. The only ones allowed through were about chipping and putting, meaning that only memories linked to these very few, selected images came out of Harrington's memory banks. And they were memories of past successes – chip and putt was his forte – and so Flood created the mental 'zone' that Harrington mentions.

What role does confidence play here? The answer is that attention cleared the way for confidence to do its work. Attention focused on a specific goal – chip this ball – which had a long history of success behind it. Bolstered by these memories, Harrington had the appropriate *can do* belief. Flood had ruthlessly focused Harrington's attention into an almost trance-like state on this tiny hinterland of behaviour. By corralling his thoughts in this way, he imposed confidence on Harrington – that is, his belief that he could chip on to the green and then putt into the hole.

Flood might just have been saying the words – but it worked. Words are powerful instruments for controlling our attention – and subsequently our emotions. And if we can control our attention and feelings, we can focus on goals that we have a chance of achieving, because they are within our circle of control. Winning the Claret Jug wasn't within Harrington's power – there were so many other factors at play – but chipping and putting at that eighteenth hole *was* under his control. He could be confident that he would achieve it by using his attention to define that goal and focus on it.

Later in the book we'll see how confidence – the belief that you can do something – empowers you mentally, physically and emotionally, and that you can learn to harness it, just as Harrington did. But the key, as learned from Flood and Harrington, is to focus your attention on precise goals, and to know when and whether you have achieved them. Lack of confidence often arises because goals are not clear and attention is not sharply focused on them.

If you're a young golfer and set your sights on winning the Open, the chances are very high that you will drop out early on, demoralized. The probabilities are so low – it is too high and distant a goal, and so is out of your control. If you play without any particular purpose – enjoying the game for its own sake – this is, of course, fine, but you're unlikely to progress much. There's a 'sweet spot' for goals, which should be both challenging and attainable. Herein lies the mental zone where confidence comes into play, both as a cause and as an effect. Believing that you will chip the ball on to the green makes it more likely that you will do it, and doing so will further increase your confidence.

But there is a further effect at play.

In successfully focusing his attention on the two shots of the eighteenth hole, to the extent that he forgot all about the Open, Harrington was achieving a remarkable feat of mental control. The pressures of playing in front of thirty thousand people, when you have just suffered the emotional turmoil of two appalling mistakes, are enormous. Attention has an incredibly difficult job of imposing order on a mind swirling with all sorts of thoughts and emotions.

This achievement of mental control would have boosted Harrington's confidence in his attention – his psychological regulator. If you have confidence in your ability to control your thoughts – and, by implication, emotions – you will perform better in any situation.

Attention and confidence are a powerful duo, and one of their most accessible tools is *language*. Flood, the caddy, might just have been saying the words without believing them, but words are potent orchestrators of our attention and confidence.

Harrington said that he was 'excited' as he made that crucial chip on the eighteenth hole – a telling word to describe his pounding heart, sweating palms and twisting stomach. But remember – a few minutes earlier, after messing up his drive, the golfer had endured the same symptoms. At that point, the word he used to describe those feelings was 'embarrassed' – anxious and humiliated – to the extent that he felt like 'throwing in the towel'.

What comes first – the word or the feeling? Well, the only way to tell for sure is to do an experiment – and that is what researchers at the University of Pittsburgh did. They asked volunteers to perform a nerve-racking mental arithmetic task in public. Before they began, participants were allocated to one of two groups. The first was asked to say out loud, 'I feel anxious,' and the second was asked to say, 'I feel excited' – regardless of how they were actually feeling. The individuals who told themselves that they felt excited performed the arithmetic better than those who interpreted their pounding hearts and twisting stomachs as anxiety. Changing just one word can make someone perform better, and I'll explain how in Chapter 5. The point here is that simply saying positive words aloud makes you better able to achieve your goal because it focuses your attention on it.

Both Harrington's and Flood's descriptions of what was said as they walked those fifty yards to take the crucial shot suggest a quasi-hypnotic quality to the language. Hypnosis is an ancient way of controlling attention. Because of this, it can work to improve confidence and hence performance by *just saying the words* in a hypnotic style.

Sports psychology researchers at two English universities confirmed this in 2010 when they compared football-kicking performance after hypnosis to improve self-confidence when performing the task. Compared to football players who just watched edited videos of professional football games, those trained through hypnotic suggestion ended up more self-confident about their on-target shots. They also hit the target much more often, even four weeks after the training.

So, how does confidence work in your mind? By helping you to pay attention to the right things, you do them better, which in turn makes you more confident, which then makes you do them even better, and so on. The words we say to ourselves bind our confidence to our attention, even if we don't fully believe those words. For example, your legs might be trembling as you stand on a podium to speak, but just saying the words *I feel excited* will make you perform objectively better and build your confidence for the next occasion.

Confidence, then, *is* the words you say to yourself, in part. And given that we can choose what we say to ourselves, we can, to some extent, control our level of confidence.

Confidence is a distorting lens

On Thursday, 23 June 2016, the people of Britain voted for Brexit by a narrow majority. They did so despite dire warnings from the

Governor of the Bank of England and others that it would cause considerable economic damage to the country. In particular, it was forecast to worsen the lot of the less well-off, who voted disproportionately to leave the EU.

In the years following the referendum, the electorate was swamped by pessimistic economic forecasts from the most respectable international economists, but also by even higher waves of optimistic promises of economic nirvana by the politicians supporting Brexit, delivered by an overwhelmingly pro-Brexit popular press.

Poorer and less-educated people voted strongly for Brexit. The more well-off and better-educated had benefited most from a globalized economy and tended to vote to remain. There was, however, one other factor that swelled the Brexit vote and precipitated the UK's most significant political crisis in several hundred years. That factor was age.

While only 27 per cent of eighteen- to twenty-four-year-olds voted for Brexit, 60 per cent of those over the age of sixty-five did so. Two years later, asked how they would vote if there were a second referendum, the proportion of pro-Brexit over sixty-fives rose to 66 per cent, while that of pro-Brexit eighteen- to twenty-four-year-olds shrank to 18 per cent.

Everyone was exposed to a tsunami of information about the impact of Brexit on the economy. While old and young may have selectively attended to different information sources, the existence of relatively impartial national broadcasters in the UK ensured that audiences would have received comparable exposure to information opposed to their views. Yet the forecasts influenced the minds of young and old in opposite directions. Why? The answer, strangely enough, is relevant to how confidence works, and reveals something incredibly interesting about the Brexit brain.

Imagine for a moment that you have enrolled for a college course and are waiting for a grade – you hoped for a B, but you open the email and find you got a C. Your self-confidence about your academic future takes a hit. Suppose now that your hoped-for B yields an A – your confidence will then surge as you update your academic self-assessment.

That's how confidence works – it gradually creeps up with every exceeded expectation or success, and sinks with each disappointed hope. So, is your self-confidence just the end result of this gradual accumulation of life's pluses and minuses?

It turns out the brain doesn't work like that. It chalks up positive scores more than negative ones, meaning that most of us end up with a rose-tinted view of ourselves and our future. Something known as *asymmetric updating.* It is the reason why most people believe that they are better than others – the so-called *superiority illusion.*

For example, most people think they're above-average drivers – a statistical impossibility. Surgeons and many other occupations tend to overestimate their professional skills, although women drivers and surgeons assess their abilities more accurately than men – something I'll come back to at a later point.

Most of us are prone to unrealistic optimism – research from Rutgers University shows that people think they are 32 per cent less likely to be diagnosed with lung cancer than the average person. They also believe that they are 49 per cent less likely to get divorced. Average students think they are 13 per cent more likely to get an award than other 'average' students. Even in something as random as selecting a card blind from a pack, people significantly overestimate their chances of picking a winner. These are examples of the distorting lens upon which a multi-trillion-dollar gambling industry is built.

How does it happen that good news shapes our confidence more than bad news? Good news – learning that your chances of being diagnosed with cancer are lower than you expected, for instance – registers in the left front part of the brain and the middle of the frontal lobes. Lousy news – discovering that your risk of cancer is higher than you thought, for example – registers more on the opposite side of the brain: the right inferior frontal gyrus.

Most of us have brains that are much more responsive to good news than bad. The more biased we are towards the positive, the stronger the connections between the left frontal part of the brain and the emotion centres, such as the amygdala and insula. Optimists, in other words, have thicker 'cabling' connecting the good-news and emotion centres of their brains. And remarkably, positive thinking also inclines you to see the past through rose-tinted glasses, shaping your memories more positively.

There are exceptions. The brains of glass-half-empty people, who find optimism a challenge, have less of a bias in favour of good news. The same is also true of mildly depressed individuals.

To be clear, we don't ignore bad news – it does shape our view of the future – but most of our brains give more weight to the good news. But there is one significant difference between good and bad news that helps to explain the Brexit brain.

How people respond to good news doesn't change much over the course of their lifetime. But the story for bad news is very different. Our brains react to negative news most around the age of forty – the response starts lower when we are children and then slowly climbs to its middle-aged peak. But then it falls off steadily through our sixties and seventies until it reaches a level in eighty-year-olds far below that seen in children.

This decline in bad-news processing is one reason the dire warnings about Brexit by economists and bankers could be so quickly waved away as 'Project Fear' by the over sixty-fives. Their brains did not respond to the bad news in the way that the younger brains did, which left the older generation in a bubble of false optimism about the consequences of Brexit. Little wonder that their views hardened in favour of Brexit while the eighteen- to twenty-four-year-olds' brains strengthened against it.

Confidence is a distorting lens that makes us optimistic in the face of contrary evidence. It is not only words, but also a mild delusion without which we wouldn't have reached the moon, created the internet or eliminated smallpox. That delusion has one other significant effect that explains confidence's workings.

Oswald the Lucky Rabbit: Confidence as an anti-depressant

In 1933, the US was in the depths of the prolonged economic crisis known as the Great Depression. Walt Disney's cartoon character Oswald the Lucky Rabbit featured in a widely viewed animated short called *Confidence*. Oswald is a farmer in charge of a happy community of egg-producing chickens. But a cowled, black Death figure rises from a stinking wasteland and casts the farm animals into a dispirited depression. Oswald makes his way to Washington, DC, where he meets President Roosevelt, who gives him a syringe of 'Confidence' to administer to his farm animals. They are miraculously revived from their sad and unproductive torpor.

Seventy-five years later, in 2008, the US and the rest of the world were shaken by another economic crisis, which came to be known as the Great Recession. Many tens of thousands of Americans suffered bankruptcy, job losses and homelessness as a result. Those who endured one or more of these impacts showed a dramatic rise in mental health conditions, such as depression and anxiety, which lasted for years after the Great Recession ended. Unlike the fortunate chickens on Oswald's farm, there was no presidential confidence serum to inject them with and lift them out of the depression. Across Europe and North America, it has been estimated that between 2008 and 2010, the Great Recession caused an extra ten thousand people to commit suicide.

Oswald's cartoon illustrates that the multi-way relationship between confidence, depression and anxiety has long been recognized. The increasing medicalization of emotions such as low mood and anxiety has tended to obscure this rather common-sense fact – bad, threatening situations tend to make us sad and anxious. These are normal responses and are not, in the vast majority of cases, diseases caused by faults in our brains. One of confidence's main jobs is in our minds: as an anti-depressant.

Confidence is also a very effective anti-anxiety drug. Here's how it works. The human brain is a prediction machine, continually anticipating what will happen in the world in a mostly unconscious way. It switches into a fully conscious mode when its predictions go wrong – when an oncoming car swerves out of the traffic and into your path, for example, or when a friend tells you he has terminal cancer.

When you anticipate success, your brain releases a powerful wave of activity deep in its reward network in the middle of the brain. The neurotransmitter dopamine is a key chemical messenger in this process. The reward network's action has natural motivational, anti-anxiety and anti-depressant effects. And, as we just saw, our brains are biased to learn more from good prediction errors than from bad, disappointing ones.

This positive bounce happens most of all when you surprise yourself with a slightly better-than-expected performance, or struggle through a difficulty and come out the other side. The brain's reward network operates by *prediction error*: a mismatch between prior expectation and actual reality. So, once you can do something easily, it no longer gives you that boost. However, if you manage to do something successfully against the odds, your brain network responds to this better-than-expected success with a gratifying pulse of positive emotion. This is the feeling of *mastery*, one of the most significant sources of confidence.

If you lose your job, your money or your house because the economy has baselined, the resulting negative prediction errors cut the activity in the reward network. This diminishes dopamine activity, sending your mood low and your anxiety levels sky high. Even without such dramatic events, economic recessions that reduce your hope for your financial future depress your mood and increase your stress levels. Most importantly, they lessen your self-confidence.

As we saw earlier, most of us are more confident than statistical reality justifies, except if we are depressed or chronically pessimistic. But rather than hitting the brick wall of fact, that strategy of self-delusion has served humanity very well. Why? Because such confidence defeats depression, smothers anxiety and makes us feel good. And when we feel good, we step out with hope in our hearts and often that pays off handsomely.

It also pays off financially. Stock markets rise and fall with the sporting success of national teams. For example, the ups and downs of the English national football team show up in the performance of the FTSE 100. Sunny days also lift the mood of investors and help the markets rally, showing that confidence and happiness are indeed the closest of sisters.

That, then, is the third way in which confidence works – it's a very natural and effective mood enhancer and anxiety diminisher. What is the most critical consequence of a good mood and low anxiety? The answer to that question points to the fourth way in which confidence works – taking action.

Doing stuff

Jo was a business consultant, successful and well paid, working typically long London hours. She was smart, exceptionally analytical, well organized, and liked by all her colleagues and bosses. She would have been on a fast track to partnership except for one problem: meetings made her anxious. Particularly with people she didn't know well, such as new clients. Even formal gatherings with co-workers would cause her face and neck to redden with an embarrassed flush she was highly aware of.

Jo's career was at risk of stalling, despite her exceptional abilities, because she started to miss meetings. She would arrive late and leave early, giving the excuse of other appointments. Initially, even though she felt anxious inside, she would have presented superbly to clients, blowing them away with her assessments of complex business issues. But as the anxiety swelled, her confidence diminished. In one particular conference with a major client, she lost the thread of her argument. So great was her distress that she had to leave work and go home.

Her boss began to allocate cases to other, less competent colleagues, who were better able to present to and socialize with clients. Jo's isolated weekend life in her studio apartment in north London spread to comparable isolation at her desk. Since she'd moved to London from the north of England her social life wasn't particularly vibrant, but even that began to dwindle as she shied away not only from work meetings, but from social ones too.

Not surprisingly, Jo's mood slipped, and she felt depressed some of the time. Her anxiety was always there, especially when she thought about meeting people. Her confidence at work had also declined. She began to withdraw from the challenging, complex tasks upon which she used to thrive. Her bosses' view of her as a rising star began to shift negatively.

In another case, Prince Harry, Duke of Sussex, also suffered problems akin to Jo's. In a television interview, reported in the *Daily Beast*, he spoke about the terrible panic attacks he began to suffer in crowded rooms after the death of his mother, Diana. He would start to sweat and his heart would pound 'boom, boom, boom, boom – literally, just like a washing machine'. His impulse was to flee, but as that wasn't an option he just had to try to hide it.

Similarly, the actor Hugh Grant also suffered from anxiety, as he told *Entertainment Weekly*. Talking about a break of several years from acting, he described how he would suffer from panic attacks that would come out of the blue and cause him to freeze when the director called 'Action', and how he would often forget his lines.

The fact Grant froze on set illustrates something fundamental about anxiety – it *stops you from doing new stuff*. Fear means you feel threatened, and when you feel unsafe, the only real alternatives are fight and flight. If you don't know why you feel anxious, or if the threat seems to come from inside you, there's nothing to fight. So flight becomes the only option, and the safe and familiar your only refuge. This might have been a factor in Grant's long absence from movie-making.

Prince Harry wanted to flee but couldn't withdraw because of who and where he was – a royal prince with public engagements and a military serviceman compelled to carry out his duties, despite suffering choking panic.

Jo had more options – even though she was aching with anxiety and low mood, she could still do parts of her job and avoid meetings, and none of her friends were going to force her out into social settings against her will. She could follow the logic of anxious behaviour and retreat into doing less stuff.

What all three individuals had in common was their urge to pull back – to stop doing stuff, to retreat. And that kind of behaviour is the opposite of what confidence does for you – urging you forward to do something that takes you beyond the familiar.

Confidence lifts our mood and quietens anxiety because it projects a successful outcome into an uncertain future. Anxiety and depression do the opposite – they project negative consequences into the future, and so drain our confidence. The result of this two-way traffic provides a clue about the fourth way in which confidence works in our minds – it makes us *do stuff* and *take action*.

A quote attributed to Woody Allen by screenwriter Marshall Brickman encapsulates this fact: 'I have learned one thing. As Woody says, "Showing up is 80 per cent of life." Sometimes it's easier to hide home in bed. I've done both.'

Woody Allen is absolutely right. If you *just turn up*, that's you taking action, moving forward. If you do it repeatedly, it will yield results that will lift your mood and boost your confidence.

People like Jo, who experience a lot of anxiety, generally do less stuff in their lives. They have fewer opportunities to experience the mood-elevating, anxiety-reducing and confidence-building effects of mastering challenges because they take less action. They also have fewer chances of experiencing success, such as meeting a compatible romantic partner or finding a new and more exciting job.

Confidence has such profound effects on all aspects of our lives because it drives us to act. It doesn't matter that our actions won't always lead anywhere – just trying out different courses of action will often pay off, if we persist.

Psychologists can treat phobias like Jo's in two main, interlinked ways. The first is to help her pinpoint what thoughts and fears are triggered by meeting other people – and to help her gradually change her thinking patterns. The second is to slowly get her to take practical steps towards doing what she is avoiding so that she can experience that crucial, confidence-building sense of mastery.

Jo was lucky to find an excellent clinical psychologist who practised this kind of cognitive behavioural therapy, and she was able to resume her high-flying career. Both Prince Harry and Hugh Grant managed to continue their professional commitments because it was harder for them to avoid doing things in the way that Jo had. Learning to be confident and learning to be less anxious usually go hand in hand.

There will be times when all of us face doing something that makes us want to run away. Confidence is the crucial ingredient that will take us forward to do what we want to avoid, and self-belief is also the primary beneficiary of that sense of mastery that comes from doing what you didn't want to do. Researchers have shown that when treating phobias like Jo's, it is the *confidence* to do the thing you fear that predicts whether or not you will overcome it. The same can be said to apply to most other areas of our lives. Confident people choose goals that stretch and improve them and, as a result, they end up more resilient emotionally.

In this chapter we have peered into the complex mental clockwork that underpins confidence, and how, in life, it can forge success across the board. But for every confidence booster there is a confidence trap, luring us into failure.

CHAPTER 3

How Confidence Declines

∷

YOU NOTICE THAT your memory – or that of your partner or a parent – is getting worse. Your doctor asks you to complete a short set of tests to measure your concentration, thinking and memory. If you are in the UK, she may use a screening test called the Addenbrooke's Cognitive Examination, devised by my former colleagues from Cambridge University, and which includes tasks such as remembering a short list of words, counting backwards in sevens from one hundred, and drawing a clockface with the hands set at a particular time. In other parts of the world, doctors use similar tests.

You finish the examination. The doctor adds up the points to yield a score out of one hundred. A score lower than eighty-two means the patient has an 84 per cent chance of being diagnosed with dementia after a full assessment in a specialist hospital clinic.

University of Exeter researchers wanted to see what happened to these test scores when people were given different information about the test. Volunteers in their mid-sixties were randomly allocated to one of four groups before being given the Cambridge test.

Half were told that they were part of a study of forty- to seventy-year-olds, and that they were the older half of the group. The remaining sixty-somethings were told that it was a study of sixty- to ninety-year-olds and that they were the younger members of the group.

The researchers then gave one of two versions of a magazine article about older brains to half the people in each of the feel-old and feel-young groups. Half read that growing old causes specific problems with memory and forgetfulness, resulting in the need to use reminders and notebooks. The other half read that growing old causes a general cognitive decline across all mental abilities, including concentration, decision-making, planning and problem-solving.

To summarize, the first group believed they were in the younger half of the overall group and that growing old affected their memory, but the use of aids could compensate for this. The second group also believed they were the younger ones, but that age caused across-the-board reduction in mental capacity. The third group believed that they were the older ones and that being old caused memory issues – but again, that could be managed with aids and reminders. The fourth group also thought they were older, and that being old caused general cognitive decline.

It's worth reiterating that the people in the four groups were the same age. The only differences were whether they felt relatively old or young, and what they had read about mental decline.

Divided into these four groups, a total of sixty-eight people took the Cambridge test exactly as they would if seeing their doctor about memory problems. The researchers then scored the screening test.

As you would expect from a group of apparently healthy sixty-somethings, only a minority scored in the under-eighty-two dementia range. Except, that is, for one of the groups. The healthy people who were made to feel older *and* who read the general cognitive decline article showed a completely different pattern. No less than

70 per cent of them scored below eighty-two, a result which in real life would have found them in a hospital memory clinic as a case of suspected dementia.

The distribution of individuals in these four groups arose from the equivalent of a throw of the dice. There could be no *actual* differences in their true risk of dementia. The *only* differences were whether they had been made to feel old or young, and their beliefs about cognitive ageing.

The word 'old' has a bunch of negative connotations we learn through films, stories and songs. The sixties band The Who, for example, famously hoped that they would die before they got old. Being told that you are old is not a neutral description. It is a sort of mental backpack, acting largely below your conscious awareness, that weighs you down with a raft of negative associations and expectations about your physical and mental abilities. This is doubly so if you believe that age causes widespread loss of your faculties, as opposed to just a specific set of memory glitches.

As we have learned, confidence is the belief that you can do something. We have seen that it can be a self-fulfilling prophecy because of the ways it works in the mind. A mental backpack such as *old* sabotages that confidence because it undermines your belief in what you can do. It saps confidence in older people's mental performance and so depresses their test scores.

There are many other such burdensome backpacks. Race, gender, religion, social class and caste can all act to sap performance. These labels that prejudiced cultures put on people – *stereotypes* – don't just exist in the biases of others. They can burrow into the brains of said badge-wearers and drain their confidence in a way that makes them behave in line with the stereotype. For example, African American students tend to underperform on standardized tests of mental function, such as the Scholastic Aptitude Test (SAT) or Graduate Record Examination (GRE), as compared to other ethnic groups.

In a famous 1995 Stanford University study by Claude Steele, African American students were tested on thirty-three verbal problems, mostly selected from the highest difficulty items from the GRE. They had been told one of two things about the research. At random, half were briefed that it concerned 'various personal factors involved in performance on problems requiring reading and verbal reasoning abilities'. Afterwards, they were told, they would be given feedback about their strengths and weaknesses. The other half believed that the study was about 'the psychological factors involved in solving verbal problems' and were promised feedback that would familiarize them with the kinds of issues they might encounter in the future.

African American students are well aware of the commonly held beliefs about their academic ability and IQ, in the same way that older people are all too conscious of preconceptions about their memory and mental agility. These beliefs can lie dormant in people's minds, and awake only in certain situations. One such situation is being tested for an ability that stereotype dictates you are poor at. Once these thoughts arise in the mind, they load it with anxieties and self-doubts. They drain cognitive ability in a way that damages actual performance and makes people conform to the stereotype.

When the African American students were told that their intellectual abilities were being tested, they scored around eight out of thirty-three on the exam. In comparison, Caucasian students scored about twelve. Many commentators have taken this sort of finding as evidence for the existence of inherent – possibly genetic – differences between racial groups in intelligence. But such beliefs are false.

We can see this in the performance of African American students who were given a different rationale about the study – namely that it was to explore how people solved problems. They scored twelve – the same as the Caucasian students. Simply thinking that their IQ was being tested sapped the other group's mental performance by a third. It was an additional mental burden, and the weight of it drained their confidence. Self-doubt flared and poor perform-ance followed. A stereotype was reinforced.

These findings also apply to gender. Women are commonly thought to perform less well on visuospatial tasks. One typical exercise to test this ability is the examination of two 3-D drawings of abstract shapes that are in different orientations. You are men-tally required to rotate one of these drawings through space until it is in the same orientation as the second. You then decide whether the structures of the shapes are identical, or not.

And yes, on average, women do perform worse than men on this test. *Yet* if female participants are 'primed' beforehand, by reading an article saying that women are better at this type of exercise than men, they perform just as well on this supposedly gender-sensitive task.

Researchers at Dartmouth College in New Hampshire used brain imaging to discover how these stereotypes change brain function. When women were made to believe that females are poor at this mental rotation task, the emotion-processing parts of their brains ramped up, disrupting clear thinking. Made to think that, on average, women are better than men on this test, their visuospa-tial brain regions boosted to allow them to perform at male levels, unhindered by stereotype.

Age, race and gender aren't the only stereotypes that affect suc-cess. Most of us have some sort of labels that others have pinned on us, and which we have absorbed into our psyche. Sometimes these can be positive, such as being physically attractive. Height also tends to increase confidence and hence success.

Confidence as a self-fulfilling prophecy

Think of a situation in which you have to do something that makes you nervous. For example, you'd like to ask your boss to keep your job open so that you can take six months' unpaid leave to go on a trip.

As you run through this scenario, try to catch your thoughts: words of explanation or entreaty, suggestions about how your work can be delivered, promises about the future. An imagined frown of surprise on your boss's face, followed maybe by a nod – or was that a shake – of her head? Impressions of what you might say and do swirl among these thoughts. You feel your face flush. *Oh no* – you stutter the opening sentence of your long-practised and supposed killer opener.

Low confidence, then, can see you defeated before you even start. High confidence, on the other hand, has the ability to sweep through these thoughts of failure like a blast of wind scattering leaves from the street. Gone is the dry foliage of doubt about what words you will use and how you will say them. Blown away are the images of disappointment and disapproval on your boss's face. All that is left behind is a dress rehearsal in your mind's eye of a sequence of actions leading to an outcome – that is what confidence does. When you rehearse an activity, your brain goes through the precise set of steps that it will execute, except for the final movement of the muscles or lips.

Everything else in your brain runs in this faithful simulation as if you are doing the act, or speaking the words. That is how imagination – confidence's chief operating officer – works. It switches on all the action circuits for the task except the very last one: output.

What this means is that your mind is uncluttered by alternative thoughts and actions – stuttering, boss's frowns, or your flushing face. Instead, it is primed and well rehearsed, like an accomplished actor behind a rising curtain. Such a cleansed state of mind, of course, makes it much more likely that you'll deliver the killer appeal in just the right tone of voice. Your sunny, confident face will reassure your boss that she cannot do without you. And because confidence leads you to anticipate success, your brain will be in reward-seeking, rather than punishment-anticipation, mode.

A 2019 Queensland University study looked at how well people processed information in a perceptual task. They received $7.50 at the start and were set the goal of achieving a certain speed and accuracy. For some periods they were rewarded with $2.50 when they met their goal; for others, when they didn't meet it, they were punished by being 'fined' $2.50. Participants responded faster and more accurately when being rewarded for success than when being punished for failure. By switching on the reward-anticipation circuit of the brain, confidence improves information-processing. This includes how well you read your boss's expression and how effectively you respond to her.

Low confidence has the opposite effect because it inclines you to anticipate punishment, just like in the Queensland study. It slows your information-processing and diverts you from your main goal with distracting alternatives – you might mumble and stutter and look away awkwardly when talking with your boss.

Without confidence, then, the brain is confused by competing actions running at the same time. Little wonder that you may never get to your boss's door or, at best, turn back and flee on the brink of entering. If you do muster the courage to go in, your shoulders will hunch, your expression will be tense, and your speech will be halting. How else could you behave given the contradictory messages and competing programs running in your brain? Confidence takes charge of this discord and orchestrates a symphony out of it. As we will see, self-belief is contagious, and a confidently delivered pitch will much more readily elicit that nod of agreement.

Confidence as a salesman

Most of us are understandably cautious about accepting all the claims of salesmen. So, if confidence is part salesman – as we will see it is – does that mean we have to be similarly wary about its claims?*

---

* I use the term 'salesman' rather than 'salesperson' here because, as we will see later in the book, this is an aspect of confidence that particularly benefits men, to the disadvantage of women.

Picture the scene. I emerge blinking into a humid American sunset after a long transatlantic flight. I haul my jet-lagged body into a bewildering thoroughfare of limos, taxis and shuttles outside the airport. A yellow shuttle brakes to a halt; people and luggage spill out. I turn to a woman beside me.

'Is this the shuttle for the car rental?' I ask her.

She frowns, and replies, 'I *think* so . . .'

I hesitate, the shuttle doors slam shut, and the bus roars off.

Another shuttle – blue this time – stops and disgorges another load of passengers. I turn to a man on my right.

'Is this the shuttle for the car rental?' I ask.

He nods firmly. 'Yeah, this is it.'

I follow him gratefully on to the vehicle, and we career into the gathering dusk. I find myself deposited, in the dark, in the furthest of faraway long-stay car parks. It takes me an hour to find my way back to the terminal and on to – yes – the yellow car rental shuttle.

Why did I not listen to the woman I spoke to first? Because she didn't seem confident. The man, on the other hand, exuded a certainty that had me abandoned on the ghastly outer reaches of the airport.

When Padraig Harrington's caddy Ronan Flood told Harrington that he could chip and putt his way to the Open Championship, it didn't matter that the caddy faked his confidence in the golfer. For Harrington, Flood's apparent faith in him was enough to help him gather the flailing networks of his brain back into the focused order needed to execute his signature strokes.

The world is a complicated, fast-moving place. To cope with this, our minds have developed some mental shortcuts known as *heuristics*. These are rules of thumb that save us from painstakingly thinking through every situation we face, particularly when making decisions when stressed or fatigued. One such shortcut is known as the *confidence heuristic*, which is what I relied on when I took the wrong airport shuttle. I made the snap judgement that the man's confidence was a reasonable indicator of his knowledge. The woman's less certain response stopped me from listening to her.

Although I was wrong in that particular case, the confidence heuristic is not a bad general rule for choosing between different sources of information. The *confidence = knowledge* heuristic is widely held, and it has the notable effect of making confident-sounding people more persuasive. Confidence, in other words, makes you an influencer and a salesman.

Persuasive people gain social kudos, which in turn makes them more confident. It doesn't matter that the confidence heuristic can be wrong. Life is usually too messy and complicated for the failures consequent on wrong advice to become apparent in time to correct them. Those who can express their views confidently are more persuasive, and influential people more often get what they want. So, when they get things wrong, hundreds, thousands, and even millions of people endure the consequences.

Thought confidence

The 2016 Brexit referendum required a binary decision on a complicated question about Britain's membership of the European Union. Many criticized the then Conservative prime minister David Cameron, who initiated the vote, for creating a damaging national schism over a question that previously had been almost entirely an internal issue within his political party.

Repeated surveys showed that UK membership of the EU was not a high-priority, widespread concern in the vast majority of people's minds. But subsequently, thanks to the rancorous political turmoil surrounding the referendum campaign – more of this in Chapter 11 – Brexit swiftly became the dominant political issue, and a bitterly divisive one at that.

When Cameron's memoirs were published in 2019, he was savagely critical of one of his successors, Boris Johnson, but he refused to express regret for having called the referendum. He insisted that it had been 'necessary' and 'inevitable'. He regretted the turmoil it created in the UK, but was insistent that he had had to make the decision.

I mentioned my surprise at Cameron's stance to a colleague who had previously been a ministerial adviser in the UK government. His reply first took me aback and then made me think. He said, 'Ah yes. You can't operate at that level in politics – and you certainly can't get to that level – unless you have a sense of certainty about your own decisions. Otherwise, the competing pressures will just wear you down.'

It made me remember a conversation I had had some years previously with a senior adviser to one of David Cameron's predecessors, Tony Blair. He was loyally defensive of his former boss, and refused to condemn Blair's disastrous decision to join in the 2003 invasion of Iraq. He praised the erstwhile prime minister's many political achievements both domestically and internationally. But his guard went down just once as he muttered, almost to himself, 'It's his constant certainty that worries me.'

At the time, I had seen this certainty as a symptom of Blair's intoxication with power. It was only years later, in my conversation about David Cameron, that I realized the certainty both statesmen had shown was a form of confidence. I had stumbled upon the concept of *thought confidence.*

Would you consider yourself to be more of an introvert or an extrovert? Now, ask yourself this: how *strongly* do you hold that belief about yourself? With that question in mind, I ask you to consider your thinking and assess your confidence in your thoughts. How confident are you that you could go back to college and learn a new profession or trade? How certain are you about what you would like to study? If you aren't confident about your choice, the chances are you won't follow it up with action. Confidence in your thoughts binds them much more strongly to concrete action, University of Madrid researchers showed in 2010. Half of the UK population wishes that David Cameron had been less confident in his thoughts about holding a referendum.

My great-grandfather was a miller on the island of Bute, off the west coast of Scotland. James Robertson's water mill, powered by a small stream called the Greenan Burn, was peacefully scenic. But it was no cash cow, and so he had to supplement his marginal income with work as a carpenter and as an undertaker. Then, one day, the biggest mill on the island – in the middle of the nearby town of Rothesay – came up for rent. My great-grandfather was, by common consent, the ideal man to run this much more profitable, higher-throughput enterprise.

The deadline for tenders to rent the mill had to be with the estate office of landlord Lord Bute – even today, it is a feudal island – by 5 p.m. on a particular Friday. All week, James Robertson hummed and hawed about taking the plunge. When Friday came, he paced about Greenan Mill in an agitated state. One minute he was decided that he would take it on, the next he baulked and focused on the im-agined downsides – of which there were actually very few. So he oscillated – in Scotland they would say he swithered. Finally, at 4 p.m., he decided to walk the three miles to town and secure the Rothesay mill. He got there just in time before the office closed.

'I'll take it,' he announced to Lord Bute's agent.

'You're too late, James,' the agent replied. 'It's gone – we thought you didn't want it.'

And so was born an apocryphal family story about the curse of procrastination.

Procrastination arises when you don't know your mind – the col-loquial phrase for lacking confidence in your thoughts. To be confident about what you can do, you have to have confidence in the *thoughts* behind the action. Decisive people make choices about courses of action without apparent vacillation, though perhaps they also to and fro in their minds before making the decisive jump. The point, however, is that they *do* jump. Some indecisives, like my great-grandfather, toss around alternatives in their minds without making the final jump. The result is delay at best and paralysis by inaction at worst. Procrastinators, by definition, tend not to get things *done* and so have many fewer successful experiences that come from goals achieved.

Confidence's sister is action, and when we lack confidence, the consequent inaction can set us up for failure. We take action through our bodies. What effect does confidence, and its absence, have on them?

The confident body

One day, a letter arrived offering me a free trial and complimentary fitness assessment at a nearby gym. I had been aware of my middle-age flab for a while, so I took up the offer. A young woman explained that we would go round the various machines together and establish a suitable baseline level for each, which would constitute my circuit.

First, she led me to a treadmill, ushering me on to it and then setting it rolling at a walking pace.

'How does that speed feel?' she asked.

'Quite slow, actually,' I replied calmly.

She increased the pace. 'Now?'

'Pretty easy, still.'

She jacked it up. 'How's that?'

Beads of sweat formed on my forehead. 'I could go a little faster.'

She upped the speed one final notch. 'That's fine for a beginning,' she said.

I shrugged, trying to convey disappointment that I had not been able to demonstrate fully my physical prowess.

She then had me sit at a piece of equipment where I had to pull down a bar to lift a stack of weights. She chose the level.

'Try that – see what it's like.'

I snapped the bar down, and the weights rattled to their limits.

'Hardly felt it,' I growled.

Weight by weight, she loaded me up. I stole a glance at her face; she was wearing an expression I couldn't quite decode, so I chose to take it as guarded admiration for an older man with the physical strength of someone half his age. And so we moved from machine to machine, calibrating the weights and speeds and resistances to my impressive level of physical capacity. At the end of the session, she wrote out my circuit for future visits to the gym, and I attempted to exit with a swagger, which didn't quite work because I'd pulled a muscle in my calf.

The next week I went back. I plucked my circuit notes from the file box and headed for the first set of weights. Choosing the rather conservative level that I had reluctantly agreed to on my trial session, I pulled the bar down towards me. It was stuck; it wouldn't move.

Typical, I thought, *you pay your subscription and then you find out that the apparatus is banjaxed*. I checked, but it looked OK, so I braced myself and pulled down again. I felt the veins bulge in my temples and groaned at the effort. No movement. I shed a five-kilogram weight. Nothing. Ten – no budging. It took the subtraction of thirty kilos before I could raise a much-diminished cluster of weights.

Moving to the treadmill, I made a mental note to complain to the manager about the condition of his apparatus. I set the speed at that agreed with my mentor and stepped on. It slingshot me back, and sent me sprawling under the bars and on to the gym floor. I found myself looking up into the eyes of the young woman who had created my circuit.

'Are you OK?'

'Yes, fine,' I responded, a little too brusquely for someone lying flat on his back.

'I thought it was too fast,' she said, 'but you insisted.'

I eased myself upright.

'The weights were . . .'

'I knew they were too heavy, too.' She smiled, with a relish that I found a little unprofessional.

I slunk away to brood about the sunk cost of my never-to-be-used membership.

The presence of that instructor at my first visit had strangely boosted my strength. I could lift weights in her presence that eluded me when I was on my own. Does this tell us something about confidence?

One popular book claims that the US Navy SEALs have a 40 per cent rule. It argues that in physical exertion when you feel you cannot continue any more, you have only reached 40 per cent of your capacity. It is an apocryphal story. I have checked with several senior SEAL commanders, who all deny that they teach this. However, there is good scientific evidence to demonstrate that increasing our confidence can enable us to boost our strength and endurance levels.

In 2007, Emory University researchers made students more or less confident about their physical strength. They measured this using a handgrip dynamometer, a metal lever which you squeeze tight against a resisting spring. The longer you hold it closed, the more challenging it becomes because your hand grows tired and sore. The researchers manipulated confidence by randomly telling some students that they were stronger, and others that they were weaker, compared to others. The two groups weren't, in reality, any different in strength.

The results were striking. The high-confidence group held the grip for 30 per cent longer than the low-confidence group. They also felt less pain and discomfort in their hands.

Researchers in Grenoble, France, used the same method with people aged between fifty-two and ninety-one. But first, they asked each of them how old they felt – many of us feel a little younger than we are, and that was the case for these French men and women. They felt, on average, 8 per cent more youthful than their real age. A sixty-year-old felt on average like a fifty-six-year-old, and a ninety-year-old like an eighty-three-year-old.

All the participants then did the handgrip test to measure their grip strength, which in itself is a good indicator of general vitality in older people. The average grip was around 25.5 kilograms. The researchers then lied to half of the group, informing them that their grip on the first trial of strength was better than 80 per cent of people their age. They told the others nothing, and both groups then took the grip test a second time.

The tired hands of people in the group who had been told nothing managed a grip that was one kilo *less* than their first attempt. But the others? Their grip was one kilo *more*. They felt strong because of the false, confidence-building feedback about their strength. Strikingly, the feedback also made them feel younger. A sixty-year-old in the confident group now said he felt like a fifty-three-year-old. A ninety-year-old now felt ten years younger. The group who had been told nothing felt the same age as previously.

While the 40 per cent rule isn't a scientific fact, what *is* true is that our expectations shape physical strength. Believing yourself to be better than 80 per cent of your peers raises your confidence and makes you stronger. My temporarily enhanced strength in the gym – perhaps caused by a deluded sense of youthfulness and a wish to impress the young instructor – was an example of something similar.

Confidence also builds endurance in the body. One grim test of endurance is cycling to exhaustion – that is, having to pedal on a stationary bike until you simply can't go on. Young fit men and women did this in one study and cycled for an average of ten minutes before having to stop. Then, half of them were taken aside by the researchers and taught to use confidence-enhancing self-talk phrases. For example, they learned to say 'You're doing well', 'Feeling good', or 'Push through this'. A few days later, when they were doing their next exhaustion test, they were instructed to say these phrases to themselves.

In the same way that 'just saying the words' worked for Padraig Harrington, simply repeating these confident words meant that the self-talk group boosted their endurance by 18 per cent – from around ten and a half minutes to thirteen minutes. They also felt less strain during the exercise than the other group, whose endurance time didn't change at all. We tend to hit 'the wall' because of pain and discomfort, but confidence reshapes these internal feelings in both our bodies and our brains.

In a University of Wisconsin study, researchers applied painful but harmless heat to the forearms of volunteers lying in an fMRI brain scanner. Half the time, they were given a joystick, which they could use to stop the pain if they had to. The rest of the time, the joystick was removed and, with it, their potential to control the pain. *Except*, however, the joystick did nothing – the researchers had lied. Their volunteers never had control over how long the pain lasted, joystick or no fake joystick.

The hot, painful feeling on their arms produced a pattern of brain activity that has become very familiar to pain researchers. Three main areas of the brain lit up as part of the pain response. These are known as the anterior cingulate, insula and secondary somatosensory cortex. But here is the remarkable thing about the study. With the same amount of heat on the same arms of the same people, the confidence given by holding the fake joystick suppressed their brains' pain response in all these three regions. The mere belief that they had control was enough to diminish the pain, even though the objective pain stimulus was the same.

Feelings of control also shape chronic pain. The more pain-sufferers feel helpless, and the more they fear the pain, the higher their disability and distress. Not feeling as if you have control over your pain worsens it, when measured objectively in the brain. Nothing eats away at confidence like fear. If you are frightened of your pain, this will ratchet up anxiety levels, erode your sense of control and multiply the pain. Feelings of helplessness follow a haemorrhage of confidence and a loss of belief that you can control it. Merely feeling confident diminishes the pain at its source in the brain.

Pain and discomfort are part of sport, so it isn't surprising that confidence can make you perform better and for longer. It is a vaccine against the pain that might otherwise make you give up.

Confident ageing

Older people – say, in their seventies – walking at a brisk pace along the street will tend to look younger, healthier and more vigorous than those who are ambling. This impression is borne out by the science. The slowest walkers – particularly men – are almost twice as likely to die in the next few years compared to the fastest.

What's more, when people slow down their walking pace significantly over a two-year period, their chances of dying in the next few years almost double. It's not easy to disentangle cause and effect in these studies. People will tend to walk more slowly if they become unwell, but also, a loss of motivation and engagement with the world may cause both slower walking speeds and an increased risk of illness and death. One way of trying to unpack these findings is by taking a very large number of people and controlling statistically for factors such as ill health.

Researchers at Trinity College Dublin did exactly this when they studied how fast more than four thousand older people – with an average age in the early sixties – walked, and how that changed over the following two years. Deirdre Robertson and her colleagues then studied how confident they felt about getting old at the beginning of those two years and discovered that people differ in their attitudes. For example, some said yes to statements such as *As I get older, there is much I can do to maintain my independence*. Others said yes to ideas such as *I have no control over the effects which getting older has on my social life*.

The walking speed of those who felt least confident about growing old slowed down by 13 per cent more than those who felt most confident. Walking speed predicts future health, and the researchers could rule out other plausible reasons for this link between ageing-confidence and walking speed.

In these same people the researchers found a similar link between ageing-confidence and changes in cognitive ability. The least confident showed a much steeper drop in their mental sharpness over two years compared to the most. Also, they showed a much more precipitous decline in their self-reported day-to-day memory.

How good you think your memory is – subjective memory assessment – is a topic of great interest to dementia researchers. Your belief in yourself matters. Almost everyone notices changes in their memory as they get older, and people who see particularly significant changes may be showing early signs of dementia. But a five-year study of around two thousand over sixty-five-year-olds in Pennsylvania makes this confidence–memory link particularly interesting. The research showed that subjective beliefs about memory appeared before changes in objective memory did.

Confidence can embed itself in your brain and in your body – and, perhaps, lengthen your life. Research on seventy thousand nurses in the US found that women who were the most optimistic earlier in their lives lived an average of fifteen years longer than the least optimistic. Optimism isn't the same as confidence – it is about the *can happen* span of the confidence bridge more than the *can do* – but it is a close cousin. Optimists agree with statements such as *In uncertain times, I usually expect the best* and *Overall, I expect more good things to happen to me than bad*. They would disagree with the following: *If something can go wrong for me, it will*; *I hardly ever expect things to go my way.*

The optimists were very much more likely to reach eighty-five than the pessimists.

So how *does* confidence work and fail?

Historically, scientists and philosophers have assumed that humans differ from other species in their capacity for language, tool use, problem-solving, empathy, or an ability to work collaboratively in groups. But through research in recent decades, these absolute distinctions have dissolved as various animals have been shown to exhibit some or all of these capacities.

There is one ability, however, that no other species shows, and where the human/non-human divide is absolute. That is the propensity for humans to imagine things that do not yet exist and then to work over extended periods towards creating that not-yet-existent reality. John F. Kennedy's moon race was a prime example of that, but every engineering, artistic, scientific or civic invention by humans depends on this ability.

The capacity to imagine something that doesn't currently exist and to create a mental model of what that might look like is uniquely human. So is the facility to create that imagined future step by step. There is, however, one essential fuel to translate that model into something concrete, and that is confidence.

We've uncovered how confidence works – and fails to work – in the mind, brain and body to help bridge that gap between imagination and the current state of the world. These ideas range from the superficial (just saying the words) to the more profound (thought confidence). I described the rose-tinted glasses that are a vital delusion for confidence. We put them on to help us get out of bed in the morning – to defy brute probabilities, and to create new ones. Pessimism handicaps because it makes you suffer the pain twice – first in anticipating the lousy result, and then in experiencing it. We can say that confidence does the opposite. It rewards you twice – once when you expect success and the second time when you get it. That is why it is a self-fulfilling prophecy.

Confidence also helps us with its pharmacological anti-depressant effects. Its energizing ability to make us do stuff helps to unfurl new opportunities that we wouldn't have encountered without it. And because confidence helps us to enact in our minds outcomes that we want, that mental simulation makes it more likely that they will happen. It makes our bodies more robust and the effort less painful. But perhaps above all, confidence makes salesmen of us and, if we have the right values, brings people together to do important stuff in and for the world.

But where does confidence come from?

CHAPTER 4

What Makes Us Confident?

:)

O N 13 JULY 2018, in the fading light of a west London summer evening, two men fell exhausted into each other's arms. They had just finished the second-longest match in tennis history. The American John Isner flailed his losing shot into the tramlines to give his South African opponent Kevin Anderson victory after a match lasting six hours and thirty-six minutes. Anderson won the final decisive set by 26 games to 24, and with it a place in the Wimbledon final.

Little did Isner know during this gruelling final set that his fate was sealed – statistically speaking – at the end of the first set, many hours previously. Anderson had won that set narrowly, in a tie-break – 8 points to 6. It turns out, according to research at Queensland University of Technology, that a very narrow victory in the first set makes it much more likely that a player will win the whole match.

The 'hot hand effect' is a basketball phrase meaning that one successful shot will lead to another, and so on, into a winning streak. Success, in other words, breeds success. Long dismissed as a sporting myth, research now confirms that hands can indeed be hot – not only in basketball, but also in other sports, such as tennis. In tennis, a wafer-thin first-set victory is most likely to happen between players of similar ability. So, victory in that set is crucial, because it elevates the chances of winning the whole match, and does so in part by boosting confidence.

Something very similar happens in professional golf, Uppsala University researchers showed in 2015. In their experiment, half-way through a tournament, players of almost identical skill were divided into successes and failures in a process known as the 'cut'. Players who scraped through and made the cut, versus those who missed it by a hair's breadth, went on to improve their performance in subsequent tournaments a great deal more. The greater the prize money in these competitions, the bigger was this winner – or hot hand – effect.

It is not just in professional sports that we see this phenomenon playing out, however. Let's say a child turns ten on 1 October, and the football team's admission rules state that the age on 30 September determines entry into a given age-stratified team. That child will be the oldest among a team of ten-year-olds, having turned eleven one day after entry. Such children are more likely to end up in national and professional football teams in the future. Their older age leads to more success experiences, and also to being spotted as 'talented' because of their physical advantages over younger team-mates. Similar effects have been seen in professional hockey.

Let's suppose that confidence isn't just the hot hand effect – the success-breeds-success and failure-breeds-failure engine that shapes our lives. If success is the fuel that helps us achieve more in life, could confidence be like an additive that tunes us into higher performance – in the same way that certain grades of petrol enhance engine performance? To answer this question, I discovered that an economist, Antonio Filippin, at the University of Milan, had researched what children think about their abilities in school and what the long-term consequences of these self-assessments are.

Schools across the world grade their children. Gradually, this feedback about their academic progress forms in their heads, giving them some idea of where they stand academically compared to their classmates. This feedback is gentle in most school systems, and variable – 'noisy' data, a statistician would say. So there is wiggle room for children to settle on their idea of their abilities, which needn't conform precisely to the grades on their teachers' desks.

Despite this mental room for manoeuvre, the economist supposed that, as the assignment and test results came in over time, this external feedback would gradually mould the children's self-assessment. Eventually, their views would converge more closely on their 'true' measured academic level. But when Filippin looked at the data, he was surprised to find that that wasn't actually what happened.

He discovered that if a child slightly overestimates her ability in the earliest years of school – in other words, she's a little more confident in her abilities than her grades would indicate – then a remarkable cascade of events happens during the course of her school years, and beyond. This more confident child – indeed, slightly overconfident compared to her actual class performance – will go on to make certain choices. For example, she may choose to work harder and to apply for more demanding courses, and that in turn will help to build her – to use Filippin's stark economist's terms – human capital of academic achievement, knowledge, and skills.

On the other hand, the child who slightly underestimates his ability will show the reverse effect. He will put in less effort and make less demanding choices, and so will steadily fall behind the more confident child. Self-belief is a multiplier that mushrooms performance over time. Look at it in terms of simple and compound interest. Confidence is a super-additive that multiplies cumulatively like compound interest over a lifetime.

Filippin's models of confidence showed that two six-year-olds of identical 'innate' ability, but with different confidence levels, will grow further and further apart in their achievements over time. Decades later, despite similar initial underlying abilities, this gap will end up as a chasm.

What is the source of this difference in confidence between two equally able six-year-olds, Filippin wondered? It turned out that social class is by far the most significant factor. Children who are born into families higher up the socioeconomic ladder have greater confidence in their abilities than the less privileged, no matter their underlying abilities.

But, as we will see, confidence is not fixed. It can be learned, even in the face of confidence-sapping external factors such as socioeconomic disadvantage.

Here is one of life's big hot hand effects – maybe even the greatest. Unlike in the Isner–Anderson tennis match, the main driver of Filippin's hot hand effect is not hormonally pumped aggression, but beliefs and expectations. What are these confidence-building thoughts? A six-year-old might not put it in this way, but I would suggest they can be consolidated into our old friends: *Can do. Can happen.*

Confidence is the belief that you can do something, and that if you do it, something good can happen. Money, status and power – all to be found in more plentiful supply the further up the social scale you go – increase your confidence. As we have just seen, these act like compound interest on further success. Filippin's phenomenon is outlined in the Bible, in the so-called Matthew effect: 'For whosoever hath, to him shall be given' (Matthew 13:12).

But your socioeconomic status can give you something else that is just as important – happiness. Happier people tend to be more self-confident. Stanford University research from 1985 showed that artificially lifting someone's mood will boost their self-confidence. While another group of researchers at the University of Iowa showed that it also makes people more confident in the decisions they make – even risky ones.

All this makes life seem very unfair. Being wealthier and more successful not only makes you more confident, but also happier. Together, these two mental states boost your chances of success and multiply in a virtuous cycle.

But the social class–happiness–confidence link might not be as absolute as it seems at first glance.

Happy Latins and dancing bears

Poor people live unhappier, unhealthier and shorter lives than their wealthier compatriots, and so do the inhabitants of poor countries as compared to those of richer ones. Except, that is, in Latin America. There, most states defy the statisticians' correlations. Their citizens stay happier than they should be, considering their wealth, the levels of corruption in their countries and the violence on their streets. Severely challenged in all three of these areas, the citizens of Brazil, for example, nevertheless manage to come close to the UK's happiness levels, while Mexico's happiness level is just above that of the US.

Why should this be? A crucial factor seems to be family and human relationships.

On average, adult Latin Americans live with their parents much more commonly (39 per cent in Mexico; 10 per cent in the US). They have family members to help with childcare (80 per cent Mexico; 46 per cent US) and, in the survey, had visited an uncle or aunt at least twice in the previous four weeks (23 per cent Brazil; 4 per cent Australia). They had also met cousins at least twice in the previous four weeks (29 per cent Brazil; 9 per cent UK) and visited nieces or nephews roughly twice as often (50 per cent Brazil; 14 per cent Finland). They also met their best friend daily, or at least several times a week (65 per cent Brazil; 18 per cent Denmark).

So, is the secret to happiness merely strong human relationships and family bonds? Do these connections protect us against the effects of harsh external realities such as poverty, crime and corruption?

Maybe – but there is more to it than that.

A quite different pattern to that in Latin America is to be seen in the former communist countries of Eastern Europe. These citizens are *less* happy on average than they should be, given their objective circumstances. For example, during the 2000s, between 80 and 95 per cent of Western European citizens declared themselves to be happy and satisfied with their lives. However, in most of the former communist countries of Eastern Europe, only a minority of people felt this (for example, 38 per cent in Bulgaria and 43 per cent in Serbia). One Polish writer, Witold Szabłowski, has tried to explain this phenomenon with a story about Bulgarian bears.

On 14 June 2007, Misho, the last dancing bear in Bulgaria, was coaxed into a cage by the five-year-old grandson of its owner, Dimitar Stanev. The six-foot bear slowly snuffled his way in, head swaying from side to side in confusion and dull alarm, and lay down to be stroked and murmured to by the boy. The gate clicked shut behind them, and the onlookers hissed at the boy to exit via the unlatched gate opposite. The boy refused and lay with the beast in feral communion. Finally, he capitulated to the tremulous, panicked entreaties from his family. He eased himself through the gate, which slammed safely shut after him.

A medieval tradition of teaching bears to dance had ended in this far corner of the European Union. Misho joined other liberated bears in the Dancing Bears Park, south of the Bulgarian capital Sofia. There, they foraged for their food, hibernated and rediscovered old instincts. But then, to the dismay of their liberators, long after the bears had entered their relative freedom, they started to dance again. In response to a human voice or a particular scent of perfume, the trained behaviour would re-emerge.

Szabłowski links these events with the response of his fellow Eastern Europeans to their freedom from authoritarian communism after the fall of the Berlin Wall in 1989. In his 2018 book, *Dancing Bears: True stories of people nostalgic for life under tyranny*, he compares the re-emergent dancing of the bears to the nostalgia for tyranny in the minds of many former Soviet Bloc citizens, and connects it to the triumph of authoritarian leaders in Poland, Hungary, Russia and elsewhere.

If your freedom of choice has been restricted throughout your life by an excessively controlling state, then there is a predictability to life that can be comforting and reassuring, even if it doesn't make you happy. Without the experience of exercising choice, suddenly having 'freedom' can be exceptionally anxiety-provoking, particularly for those less equipped by education and confidence to take advantage of that liberty. Szabłowski's nostalgia for tyranny may be driven in part by a desire for predictability that assuages anxiety in those with little experience and skills in exercising choice. Alleviating anxiety has intensely rewarding effects in the brain and so boosts the emotional appeal of authoritarian leaders to large numbers of people.

What could be behind these two outliers – happy Latins and gloomy Eastern Europeans – who refuse the typically robust relationship between wealth and happiness? And, more importantly, can this tell us anything about confidence?

The happy brain

Take out your phone and open the photos app. Scroll to a photograph of someone close to you who warms your heart. Gaze at that photo for a few moments and let the lovely memories, feelings and thoughts about that person flow through your mind. Notice how you feel; be aware of that glow of pleasure. That sensation arises deep in your brain in a network of areas around a part called the ventral striatum. The well-known neurotransmitter dopamine is the essential 'fuel' in this emotional circuit. Its release is both a cause and an effect of the pleasure you feel while looking at that photograph.

We only have one such 'feel-good' centre in the brain, but the bustle of our lives revolves around it. Its up-and-down fluctuations depend on what we do, think and aspire to. Could these fluctuations in the activity of this feel-good network merely be the transient marker of momentary pleasure rather than having any link to our longer-term happiness and wellbeing? No, the greater your wellbeing and happiness, the higher the level of dopamine activity in this circuit. This is true not just for minutes or hours, but for days, months and years.

This pleasure-related brain activity is a natural anti-depressant and, as you might expect, depressed people have much lower levels of it. Equally importantly, dopamine-driven pleasurable activity dramatically reduces the amount of the stress hormone cortisol that your body makes. And, as we saw earlier, happiness breeds confidence, and vice versa.

This isn't surprising, since both of these psychological states have a common basis in the brain's reward network. The effect cocaine has on people is perhaps the most prominent and extreme example of this happiness–confidence symbiosis – both surge (temporarily) when you take the drug. But even without cocaine, neurologists can create similar psychological states by electrically stimulating the reward network. Great national sporting victories also have a similar effect on the mood and self-confidence of millions of people. This is because – as researchers from the University of Utah showed during the 1994 World Cup Final between Italy and Brazil – they boost dopamine levels in the brains of supporters via increases in the hormone testosterone.

Confidence and happiness are interlinked, mutually reinforcing each other via the brain's dopamine reward system. Happy, confident people perform better in many areas, as well as being more motivated and resilient. They are also less stressed because of lower levels of cortisol. Conversely, people with low confidence and lower levels of happiness have higher cortisol levels. While cortisol is excellent as a short-term emergency fuel to get through a crisis – it helps to regulate a body's response to stress – when it circulates at high levels for long periods, it can do a lot of damage.

Is this one important reason (among many others, such as diet and exposure to pollution) why individuals higher up the socioeconomic ladder are less sick and live longer than those lower down? Do we know that the brains of people lower down the socioeconomic scale show any less activity in these pleasure circuits? And where do the happiness levels we see in Latin Americans, but not in the citizens of the former communist countries of Eastern Europe, fit in?

New York, like most of the world's cosmopolitan cities, is a place where the rich and poor rub shoulders. This is particularly true on the Upper West Side, where Columbia University's Department of Psychiatry sits, deep in Harlem's disorienting mix of poverty and gentrification, on West 165th Street. There, in 2010, Professor of Psychiatry Diana Martinez and her colleagues slid volunteers from different socioeconomic backgrounds into their gleaming PET (positron emission tomography) brain scanner to try to find out whether the brain's pleasure centres do mirror economic reality. Are the global surveys about the relationship between happiness and wealth accurate? Martinez wanted to know.

She found clear evidence that the higher a person's social status, the more molecular receiving stations for dopamine there were in the brain's pleasure centre.

Martinez further asked her volunteers about how much social support they could expect from family, friends and the community. As we have seen, Latin Americans' strong family relations and friendships seem to offer a healthy buffer against the mentally depressing effects of low income. This was also reflected in the New Yorkers' brains. Social support had a similar boosting effect on dopamine receptor levels to that delivered by socioeconomic status.

We know that confidence and happiness are interlinked in the brain, and both reduce anxiety. Very socially anxious people who receive cognitive behavioural therapy for their problems show steady increases in brain dopamine activity. This goes up as their anxiety declines and as they become more confident in social situations.

What, if anything, can we do about the fact that confidence leads to privilege, then further confidence and so on? Is our status at birth, with its effects on our happiness and confidence, simply a fact of life? Thinking again about the Bulgarian bears, might there be something more fundamental going on behind the happiness–confidence research that might help to answer this question?

Our greatest need

On 9 November 1989, a man hunched into a thick grey greatcoat, with a pistol at his hip and a peaked cap pulled low over his eyes. He squared up to a chanting, swaying crowd of his fellow citizens. This man was Harald Jäger, and the forty-six-year-old border guard just wanted his night shift at Berlin's Bornholmer Strasse border crossing to finish quickly. He was in charge of thirty guards and three border crossings, but his world was beginning to go a little crazy. It had started at around 7 that evening, just as he and his men were pulling on their lumpy coats and checking their guns.

An East German government official by the name of Günter Schabowski appeared on the grainy TV screen in the guardroom. He announced – in an expressionless tone of tedium typical of East German broadcasting – new travel rules for its citizens. Harald's eyes were fixed on the screen. He could hardly believe what he was hearing. Schabowski, almost offhandedly at the end of his speech, announced the immediate opening of the East German border. Harald was stunned, and the world warped suddenly before his eyes into a torsion of confusion. 'Then things happened, that I would have never imagined even in my worst dreams,' he told a Deutsche Press-Agentur reporter.

At first, there was just a handful of East German citizens at his crossing point, but more and more arrived by the minute. The numbers grew swiftly from hundreds to thousands. 'They chanted, "Open the gate!"' Harald said.

'We stood just an arm's length away from the masses, who were separated from us by just a closed crossing gate,' he told the reporter, saying that mass panic was what he feared most. He was aware that he and his colleagues no longer had the situation under control. He kept trying to phone his superiors for orders. 'But higher up, chaos reigned just as it did for us.'

Around 9.40 p.m., he finally got his order – he and his men were to let exceptionally provocative citizens through the gates, but were not to let them back in again. This attempt to relieve the pressure failed.

Harald recounted to the DPA reporter that at 11.20 p.m., 'I then ordered the crossing gate to be opened and to allow everyone to leave without inspecting their papers.' That night around twenty-five thousand people flooded through the wall into West Berlin.

'In the first moment, something was really empty inside me. I didn't understand the world any more,' he told his interviewer on the twentieth anniversary of these events.

No wonder Harald didn't understand the world any more. When, on 7 October 1949, the German Democratic Republic was founded, Harald was six years old. He had just started school under the newly established education policy of the GDR. In Harald's first class there were meetings several times a day called class collect-ives. There, the teacher would publicly tell the children how well or badly they had performed in their school work. This was tough, because the new communist regime strictly controlled the content and pace of teaching in a fixed curriculum. It meant that children who were slower to learn than others would receive progressively more negative public assessments of their performance.

Some GDR schools also had meetings called learning conferences. There, pupils had to stand up and evaluate themselves in front of the whole class. The less able were compelled to confess their poor performance and explain how they were going to improve.

For Harald and the other children, this relentless scrutiny didn't end at the school gate. They weren't just forced to confess their academic sins in front of their classmates and listen while their teacher publicly assessed them. They also had to sit through similar events at parent–teacher meetings, in after-school youth organizations, and even in their parents' workplaces. Parents had to 'confess' before their colleagues why their child was doing worse than their peers.

The educational aim was to mould 'harmoniously developed socialistic personalities'. At the core of this was training children to accurately self-assess – continually and publicly. In reality, this meant conforming to their teacher's assessments. In other words, drilled into Harald's brain was an externally imposed and supposedly objective assessment of his character and his abilities. This left little room for any dreamy self-enhancement or 'unrealistic' ambition – the kind of mental leeway crucial for confidence to do its work as a fuel additive. The communist regime, by extinguishing the mental wiggle-room that confidence requires, doomed generations of its citizens to unhappier and less fulfilled lives than those of other countries.

Not all children mentally succumbed to this regime, however. A researcher called Matthias Jerusalem showed this just weeks after the Berlin Wall fell in November 1989. His team located 124 eighteen- to thirty-year-old men and women who had just made the crossing from East to West, and then watched how they progressed over the next two years in their attempts to set up new lives.

Unsurprisingly, many found it hard to adjust to the West, as might be expected in light of the dancing-bear discussion. But some fared better than others, and the researchers wanted to find out why. As these individuals looked for jobs and apartments, it became clear that those who had partners fared better. They felt healthier and were less anxious. They also held a more optimistic outlook and were more likely to see their new life as a challenge, not a threat. And, just as unsurprisingly, those who found jobs were doing much better in these respects, too. But there was one other factor – independent of work and relationships – that hugely shaped these people's health, anxiety and sense of optimism: a feeling of control.

The young men and women who had managed – perhaps because of their family background or some other reasons – to avoid the overwhelming mental control that their upbringing under a Stalinist regime had imposed on them were noticeably healthier and happier than those who had not. This applied whether or not they were in a relationship or had a job. Feeling in control of their own lives translated into an empowering sense of *can do* confidence. For example, they were more likely to agree with statements such as *No matter what comes my way, I am usually able to handle it*, or *I remain calm when facing difficulties because I can rely on my coping abilities*.

Such confidence made people healthier and happier in every situation over the two years of the study. There was one exception, though. If, by 1991, they had found a job and a partner, then those factors alone made them happier and healthier. In other words, if life was going well, they didn't have to call on confidence to see them through the harder times.

A sense of control – this fatalism-destroying confidence that can influence your destiny – can be a psychological buffer against all sorts of external pressures. Could this explain the happiness gap between the Eastern Europeans – who had too little of the antidote – and the people of Latin America? Did they have a sense of control stemming from the fact that they felt part of a tightly knit, integrated family and community network?

There is abundant research showing that a sense of control buffers people against the stresses of life.

In 1999, Margie Lachman and Suzanne Weaver at Brandeis University in Massachusetts sifted through the data from a longitudinal study of almost six thousand people in their forties whose health and happiness had been measured over earlier years. Like many others before, Lachman and Weaver found that socioeconomic status, health and happiness were all tightly linked. The further down the social scale a person went, the more likely they were to be depressed, have low life satisfaction, and be in poor health. Yet this applied only to some. There was one group of low-income individuals who were just as happy and satisfied with their lives, and who rated themselves as being as healthy as the richest group. These individuals were the ones who rejected statements such as *I have little control over the things that happen to me.* A sense of control could indeed break the malign grip that poverty can have on mental wellbeing.

Feeling in control means that you believe you can act and that there will be consequences of that action. That is confidence.

The Eastern European happiness gap becomes more understandable in this context. In the absence of a feeling of control and the confidence this inspires, a person feels defenceless against the vagaries of economics, politics, corruption and social forces. Relatively few modern states have tried to eliminate the sense of individual control that is so crucial to human happiness and confidence in the way that the communist regimes of Eastern Europe did. This policy left tens of millions of people mentally naked in the face of stress, economic change and unpredictability in the world. Bereft of the crucial antidote of control, their happiness and confidence were stillborn.

So, for children who are born into less fortunate circumstances, there is at least one escape route from the meat-grinder of economic fate. Those who feel as if they have some control over their abilities and/or environment can use this additive to do better in school, and it is irrespective of family background, parental expectations or social history. Separate reviews of scores of international studies have shown that early education programmes are particularly useful at staving off some of the effects of economic disadvantage far into adulthood. Increased confidence is one element of what such programmes provide.

The need for control is one of our most basic drives. If you offer an animal an equal reward for doing one of two different things, they will choose the action where there is a degree of choice, even if the payback is the same. Having choice feels particularly good for humans. Researchers from the University of Leeds showed that people would go for 'choose to choose' over no-choice situations in opting for which nightclub to go to or which bank to select. They preferred to exercise choice (and therefore some form of control) even when that had no influence over the quality of the product or experience. The desire to make choices, and so to feel in control of our lives, is hard-wired into our brains. That is why exercising control switches on the same dopamine-linked reward network as happiness does.

Confidence harnesses a deeply ingrained need for control. It does so because it makes you believe that you can do something that has an effect on the world. That is the essence of control. This is not just a feature of wealth or specific cultures. It applies across the globe, as shown by the World Values Survey, which is given to thousands of people in more than a hundred countries every year.

One question from this survey is this: *Are you satisfied or dissatisfied with your freedom to choose what you do with your life?*

Across the world, if you answer *satisfied* to this question, you will, on average, have higher levels of positive emotions and lower levels of negative emotions. As we saw in Chapter 3, feeling that you have control is a crucial ingredient in confidence. So it isn't surprising that control–confidence–happiness mutually reinforce one another.

This triumvirate of psychological states also leads to economic growth. Happy, confident people who feel they have control over their lives take more investment risks, University of Illinois investigators discovered, and your happiness predicts your personal wealth independently of your socioeconomic status.

Across the globe, the confident feeling of having some control over your life predicts your life satisfaction better than your health, work, wealth, marital status or religion. This is true both within and between countries. Escaping from disadvantage and improving your life chances needs both spans of the confidence bridge, the *can do* and the *can happen*. Once in place, such confidence strongly predicts how well individuals – and, as we will see later in the book, whole economies – will perform.

Simply believing you have control won't, of course, automatically change your circumstances, but it can change your longer-term outlook. Latin Americans can't change crime levels or economic inequality just because they feel a sense of control. However, having a sense of control within their community has a positive effect on their happiness and, hence, confidence.

If it follows that feeling in control makes me happier, how do I know if I am happy or not?

The unhappy silver medallist

It turns out that my subjective sense of how rich or poor I am is as important in predicting my happiness and longevity independently of how objectively wealthy or poor I am. Something similar applies to my subjective versus objective physical health.

A 2020 study from Duke University and King's College London of over two thousand pairs of British twins confirmed this. The twins came from a range of backgrounds, from the richest to the most deprived areas of the UK. At the age of eighteen, their involvement in work, education, drugs and crime as well as their depression, anxiety and optimism were all assessed. The twins, from the poorest to the richest, were then asked to place themselves on a social status 'ladder' relative to other people in the country.

Remarkably, among adult twins, those whose perception of their social status was lower than that of their twin suffered worse on all these indices, from crime to education to mental health. This was true even with the objective levels of socioeconomic status, intelligence and other variables equalized. And significantly, this wasn't true when the twins were aged twelve, so it couldn't be the case that there were some pre-existing differences between the twins.

Rather, something happened during adolescence that made some of the twins *feel* that they had lower social status than their sibling. Once they felt that, their behaviour, mental health, education, job and optimism suffered accordingly.

Could Olympic-medal winners' reactions to victory help us to understand this powerful effect of perception on health and well-being? Research shows that silver-medal winners are on average less happy with their achievement than gold-medal winners. This would be an unsurprising finding, except that they are also less happy than the bronze-medal competitors they beat.

This happens because your happiness depends upon who you compare yourself with. Silver medallists tend to 'dream upwards' – *A little faster and it could have been a gold*. Bronze medallists are more likely to 'dream downwards' and sigh with relief – *Phew, I scraped a medal, I could so easily have had no place*. And so it goes with deciding how rich or poor – or, indeed, how happy – I am. To all intents and purposes it is up for grabs, depending on who I choose to compare myself with.

We can see the effects of such social comparisons in the MRI scanner. Klaus Fliessbach and a team from the University of Bonn showed how the brain's reward network is involved. Our reward system is switched on not only by our own rewards but, crucially, even more so by what other people are getting. In Fliessbach's study, pairs of volunteers lay in adjacent fMRI scanners, playing a simple game, making quick decisions about the number of dots on a screen – and, importantly, they were paid for correct answers.

Winning boosted the level of activation in a critical part of the reward network – the ventral striatum. But what happened if, on some rounds, your partner received more reward than you did for the same correct answer? After all, you still got a reward, so shouldn't the ventral striatum be active? It is, but much less so than before because, in comparison with the other person, you won less. Your sense of whether you feel rich or poor, thriving or struggling, is similarly based upon who you compare yourself with.

So far, then, we've discovered that confidence arises from success, higher socioeconomic status and happiness. Having a sense of control and feeling advantaged in comparison to others also have important effects on how these big variables play out in our lives. But there are yet more factors at play in shaping confidence.

CHAPTER 5

Failing Confidently

: :

E ARLY ON 27 November 2009, an SUV accelerated away from the driveway of a Florida house. Swerving on to a neighbour's lawn, it collided with a tree before careering to a metal-grinding halt against a fire hydrant. Police officers arriving at the scene found the driver lying unconscious on the street.

On 17 August 2017, police found the same man – unconscious again – in the driving seat of his erratically parked and badly scraped Mercedes-Benz. Blood tests revealed five different drugs in his system, including THC (a key component of marijuana), two sleeping medicines and two heavy painkillers. The police mugshot showed a heavy-lidded, unshaven man with bloodshot eyes staring blankly into the camera. He pleaded guilty to reckless driving.

At the time of his first accident, Tiger Woods was the most successful golfer of all time, having been ranked first in the world for eleven out of twelve years between 1998 and 2009. However, both his personal life and his career went into a tailspin after that accident. Divorced by his wife on grounds of serial infidelity, he plummeted from first in the golf world in 2009 to 1,199th in 2017.

Multiple surgeries for back problems left him in chronic pain and, at times, so disabled that he was barely able to play with his young children.

Then, on 14 April 2019, something remarkable happened: a white ball dropped with a soft plop into an Atlanta eighteenth hole, winning Tiger Woods the 2019 Masters Championship. His rise to fifth in the world was, for him, a remarkable rebirth after nine years of sporting and personal failure. How did he do it? On what inner resources did he draw to reach the summit of his sport again?

According to some 2017 research from Bangor University, super-elite performers, as compared to merely elite athletes, have experienced an early sporting victory, a 'foundational' success experience that fuelled their self-belief at a young age. Tiger Woods was fifteen when he became the youngest ever winner of the US Junior Amateur Golf Championship. There is, however, a second ingredient that distinguishes super-elite from elite sportspeople. All the super-elites also had something bad happen to them in their early lives. For example, their parents divorced acrimoniously, there were other serious relationship problems at home, or they were bullied and lonely. However, these negative experiences were followed by a subsequent 'career-turning' event that focused their minds on their sport and motivated them. Examples of such events are being selected for a prestigious squad or inspired by meeting an Olympic medallist.

In the depths of Tiger Woods's lowest period in 2015, the parents of a sixteen-year-old boy with a severe stutter, who had attempted suicide because of bullying and isolation, contacted the golfer. Woods wrote a letter to the boy revealing for the first time that he, too, had endured the loneliness and bullying that come from having a stutter. That is, he, too, had suffered from a profoundly negative experience at a young age.

Why are tough early life experiences so common in super-athletes, and how does that seem to help them?

'I wish someone had told me it's OK to be anxious'

These were the words of writer and child actress Mara Elizabeth Wilson when talking about the anxiety she felt as a child and as a teenager. This highly successful young woman, who played roles such as Matilda Wormwood in *Matilda* and Natalie Hillard in the award-winning *Mrs Doubtfire*, was prone to that most twenty-first-century of ailments – anxiety. This problem mushroomed after she finished filming *Matilda* at the age of nine in 1996, when she lost her mother to cancer. Plagued with anxiety and other problems for years afterwards, she wishes that someone had told her that it was 'OK to be anxious'.

But what does she mean by that? What would it signify if Mara and the millions of other people who suffer from anxiety felt that it was 'OK to be anxious'? Why would that help? Believing this implies a few things. First, it suggests that feeling that way isn't dangerous – nothing terrible will happen because of it. Second, it means that the anxiety isn't permanent – it won't last for ever. And third, it detaches you from the fear, helping you to see it as something external and temporary, like a passing virus.

Super-elite sport is a high-wire act of failure, self-doubt and injury, as well as of heady success and acclaim. Top performers like Tiger Woods play for high stakes, and this inevitably entails great ups and downs of emotion. But super-elite performers who have put tough early life experiences behind them have already endured the downside of these emotions. They have already learned that, while they are painful and unpleasant, they are also temporary, controllable, and not central to who they are.

What Mara Wilson was talking about is fear of fear. She was suggesting that if you eliminate it, what remains is something that, while being unpleasant and uncomfortable, can be contained.

Being bullied as a child would make most people feel anxious and miserable. But suppose that something positive happens to you, like someone you admire praises you, or you win a competition? Such experiences release a chemical messenger in our brains. This is the mood-enhancing, anxiety-depleting, motivation-boosting natural pharmaceutical – dopamine. Woods's success on the golf course would have moderated his misery at school. In the process, he would have learned three things.

Anxiety was only a small part of who he was; otherwise, he would still be nervous on the golf course, which he wasn't. Anxiety passes. Anxiety is controllable by action.

In Mara Wilson's case, by simply naming it, she had netted her anxiety like a fish. This creature wasn't part of who she was. Instead, it was something outside of her that was defined and changeable, and therefore less scary. And so, yes, success builds confidence, but that success becomes supercharged if you have been through tough times of anxiety and depression. Succeeding pushes the happiness button in your head, expelling fear and lifting mood. It also helps you to learn the three critical lessons about negative emotions, just as Tiger Woods had.

Stanford University researcher Albert Bandura viewed the sort of experience Tiger Woods had as one of the most potent sources of personal confidence. The feeling of having got through – mastered – painful or difficult experiences swells self-belief like little else.

Until she was ten, Venus Williams lived in Compton – a poor, gang-ridden city south of Los Angeles. According to a 2012 article and interview with Williams in the *New York Times Magazine*, she and her sister Serena knew to lie down on the public tennis court when they heard gunshots in the neighbourhood. Serena remembers practising as a seven-year-old when white children, unused to seeing non-whites playing tennis, came up to her and her sister, and chanted 'blacky' at them. In 2003, Venus and Serena's oldest half-sister, who was also their personal assistant, was murdered in Compton.

Venus, then, fits the pattern of a confidence forged in the kiln of adversity. But there is a further factor – her father. He had a remarkable faith in the sisters' future tennis greatness. 'First you had the belief, and then you had the training,' Venus told the *New York Times Magazine* interviewer, and that belief came from her father, Richard Williams.

His unwavering confidence in them and his single-minded dedication and coaching must have embedded itself in Venus and Serena's minds to such a degree that it felt like an inner conviction.

Research shows that children who have a robust and secure attachment to one or both parents end up more self-confident, particularly in their relations with other people. Capable parents kindle confidence so that their children feel embraced by it, not excluded from it. However, some successful parents either consciously or unconsciously seek admiration for their own accomplishments. They may exude a narcissistic air of 'specialness' that makes their children feel they could never match their achievement. This perception, by contrast, is very damaging to a child's self-confidence.

Such adverse effects can happen even when there is a warm relationship between parent and child. A parental focus on ranking, rather than on individual progress against past achievements, risks sapping a child's self-confidence. Always looking over one's shoulder at how others are doing is a recipe for breeding fear of failure in a child. And, as we will see, fear of failure is a significant obstacle to developing self-confidence.

Parents and mentors – as well as friends, siblings, colleagues or bosses – can also try to build confidence in a person by persuasion. *Go on. You can do it!* Depending on the relationship, that can prompt a child to try something that she wouldn't otherwise have done. Woody Allen's quip that 80 per cent of success is showing up is often true, because merely doing stuff can give a person a sense of accomplishment that feels like success.

If taking action is key to confidence-building, then it isn't surprising that people prone to anxiety tend to be less self-confident. Avoidance deprives them of the confidence-building effects of small daily successes, which have natural anti-anxiety and anti-depressant effects on the brain.

Anxiety is something we feel in our gut that influences the decisions we make. *Will I? Won't I?* It feels so acute and compelling that it can often override rational thoughts such as *There's no reason why I can't do this*. It also often trumps exhortations from family, friends or colleagues – *Come on, you know you can do it*. You may know rationally that you can do it. But if your stomach is churning, your heart is pounding and your skin is damp with fear, these powerful feelings often win out. They persuade you that danger and failure await any step into this particular unknown.

Our guts, then, are potent dictators of confidence. But can we trust them?

Trusting my gut

In 1998 I decided to leave my tenured research-only post at Cambridge University for another at Trinity College Dublin. I did so on a gut feeling that it was the right move. And so, over two decades later, it has proved to be. When I compare how I made this big decision to how I decide on the small stuff, such as where to go on holiday or what sort of computer to buy, it couldn't be more different. These sorts of choices incline me to an extended, agonized weighing up of costs and benefits, in stark contrast to a feeling of settled confidence about the big decisions that seems to arise from somewhere deep in my gut.

So, does confidence come from the belly? In a way, it does.

When you choose to do one thing over another, it isn't just your rational brain that registers whether you made a right choice. You also have an emotional response to what happened – pleasurable if it was correct and painful if it wasn't. Anxiety can register as a tightness and twisting in the stomach. Muscles tense, particularly in the neck and shoulders, and your breath comes faster.

Your brain keeps a running tally of the outcomes from decisions you've made in the past. But it doesn't just store them like a dispassionate audit of good and bad calls, in a purely cognitive way. It also stores up memories of the physical sensations associated with different types of decision. It does this in a part of the brain just above and behind the eyes, called the ventromedial prefrontal cortex. These memories then orchestrate the drawing of a map of internal feelings in another part of the brain called the insular cortex, which dictates the pattern of bodily sensations you experience from moment to moment.

I remember being a fresh-faced graduate student at my first international conference, agonizing over whether to put a question to an eminent speaker. I still remember the will-I-won't-I anxiety about whether to stand up in front of hundreds of people and risk making a fool of myself. Finally, I took the plunge and asked a question which, though not unveiling me as an undiscovered genius, was at least answered thoughtfully by the speaker.

I remember a sense of relief and nervy satisfaction flooded through my muscles, lungs and belly as I sat back down. These feelings soon passed, of course, and I forgot all about the anguished decision-making process and its outcome. Soon afterwards, however, there was another conference at which I wanted to ask a question. This time I didn't feel quite as tortured as I steeled myself to grasp the microphone and again risk exposing my ignorance. The process was easier because my brain had stored the emotional outcome of the last occasion, which was positive. So, as I wrestled with the will-I-won't-I decision, the emotions linked to

the previous outcome replayed like a musical riff of physical sensations that, for me, was a positive – if a little nervy – gut feeling.
And that's where my confidence to ask the second question came
from.

With every new conference, the gut-feeling memory for speaking out in public became stronger. It continued until there no
longer seemed to be a decision to make if I wanted to make a point
or ask a question. Whenever it occurred to me to speak out, my
brain would replay the bodily melody that was the central theme
running through my confidence. I had learned to feel confident in
this situation.

Gut feelings can also push confidence the other way, of course.
Had I garbled my question or felt humiliated by the response, my
brain would have played an unharmonious melody of sensations,
which would have created a gut feeling of *No, you can't do this*. If
this were to happen a few times, then a no-go decision, with all its
confidence-sapping effects, would have become my default option.

Deciding to leave Cambridge must have been easy for me
because my brain replayed in my body the theme tunes of big decisions I had made in the past. And because I have been quite lucky
in life, in the main, these tunes have been relatively melodic, and
so have made me confident to follow them. But I know full well
that it could have been very different if I hadn't been so lucky. My
gut could have learned to tell me to play safe and not risk change,
and the more I did that, the more this negative gut feeling would
have dominated my decisions in life.

Is this, in effect, a circling back to the hot hand effect? There,
successful decision breeds successful decision, with confidence
simply being a cumulative read-out of life's lucky breaks. But it
isn't as simple as that. This is because, as we saw with the super-
elite athletes, tough experiences in life reinforce success. As Mara
Wilson ruefully reflected, how we think about the bodily sensations we call anxiety can also shape our confidence.

Talking to my gut

One Saturday afternoon a few months ago, I was sitting at home, my stomach in a knot. My breathing was fast and shallow, and my palms were sweaty. I was so racked with tension that I could hardly keep still because of a nagging restlessness. What was making me so anxious? Ireland's rugby team had just beaten the New Zealand All Blacks 16 points to 9 in Dublin's Aviva Stadium for only the second time in a century. I wasn't anxious at all. I was excited.

So, here is the puzzle. My symptoms of excitement were identical to those of a different emotion – anxiety. With the same physical sensations for two such opposite emotions, how do I know which one I am feeling? It is a more difficult question to answer than it sounds, because we only know from its context. In this case, I knew I was excited because I was watching a match, and my team was winning. But if I had been on a plane that suddenly lurched in mid-air, I would have experienced the same bodily symptoms, but as anxiety.

Listen to Tiger Woods again: 'I've always said the day I'm not nervous playing is the day I quit.' Woods says he needs to feel nervous – a mix of anxiety and anticipation – to play well, and there is a good scientific reason for this. When you feel nervous, your body prepares for action by making your heart pump more blood to your muscles. It coats your skin in sweat, quickens your breathing and de-prioritizes digestion, causing your stomach to churn. The brain produces more of a chemical messenger called noradrenaline, which, in the right doses, synchronizes your brain functions to make it perform better. Too much of this chemical spoils this synchronization, as does too little, so there's a sweet spot where you hit a zone of peak performance.

Tiger Woods needed to be in that zone to play his best but, more importantly, he interpreted these feelings positively – as an energizer of his performance, not an obstacle.

If my gut tells me how confident I am, does this mean that it can mislead me and sabotage my confidence? The answer is yes. But we don't just have to sit back and listen to our gut. We can talk to it and transform one emotion – anxiety – into another – excitement – by reframing how we think about it. This is exactly what Tiger Woods was talking about. He interpreted his gut feeling, his nerves, as excitement – that is, a positive, energizing emotion.

The science is clear: it is possible to talk your gut into changing anxiety into excitement. In Chapter 2, people who were performing a nerve-racking mental arithmetic task in public were told to say out loud before they began either *I feel anxious* or *I feel excited*. Those who said the latter phrase not only shaped their confidence with these words and performed the arithmetic better, but they also made a Tiger-Woods-type positive interpretation of these sensations. They lowered their noradrenaline levels to nearer the sweet spot for optimal mental performance. Good performance makes us feel more confident, which inclines us to try again, and so on in a virtuous circle.

But this raises yet another question. If you can harness a gut feeling to boost your confidence, why do some people learn to do this, and others don't?

Your theory of you

Take a moment to think of a stressful situation that you may be encountering soon. Perhaps it's an awkward conversation you are due to have, or a presentation you need to give, or a job interview. Now close your eyes and try to 'feel' yourself into that situation, as if you were already there. By visualizing the details of the encounter, you will probably feel your body – and in particular, your gut – react.

What feelings do you notice? Are there sensations in your abdomen? Is your heart beating faster? Or maybe you can feel your neck muscles tensing? Hold these in your mind and then ask yourself two questions: *Is stress harmful and to be avoided wherever possible?* And then this: *Can stress be good for me by making me more productive and energized?*

If you answer no to the first question and yes to the second, then your theory of stress is like Tiger Woods's. You see it as something positive, and you will, because of this, perform and feel better. Your adrenal glands will produce more of one of the body's most import- ant naturally occurring steroids: DHEAS (dehydroepiandrosterone sulfate). This substance has several positive effects on the body and brain, including improved mood and better physiological resilience.

Thinking positively about stress is a plus. Why, then, do so many people worsen their anxiety by being frightened of it? Or, to echo Mara Wilson, why do some of us think it is OK to be anxious, and others not? Is this perhaps to do with how we have learned to think about ourselves more generally? Stanford psychologist Carol Dweck discovered that the ideas we hold about ourselves have pro- found effects on both our bodies and our minds. If we have fixed ideas about our personality, intelligence or emotional state, she argues in her book *Mindset*, then these seem unchangeable, as something we have inherited, and therefore out of our control.

Having a fixed theory about yourself can help your confidence if you have a history of success. However, it is a fragile confidence because any setbacks or failures can seem like evidence that your fixed idea is wrong. This is alarming because, by definition, you can't do anything to remedy a fixed ability – it's something outside of your control. With a growth mindset, on the other hand, failure is just part of the complex, multi-stranded nature of learning. It is not a threat to your views of your abilities, because they can be changed.

What about your personality and emotions? Consider this. Do you think that these are preset and something you have to live with, or something that can at least be changed partly – by experi- ence, learning, example or outside help? That is, do you have a fixed or a growth theory about personality and emotions?

Adolescents who have a fixed theory find it hard to cope with the sort of exclusions from social units common in their age group. Because of their fixed ideas about themselves, they take any rejection as evidence that there is something wrong with them. This draws them into a vicious circle where they are more likely to withdraw. Dweck's research group showed in 2013 that these adolescents are also less likely to make an effort to forge new friendships, and so they tend to become even more isolated and unhappy.

Research suggests that people like the young Mara Wilson are frightened by anxiety because they hold fixed theories about themselves. They see these feelings as something settled and unchangeable that they have inherited, and so feel they can't control.

Ask yourself this question: *Can I change how anxious I am?* And this: *It doesn't matter what I do, I can't help my tendency to be anxious.* If you answered no to the first and yes to the second, then you have a fixed mindset about your anxiety. People with a fixed mindset find it harder to cope with stressful life situations, such as splitting up with a partner or losing a job. Fixed beliefs such as these expose you to a repeating double whammy of having feelings in your gut and body that a) you are frightened of, and b) you don't believe you can control.

Life's stresses are hard enough without having to face down these seemingly alien, uncontrollable feelings. However, the important news is that they are controllable. People who don't cripple themselves with a fixed mindset about their anxiety cope much better with life stresses. They respond much better to psychological help if they need it than those with fixed views. After all, if you think that your anxiety is fixed and unchangeable, you are hardly likely to take your therapist's advice about how to manage it.

Where do my theories come from?

An old friend of mine had two children – a son, and a daughter, Kim, who was a year and a half younger than her brother. The brother was always top of his class in school and continued that way right through to university. My friend's daughter didn't do so well academically but progressed well in the middle rankings of a quite competitive school.

I found her parents' response to their daughter's test results strange. If Kim came home with a B or a C grade, they would sometimes comfort her, saying things like, 'Ah, never mind – it's not the worst thing in the world.' But they also compared her results with her brother's, worrying that she wasn't doing so well in school, by their standards. They even seemed to pity her, saying to friends like me, 'Poor girl, she just isn't academic like her brother.'

Kim's school performance was just fine, but against her brother's effortless supremacy, she was doomed. On each school report, her mediocrity was spelled out starkly. Despite the constant reminder that she wasn't the best student, she got into university but dropped out after a year and took a clerical job in a solicitor's office. The girl I knew was intelligent, charming and witty. I could never understand why she left university and then didn't progress very far in her career – until I began my research into the question of where confidence comes from.

In Kim's parents' eyes, every exam result, every school report was a failure, because her brother was the benchmark. Perhaps Kim also saw herself as a failure at school, which sapped her confidence and, hey presto, that's why she didn't thrive in her career? Partly. But it is a little more complicated than that. It wasn't her supposed failure itself that ended up mentally handicapping Kim. It was the mindset that it created in her: *My abilities are fixed, and therefore there's nothing I can do about them.* She took that feeling from school into the workplace. Where did this mindset come from? From her parents' response to her 'failures', which, in turn, arose from their theories about failure in general.

If you are a parent, think about your responses to the following statements. If not, think how your own parents might have answered:

You can use failure positively in your life.
Experiencing failure can help you to develop and learn.
I think experiencing failure can help me do better.
Failure hinders my ability to learn and develop.
Failure makes me much less productive.
You should try to avoid failure because of its bad effects
    on you.

If you agree with the first three statements and disagree with the last three, then you have a positive mindset about failure. Your children will more likely have a change mindset of their emotions and abilities. If you answered the other way round, then your children are more likely to have a fixed mindset, with all the potential risks to their confidence and performance that this entails, as Dweck's group showed. If you answered for your parents, think how their mindset is shaping *your* approach to life.

In Kim's case, her parents saw her middle-of-the-road grades as failures. Their fear of Kim's lack of success burned itself into her growing mind, and branded it with a fixed theory of her abilities. This spread far beyond her schoolwork into her self-confidence about relationships, her independence, and, above all, her emotions. Throughout her adolescence and young adulthood, Kim was treated for anxiety and depression by doctors who also held negative views of her apparent failure in life. Their mainly medical treatments cemented her fixed, confidence-sapping picture of herself. Fortunately for her, she eventually met a clinical psychologist who was able to coax her out of this fixed mindset to realize that change was possible.

Kim's lack of confidence stemmed in part from her parents' beliefs about failure. Our confidence depends very much on our close relationships. Ask anyone who has experienced sibling rivalry how a brother or sister can boost or sap your confidence. And, of course, our parents affect how confident we feel in several ways, including via their beliefs about failure. Later in the book we'll come back to Kim and how she learned to build up her confidence. And in the next chapter, we'll come back to the question of relationships and confidence, including those linked to gender.

Confident failure

Confidence may come from success – the hot hand effect of life – but the most robust confidence comes from mastering adversity and embracing failure. Facing up to difficulties gives a confidence-boosting sense of mastery. Feeling this strengthens a sense of control and weakens the false belief that your emotions and abilities are fixed. That's why your theory about yourself and your beliefs about failure are so crucial to whether you can benefit from the success of mastering difficulty.

After all, confidence is a belief about the future – about whether you *can do* something, and whether something positive *can happen* as a result. Self-belief might seem to come out of the blue, but often it arises in the gut. As the gut is a rather simple beast that doesn't discriminate between excitement and anxiety, it means it's possible to harness these feelings positively to give oneself the right 'gut feeling'.

Confidence is a remarkable fuel additive for life, and its crucial partner is a sense of control. If we don't feel in control, then we will feel less happy and less confident. Success also makes people more confident and happy. That includes all the various levels of success that our social class confers on us. This is mirrored in our brains, deep in the reward network. There, the primitive dopamine-linked systems that underpin happiness, confidence and control ramp up and down depending on what is happening to us in our family life, work life and, on a bigger scale, in our countries.

However, strong bonds with our family members, friends and communities, along with a sense of control, are potent antidotes to the otherwise overwhelming effects of socioeconomic fate on our happiness and confidence. Many (maybe most) of our human relationships are shaped by power and the dominance – and hence confidence – that power offers. Human hierarchies are everywhere – from families to teams to communities to corporations – and those higher up the hierarchy have more power and control, and hence more confidence.

Wherever there is a group of people, there will be a more or less subtle jostling for dominance, with all the psychological and material advantages that dominance offers. Every family has such struggles, and seldom is there an even playing field. Older siblings have an advantage over younger ones because they are usually bigger and, for a while at least, smarter. Males are privileged over females by size and strength, and because they are conferred a higher status in many cultures. Confidence is a precious resource, like gold. And, like that precious metal, people will fight for it, steal it, hoard it and envy it in others.

Nowhere is this struggle more complicated and brutal than where gender is concerned.

CHAPTER 6

The Confidence Saboteurs

: :

L OUISE, AT THIRTY-TWO, was sailing through life. She was soar-ing up the tech company promotion ladder, happy with her friends and her social life, and in love with Mark, her live-in boy-friend of seven years. He would, she was sure, be proposing very soon. Louise's company had excellent parental leave policies, as she had been careful to establish when she accepted their offer some time ago.

Then, one day, Mark told her he was leaving.

It might have been a coincidence, but his announcement came the day after she had received a further promotion, and a salary increase to match. Mark was a civil servant, and neither his pros-pects nor his pay had improved for several years. When Louise tearfully asked him to explain his decision, he didn't say it was about her career. However, intuitively, she felt it played a part.

Many – not all – men find it very hard to be with a partner who is more successful and earns more than them. Mark was neither articulate nor honest, but the same could not be said for Dave Peters, a forty-nine-year-old from Detroit interviewed for *Mel* magazine. When asked to describe his reaction to his wife's career seniority, Peters said that he wouldn't advise having your wife earn more than you, because it means she has the power and is the dominant person in the relationship.

Research backs up this view. Joanna Syrda of the University of Bath sifted through data from over six thousand US households, looking at the link between psychological distress in husbands and their incomes relative to their wives'. The men's stress levels dropped as their wives' incomes rose – science confounding the anecdotes, you might think. Except for the remarkable fact that this was true only up to a point – where the woman earned 40 per cent of the joint income. Once above 40 per cent, their partner's distress escalated with each percentage point. By the time the wife was the sole earner, the men's upset was hugely higher than when their wives were earning nothing at all.

However, there is one crumb of comfort for ambitious women in this study. These findings didn't apply to couples who had started married life with the woman earning more, and when that was clear to both parties in advance. Maybe these couples began life without being embroiled in the struggle for dominance that Dave Peters from Detroit experienced. For what seems to be at play is that many men have a deep need to be top dog in their relationship – a requirement that becomes threatened when their wives earn more than them, as we will see below. Equally, many men do *not* have such a need, we should note.

The higher-earning a woman is, the less likely she is to get married, the US National Bureau for Economic Research has shown. They identified another cliff – 50 per cent this time. Once it looks as if a woman is going to earn more than half the household income, her likelihood of getting married declines dramatically. And when she does marry, she is more likely to end up not working than other less high-earning women whose husbands earn more. When she does work, it is likely to be below her potential. Marriages in which the wife earns more than the husband are, on average, less satisfying to the couples and more likely to end in divorce. Oh, and the woman will often try to compensate for being top dog in earnings by doing a larger share of the housework than in more financially equal homes.

Dominance is the struggle for power, and power is the ability to control what other people want, need or fear. Dominance is a major source of confidence because of the sense of control it gives a person. Many men in heterosexual relationships find it difficult not being dominant; others less so. A 2012 study across twenty-seven countries showed that a greater need for dominance among men was associated with higher levels of sexism and female disempowerment. Women's confidence will always be a victim of this unequal struggle when their partner has this need.

Here is a key point that I'll present in more detail in the next chapter: where confidence is concerned, men and women are playing by different rules. A woman's self-esteem depends more on her relationships, including that with her partner, than a man's does on his. Men's self-esteem depends more on their individual achievements – their lonely individualism allows them to compete for dominance much more unambiguously than is the case for women.

Evolutionary psychologists argue for a profound biological basis for these sex differences in behaviour. One of the critical hormones involved with dominance is testosterone, which circulates in men's bodies at up to ten times the level of women. In 2019, the Court of Arbitration for Sport made a ruling about women with unusually high naturally occurring testosterone levels due to abnormal sexual development. They would have to take medication to reduce those levels before they would be allowed to compete internationally at distances between 400m and a mile. The case of the South African female athlete Caster Semenya was a trigger of this ruling, showing how important testosterone is for dominating the field in athletics.

Higher levels of testosterone make people more competitive

generally, not just in sport. High levels also increase confidence, and women are more sexually competitive with other women when their testosterone levels are higher. Parents of schoolchildren in Shanghai competed in a tournament in which they were rewarded for how well they could solve a series of arithmetic problems. The rewards were either cash, or vouchers to buy educational books for their children. In line with research on sex differences that, again, we'll come back to in the next chapter, the men were more competitive than women when playing for cash. However, when the contest was for educational vouchers for their children, the women were more competitive and performed better than the men.

Women can be just as cut-throat competitive as men, but it depends on what is at stake. Biological differences between men and women don't translate directly to aggression and competitiveness, though, as a number of studies have shown. While men are more aggressive than women in response to violent images or signals, for example, women are just as aggressive as men when they are provoked.

There is, therefore, nothing biologically inevitable about women's confidence being diminished by dominant men. It is less the biological differences than the social rules – saying that men should earn more than women, for example – that determine confidence. Such norms evolved in a very different society from today – one in which physical size and strength mattered. These early primitive advantages allowed men to accumulate power, wealth, status and confidence. Such assets multiply over time and across generations in the manner of compound interest, as we saw in Chapter 4.

As any power-heeled woman or small-statured man will tell you, height still matters. Women *are* smaller and less physically strong than men, and height, like it or not, is a common, if shallow, source of confidence, according to our social norms. Taller men are, on average, esteemed more by others, are more likely to become leaders, have higher self-confidence – and earn more. This is also true for taller women. Given that men are taller than women on average, this primitive source of confidence gives men a distinct edge in the competition for who becomes top dog. There are, of course, many highly confident women with a disdain for height prosthetics, and men who try to steal an advantage with concealed heels.

In the developed world, where height and strength are now irrelevant to most human activity, the early advantages of these primitive assets still live on in the social rules they have spawned and the accumulated power that they have given to men.

Choosing the captain

On 7 June 2008, Hillary Clinton announced that she would step down from the nomination race for the US Democratic Party and endorsed her rival, Barack Obama. A week earlier, 681 five- to thirteen-year-old Swiss schoolboys and schoolgirls, who knew little or nothing about US politics, played a computer game involving a voyage from Troy to Ithaca. They then had to imagine that they were about to embark on this adventure in real life. They were shown two faces and asked, 'Who would you choose as the captain of your boat?' Overwhelmingly, they foretold the result of the nomination contest by choosing Barack Obama as their captain.

These Swiss children didn't have this uncanny ability only with such well-known faces. They were just as successful at predicting the winners in the French parliamentary elections. Based on nothing other than glimpsing two candidates' faces, they chose the eventual election winner as their ship's captain with 71 per cent accuracy.

Both boys and girls were as good at choosing the winner between two men as they were between a man and a woman such as Obama and Clinton. What's more, adults behaved in the same way as the children. Before the 2004 US congressional elections, people had to rate the relative 'competence' of two unfamiliar politicians' faces flashed up for a mere second on a computer screen. With just this sliver of information they were able to predict election victory with approximately 70 per cent accuracy. What was it about the winners' faces that meant both children and adults could predict their electoral victory so well?

The appearance of competence is crucial to being chosen as a leader, a judgement based on something fleetingly detected in the face. What is it? This primitive and error-prone mental heuristic is particularly important for understanding female confidence, because how other people see you shapes your self-confidence. The news is not good for women.

In general, people tend to rate men as more competent and confident than women, with women being just as guilty of this bias as men. Those with a facial façade of competence end up as CEOs more often and are paid much more. It's important to note that they don't perform better than less competent-looking people. Their looks take precedence over actual outcomes, something that also happens with politicians. Unfortunately, this man-favouring bias in assessing confidence and competence happens across almost all cultures.

We elect politicians and appoint CEOs who look capable and confident based on a one-second glance at their facial appearance. But these superficial assessments that are so successful in elevating people – particularly men – to high places are of little use in predicting *actual* performance in the job. This is something of a problem for the world, and we badly need to understand better what is going on in these faces that they provoke this reaction.

Researchers at Princeton University have begun to unravel this puzzle of the competent face. They did so first by creating computer-generated faces that varied in apparent competence, based on ratings by volunteers. They did the same for the attractiveness of these faces and found that the more attractive a face was, the more competent the person was judged to be.

They were then able to create a series of equally attractive, computer-manipulated faces that differed only in how competent they looked. With attractiveness equalized, they discovered that a face judged to be more competent-looking was also rated as being more masculine- and confident-looking. The researchers asked people to judge whether faces of different levels of competence were men or women and sure enough, the more competent a face looked, the more likely it was to be judged as male.

So, competent faces look confident, attractive and masculine. Can we then boost our chances of being seen as competent by photoshopping our real photographs to look a little more masculine? Indeed, we can – or at least men can. As the Princeton researchers made men's faces look more masculine, so they were rated as more competent. Women altered in the same way suffered a backlash. Up to a point, making their faces look more masculine made them seem more competent. But then the benefits of increasing maleness in a still-feminine face reversed. Beyond this point, the competence ratings slumped.

It is little wonder then that women are often reluctant to aim for the most senior roles in organizations, business and politics. Not only do men see them as less competent and confident on average, but so do other women. And if they try to counter these views by adopting a more masculine – and hence confidently competent – appearance, they risk tipping over into being seen as less capable.

It's true that the more attractive a woman is, the more competent she will appear to be. But her femininity will cut across that because of the masculine–confidence–competence link in people's minds – a connection that is largely unconscious, deeply embedded and so hard to change. The tension always remains that confidence and competence are so strongly associated in people's minds with masculinity that this penalizes women who are both highly competent and feminine. Ever looming is the potential double whammy of being seen both as less attractive because of being perceived as too masculine *and* being seen as less competent for the very same reason.

Some women defy gender stereotypes by adopting the self-promoting style that serves men so well. They tend to be rated high in competence by both men and women, but at the cost of being seen to lack social skills. Given that confidence inspires self-promotion, confident women who are seen as competent self-promote at the cost of being liked less. Likewise, men in similar situations who are modest in their demeanour are seen as less competent because they are not behaving according to their gender stereotype.

It is little wonder, then, that so many women managers say they feel like impostors. They face the dominance contest with men, but both sexes unconsciously see them as less competent than men within a second of meeting them. But if they adopt the confident, self-promoting behaviours that work so well for men, then both sexes will tend to like them less and view them as less socially skilled.

Perhaps this is one reason that women inadvertently sabotage their promotion prospects in organizations by more often taking on good-citizen but un-CV-friendly duties such as sitting on committees: research shows that, on average, they value relationships and tend to be less selfishly individualistic and self-promoting than men. But perhaps behaving *nicely* also offers relief from a constant straining in the face of hair-trigger prejudices against the perceived competence in their actual faces.

This one-second effect means that these attitudes are buried deep in the brain, and women must necessarily be subject to these same unconscious prejudices when applied to themselves. It seems that something happens to girls at around age six that helps to cement this self-deprecating prejudice into their brains. In 2017, researchers at the University of Illinois told five-year-old children a story about a person who was *really, really smart*. The children then had to guess which of four adults – two men and two women – was the person in the story. The girls chose one of the women mostly, and the boys one of the men.

But in six-year-olds, something strange happened – the girls' preferences became boy-like and, more often, they began to choose a man as the very smart person. They were then asked to choose between two new games, one of which was for children who were *really, really smart*, and the other for kids who *tried really, really hard*. Those girls who had chosen men in the first experiment were less likely to select the new game for really smart children.

As the girls entered their sixth year and abandoned their innocent impartiality about brilliance, so another idea about femaleness replaced it. When asked to choose someone who was *really, really nice*, the six-year-olds opted much more often for a woman while the five-year-old girls did not.

All this means that tough forces are acting against women's confidence – ones embedded in their own and others' brains from an early age. Is there any remedy?

The stiff headwind of stereotype

On 2 March 2011, a newly elected member of the Irish parliament, Mary Mitchell O'Connor, was driving out of its car park. A talented former school principal who would soon rise to ministerial rank, she was exhilarated after her first day in the centre of government. But she was unfamiliar with the car park layout, and managed to bump her red saloon down a few shallow steps on the parliament forecourt, to the exquisite delight of a group of male photographers who were watching. Her brilliantly blonde hair, vibrant lipstick and ultra-feminine manner did her no favours in this minor mischance. A torrent of masculine celebration followed, confirming a long-held belief about women's spatial navigational abilities.

Men and women differ most on spatial thinking cognitive tests, a fact that has fed into popular theories about female competences. Their apparent validity at the hands of Mary Mitchell O'Connor spread with gusto among men in bars and locker rooms far and wide.

One spatial thinking test shows a top-down view of a circle of objects – a car, a tree and a flower. In the middle is another image – say, a cat. After looking at this, you are given a blank circle on which you have to draw a line to show where one object on the circle – say, the tree – is located in relation to the cat in the middle. This is a classic, map-reading-type task in which you locate places in relation to each other independently of the direction you are facing.

In 2016, researchers at the University of California, Santa Barbara, gave participants an explanation about what the test measured, saying, 'Perspective-taking ability can be thought of as a measure of spatial ability. Spatial ability is a cognitive ability that is defined as understanding the relations between objects in space and being able to mentally manipulate them and respond correctly. Males often score higher on measures of spatial ability.' After they finished the test, the researchers showed that the women volunteers were indeed poorer at this task, scoring at least half as well as men.

But then they tweaked the test a little. Instead of a cat in the middle of the circle, they drew a top-down, head-and-shoulders view of a person. And they also gave a different explanation of the test, as follows: 'Perspective-taking ability can be thought of as a measure of empathetic ability. Empathetic ability is a social ability that is defined as being able to identify with and understand what another person is seeing or feeling and respond appropriately. Females often score higher on measures of empathetic ability.'

A second group of men and women did precisely the same visuo-spatial test as before, except with the person instead of the cat, and the different explanation of the test. How did the women perform in this identical spatial task? They scored just as well as men, with no difference in ability.

The investigators reached the same findings with a different map-reading task. In this, you look down at a route through the streets of a town. You then have to say whether to turn right or left at each of the turn points. Again, the men–women differences melted away when the task was presented as a human one connected to empathy rather than an abstract spatial test.

Women like Mary Mitchell O'Connor know very well that they are supposed to be mediocre at spatial tasks such as map-reading, driving, engineering – they have been told this throughout their lives. This means that when they are watched closely in a test or a parliament car park where spatial thinking is required, they become more anxious. Anxiety makes it much harder to think clearly. What's more, they need to summon up additional mental energy to keep these negative stereotypes in their brains at bay, which makes it even harder to keep their minds on the task at hand. And so they perform more poorly on tasks where they are supposed by all – including themselves – to be less competent.

This is the stiff headwind of stereotype-threat that all women face. It blows inside their brains as much as it blusters outside. One way to reduce this threat is by portraying or reframing the task as something that women are supposed to be – and actually are – good at, such as empathy.

Women are much less inclined than men to spend time trying to kill virtual others in a simulated war game such as *Medal of Honor*. This video game requires you to locate yourself and your adversaries in various 3-D bombed buildings or other apocalyptic scenarios, to stalk your opponents and shoot or otherwise maim them. In my limited experience of such games, my lifespan can be counted in seconds before I am blasted lifeless into the virtual rubble.

Games like this stretch your brain's ability to create mental maps that allow you to see your spatial position relative to other players. Women don't play these games nearly as often as men, and so don't get to exercise their spatial thinking abilities as much. Our brains are quite plastic, meaning that they change physically depending on what we do with them, and spatial thinking is no exception to this.

Hence the decision of the University of Toronto researchers to test women's spatial thinking before giving them ten hours of playing time on the killing fields of *Medal of Honor: Pacific Assault*. The volunteers' spatial reasoning – notoriously lower in women – was measured before and after this training, and compared with women playing a non-spatial computer game, as well as with men playing *Medal of Honor*. They found that playing the game made the male–female difference disappear. Women's spatial abilities rose to men's levels when they felt inclined to practise them.

Just mentioning gender in a situation in which women are being assessed for their spatial thinking makes them perform more poorly. Simply raising the gender issue makes the prejudices and stereotypes about their abilities rise out of the depths of the mind like lurking monsters. This happens with other stereotypes such as age, too. And the same is true for race. The headwind of stereotype-threat blows away mental resources and creates a self-fulfilling prophecy.

In 2005, Harvard University president Lawrence Summers raised a storm. He declared that there were genetic reasons why there were so many more men than women in science and engineering professorships at elite universities. Spurred by this controversy, Canadian researchers decided to investigate whether beliefs in genetic causes of ability affected performance.

They gave women two mathematics tests of the type used in the Graduate Record Exam (GRE), interspersed with a reading comprehension test. Unknown to the participants, they were randomly assigned to four groups who read four different essays after the first test. One essay stated that there is no difference in maths abilities between men and women, while a second simply raised the issue of gender without mentioning the subject of maths. A third proposed that genetic factors caused supposed male–female differences, while a fourth said that such differences existed but were due to different experiences.

These essays made a considerable difference to how the women fared on the second maths test. The women who had read that there was no male–female difference scored an average of 15, and that compared with 7.5 in the just-raising-the-topic-of-gender-in-general group. Gender stereotype reduced the women's mathematical ability by *half*. But what about the two other essays – the genetics versus experience groups? The experience group scored an impressive 17 on the test, but those who read that women were poorer at maths for genetic reasons saw their scores plummet to an average of 6.

If your group – sex, age, race – is supposed to have low ability in something, then believing that genetics causes this will sap your confidence in doing it. Low confidence means low performance. In most countries, women are just as good as men at mathematics, but they have far less confidence in this ability. Countries with less gender equity – as measured by sex differences in school enrolment, parliamentary representation and research positions – have much larger male–female gaps in maths ability because women are less maths-confident. High gender equity in a society reduces the negative impact of stereotype on maths performance.

As we saw in Chapter 5, some of us believe that our abilities are fixed by genetics or other factors. Others believe that a mix of effort, chance, experience and inheritance shapes what we can and cannot do. On average, girls have lower self-confidence than boys. That gap is much more prominent if the girls have a fixed genetic theory of their abilities. When the headwind of stereotype is diminished, or the genetic theories behind it are weakened, women's performance improves in domains where they are typecast to be weaker, often up to the level of men. But while confidence differences can shrink, they are hard to eradicate unless societies can, through education and policy, gradually eliminate these damaging and inaccurate stereotypes.

Nothing quite eats away at confidence like feeling anxious. That's because anxiety makes us search the world – and, indeed, our memories – for bad things that threaten us. And that makes it much harder to anticipate success in the future – that is, be confident. Girls and women are more prone to anxiety than boys and men. The usual and easy explanation for this is genetics, biology or hormones: women are naturally more anxious; anxiety hurts confidence; thus, women are naturally less confident.

This theory runs into a problem outside the West, though: studies have shown that Japanese and black South African women, for example, are no more anxious than men. It appears to be cultural stereotypes and discrimination, then, that shape these differences in anxiety. A common Western stereotype of a woman includes cautious nervousness, a lack of assertiveness, and a substantial imperative to be *nice*. To the extent that women are socialized into conforming to this stereotype, it saps their self-belief because such behaviours are antithetical to confident behaviour. Male stereotypes of self-asserting dominance, on the other hand, offer advantages of boosted confidence to those men who conform to them.

Doing it together

In November 2018, the Democratic Party took back control of the US Congress, largely due to successful campaigns by women candidates. Their numbers surged from 312 in 2016 to 592 in 2018. During that same period, the number of women expressing an interest in running for office rose from 920 to 42,000. This was a remarkable turnaround from a pessimistic 2014 study, which found a big gender gap in political ambition in high school and college.

Researchers concluded that an important factor causing this gap in political ambition was women having less experience in competitive activities such as sports. More boys and young men are encouraged and socialized to take part, and women are therefore less confident in competitive arenas.

So, what could explain this surge in political confidence and activity among women in the US? There are clear political reasons for this – notably in the policies, statements and behaviour of the then president – but other potential factors are at play that might help us to understand female confidence further. The first is that, as research has shown, women are more collectively minded than men. This serves to handicap them when it comes to their individual confidence, but might be an advantage to them when it comes to the collective confidence of a movement.

For several reasons, then, between 2016 and 2018 women were galvanized into a political movement that allowed them to gain confidence in a collective way. Such collective confidence has many, if not more, of the benefits of individual confidence, and the 2018 midterm election results were evidence of this.

A second factor in the surge in women's political confidence could be *action*. The 2016–18 period was characterized by events such as the 2017 Women's March in Washington, DC, which almost half a million people attended. A 2018 report by the Brookings Institution think tank concluded that indeed, over the previous twelve months, young women were much more likely than young men to have engaged in one or more political activities. The report concluded, 'This may be the first time in American history that an entire cohort of young women reports greater political engagement than their male peers'.

And as we will see now, there is evidence that planning for action builds women's confidence much more than it does in men.

Think about a should-I-shouldn't-I problem you are currently grappling with. This could be *Should I change my job? Should I move to a new house?* or similar. Take a few minutes to think through the pros and cons of each avenue. Doing this exercise puts you into a *deliberative* mindset, one in which you are weighing up options and are not yet fixed on a clear course of action.

Now bring to mind the most important personal goal you intend to achieve in the next few months – for example, *I plan to find a new apartment*. Thinking about this for a few minutes will put you in what is known as an *implemental* mindset. In this frame of mind, you made a decision, you know what you are doing, and you are moving forward towards a clear goal.

These two mindsets make you feel, think and behave quite differently. Deliberating makes you consider both upsides and downsides, and your mood and confidence fluctuate as you do so. On the other hand, thinking about how to implement a specific goal lifts your mood, and your mind closes in on that goal, ignoring irrelevant information. This focus of attention on reaching your goal makes you feel more confident in achieving it. In turn, this makes you feel even more positive.

In 2014, researchers at the University of Cologne induced either a deliberative or an implemental mindset in a group of volunteers and then gave them a general knowledge quiz. The women who had deliberated thought they had done much worse on the quiz than their true scores revealed. At the same time, the men, typically, believed that they had done better than they actually had. But the underconfidence of the women in the implemental mindset group disappeared – they became accurate, and neither under- nor overconfident. The implemental men's overconfidence, however, surged to even higher levels.

Focusing the volunteers' minds on taking action dramatically shrank women's underconfidence. That's why ensuring women have access to positions of power and responsibility in which they can take action is a powerful way of boosting their confidence – and hence their performance. As men and women tend to play by different rules where confidence is concerned, the issue is that he who sets the rules wins the game. Women's confidence is shaped hugely by the behaviour of men and by their relative powerlessness in most societies.

How does this play out in terms of sex differences in how confident people are? Men have the wind behind them when it comes to the competition, while women are battling against those headwinds of stereotype, dominance and biased perception. Fortunately, none of these is inevitable or irrevocable.

CHAPTER 7

The Gender Gap

I N JULY 1967, a young Cambridge graduate student in astrophys-ics was poring over charts of data when she noticed a strange, repeating pattern. These signals were produced by a radio tele-scope that she had helped her PhD supervisor, Anthony Hewish, and his colleague Martin Ryle to build. When she first told Hewish about the signals, he dismissed them as mere radio interference, but she kept working on the evidence to persuade him that they were real. Over the coming months, the three scientists ruled out explanation after explanation for these signals until they finally concluded that they had discovered the regular radio pulses from a completely new type of heavenly body – a neutron star, which they named a 'pulsar'.

The paper they wrote together and published in the science jour-nal *Nature* caused a sensation, not least because a twenty-four-year-old woman was named as second author in this heavily male-dominated field. In 1974, to great acclaim, the team was awarded the Nobel Prize in Physics – except Jocelyn Bell Burnell, the woman credited with the discovery, who was ignored by the Nobel committee. This huge injustice can be explained by the sexism prevalent at that time. The unfairness of the decision was recognized more than four decades later through Bell Burnell's award of the $3 million Breakthrough Prize in Fundamental Physics in 2018.

The immense challenges to women's confidence arising from discrimination and domination by men mean that their confidence, by necessity, has had to take a different shape from that prevailing among men. One such difference was revealed by Bell Burnell as she expressed her feeling of being an 'impostor': 'It was a very, very small signal. It occupied about one part in 100,000 of the three miles of chart data that I had. I noticed it because I was being really careful, really thorough, because of impostor syndrome.' What is this 'impostor syndrome'?

Impostor syndrome

Take a minute or two to think about how strongly these statements apply to you:

> I tend to do well in tasks that I previously thought I
>   couldn't do.
> I try not to be evaluated by others if at all possible.
> I think people might find out that I'm not as capable as they
>   believe.
> It's difficult to accept praise about things I've done well.
> Others often seem to be more capable or intelligent than
>   I am.
> Most of my achievements have been a matter of luck.

Many people feel like Bell Burnell – namely, that they are less able than others think they are. This is the opposite of the distorting lens phenomenon and self-inflating strategies we saw in Chapters 2 and 3. With these strategies, it's normal for people to overestimate their own abilities, including a reluctance to downgrade their self-regard in response to negative feedback. And as we saw, the distorting lens is part of the machinery of confidence.

The more strongly you felt the statements above apply to you, then the more impostor-like you feel, and are plagued by doubt about your true abilities. Given how widespread *overestimation* of one's abilities is, maybe a little bit of *underestimation* keeps us closer to reality? However, overestimation is part of confidence, and confidence helps you perform, persist and persuade, so it's not easy to give it up.

This is the nub of something very important for the world. Women, on average, show less overconfidence than men. In 2011, for example, the London-based Institute of Leadership and Management surveyed three thousand managers across the UK. In response to being asked how they would rate their level of personal confidence, 50 per cent of women answered either that they had a high level of self-confidence with rarely any self-doubt, or quite a high level with an occasional few doubts. But 70 per cent of men selected one of these two options.

The response which might seem the most accurate and reasonable for most people – feeling quite self-confident but with some doubts – was chosen by 41 per cent of women but only 25 per cent of men. These findings suggest that women may be underconfident compared to men. A more realistic assessment might be that men are more overconfident than is reasonable in a complex world.

Students at Cornell University were asked to answer the question *Am I good at science?* The men scored themselves 7.6 out of 10 on this scale, and the women 6.5. Much later, their scientific reasoning was objectively measured, and the women performed the same as the men. After the objective test, when asked how they thought they had scored, the women guessed 5.8 out of 10, on average, and the men 7.1 out of 10.

Men oversell themselves compared to women. In the UK study

of three thousand managers, in response to the question whether when they started work they expected to take on a management or leadership role, 35 per cent of men answered that they fully expected or hoped to. How many women responded this way? Twenty-three per cent. In the adult job market, women become progressively more of a minority at more senior levels. In negotiating with their bosses, they expect, and ask for, much smaller salary increases than do men of the same status and ability.

So where does this all start?

It's easy to assume that the differences in confidence between the sexes would be lower in advanced developed countries with a strong gender equality agenda and relatively better provisions for maternity and childcare. But it's not as simple as that.

A survey of almost 1,400 Americans aged eight to eighteen discovered that between the ages of eight and fourteen, as they are entering the adult world, American girls show a 30 per cent drop in self-confidence, while boys of similar ages show no drop.

A study of over two thousand eleven- to thirteen-year-old Norwegian schoolchildren found that, despite showing better academic achievement, girls had less confidence in their academic abilities than boys. They also had lower self-esteem. Self-esteem doesn't guarantee confidence, and this study showed that confidence – not self-esteem – was key to school achievement. Low self-esteem, however, means that it's harder to feel confident, and so sex differences in this are very relevant to women's confidence.

A remarkable study of around a million people in forty-eight countries discovered that women globally have a lower level of self-esteem than men. Rich, egalitarian, individualistic countries with greater gender equality, lower adolescent birth rates and a later age of marriage – the UK, US, Canada, Spain and Norway, for example – had *higher* teenage gender gaps in self-esteem. This was when compared to poorer, developing, collectivistic countries with greater gender inequality, higher adolescent birth rates and an earlier age of marriage – India, Indonesia, Thailand and the Philippines, for example.

In the wealthier, individualistic countries that had gender equality measures in place, the gender gap decreased as teenagers grew into adults, but it was not eliminated. However, it *increased* in the poorer, collectivist countries that did not have such measures. This shows that policies to reduce discrimination against women do, eventually, have some effect on their self-esteem. So why would these richer, individualistic countries have *bigger* gaps in self-esteem between teenage boys and girls, as compared to the poorer, collectivist ones?

Playing by different rules

Here is Jocelyn Bell Burnell's response to feeling like an impostor, having been awarded the $3 million Breakthrough Prize: 'I'm a bit of a fighter, so I decided that until they threw me out I would work my very hardest. Then, when the time came, I wouldn't have a guilty conscience. I'd know I had done my best.'

This is the mindset of someone who doesn't want to let others down – avoiding a guilty conscience – more than of someone seeking personal glory and success. And it gives a clue to one way in which women's experience can lead them to learn, use and experience confidence differently from men.

Below are five statements. Think about how strongly each of them applies to you:

> I like not to be the same as others in lots of ways.
> I am inclined to get on with what I like doing no matter what others think.
> I like being singled out for special mention or praise.
> I act much the same irrespective of who I am with.
> Looking after myself and being good at what I do is a number-one priority for me.

Now consider how strongly you'd agree with these five statements:

> I tend to show respect to modest people.
> What happens to me is closely linked to other people's destiny in life.
> My achievements often come second to my relationships with others.
> I tend to fit in with others' wishes, even if I would prefer to be doing something else.
> My happiness depends greatly on the happiness of the people around me.

Which group of statements most applies to you? If it is the first, then you have a more *independent* mental model of yourself – you see yourself very much as an individual. If, on the other hand, the second group of statements applies to you more strongly, then you have more of an *interdependent* self-view – or *self-construal*.

Independence-inclined people – let's call them individualists – tend to prioritize expressing, sustaining and promoting themselves. They struggle for a sense of uniqueness and spend a lot of time trying to influence other people, rather than adjusting to them. They see the world in terms of individuals and their traits – heroes and villains, for example – and are not inclined to interpret people's behaviour in terms of its context, or relationships. One phrase you're unlikely to hear on the lips of an individualist when he's asked what he thinks of some other person's behaviour is, 'Well, it depends on the circumstances.'

What's perhaps most striking – and most relevant for thinking about confidence – is that individualists have a more powerfully distorting lens. With the *superiority illusion* (see Chapter 2), we tend to overestimate our abilities and chances in a way that can act as a self-fulfilling prophecy. Our brains achieve this by *asymmetric updating* of good versus bad news about ourselves, which builds and protects the ego, and so boosts confidence.

Individualists have a bigger superiority illusion than people who endorse the second set of statements. They overestimate their own chances of success compared to others.

More interdependence-inclined people prioritize social harmony, relationships and social duties. This makes them inclined to try to adjust to groups more than to influence them. They are concerned less with the struggle to be unique, and more with the effort to keep relationships strong and functioning. They are less likely to pump themselves up in terms of their abilities, achievements and success.

Individualists spend much of their mental energy getting what they want, asserting their rights and striving for their goals. They are more optimistic than interdependent-minded people about succeeding, because they think they are much better than they objectively are – a result of their big superiority bias.

This goes some way to solving the puzzle that richer countries have a bigger self-esteem gap between girls and boys than poorer ones. On average, wealthier, developed, Western countries have a more individualistic, independent-minded style of thinking than less well-off nations that tend to foster a more collectivist mindset.

But here's the rub – women and girls across the globe are less inclined to be individualistic in their thinking styles than males. There is, therefore, a bigger *mismatch* between rich countries' preferred thinking style and that of their young girls. Adolescent girls tend to think about themselves more in terms of their relationships than boys do – that's what they are taught to do from an early age. It is what most relatively powerless people – male or female – have to do, because having less control over your life means that what happens to you is more dependent on the actions of other people.

In school, teenage girls are faced with an army of boy salesmen, trained to exaggerate their personal offerings. This is part of an ego-driven self-confidence that, as we have seen, drives a certain type of success through making people more persuasive and better-performing. The boys have more of this confidence fuel additive that multiplies its effects over time. This higher than average self-confidence in boys not only makes them more likely to succeed in sport, but also builds their self-esteem.

This is a challenge for most girls. Because their upbringing fosters a less individualistic frame of mind, *they* draw their self-esteem less from personal individual achievement, and more from a sense of connectedness with others and from a shared pleasure in the success of close others. The goals of family and close others are often as important as the females' own goals, which is less true of males.

What this average difference *does* mean, however, is that there isn't a level playing field for confidence among boys and girls. Each sex is playing by different rules. Girls see boys with a confidence that makes them better salesmen, persuaders and performers. These benefits depend on an individualist mindset, the focus of which is on ego-boosting personal achievement.

Such an outlook means that for many – but not all – boys, relationships are an opportunity to compare and distinguish themselves – a means to an end rather than an end in itself. With the more collective mindset that girls tend to have, close relationships *are* that end and shape self-esteem, unlike for the individualist, whose independent achievements are the prime driver of his self-esteem.

The research on individual versus collective mindsets suggests that confidence plays by different rules in the two sexes, and there is support for this view from the world of sport.

In Chapter 2 we saw that the winner of the first set in a closely matched major tennis game is more likely to go on to win the match – the hot hand effect. But you see this only in men, not in women, a 2017 study found. And while individual confidence very strongly boosts sporting performance in men, in women it plays hardly any role at all.

Something similar happens in the school classroom. Boys are more likely to boast about their abilities than girls are. Girls don't make nearly as many self-congratulatory comments as the opposite sex. And just as happens in sport, the more confident and self-praising comments the boys make, the better their school performance tends to be. But for girls there's no such relationship. Girls are more inclined to make positive comments about other children's performance than about themselves.

All this makes self-confidence a double-edged sword for girls. If they talk themselves up, their more connected mindset makes them more aware of the potential emotional collateral damage to their relationships and self-esteem. The boy with the more independent mindset, however, has fewer qualms about such consequences because his self-esteem is driven more by his personal accomplishments than by relationships.

So here's a possible answer to the puzzle of why there's a bigger boy–girl self-esteem gap in richer countries. We know that such cultures foster an individualistic mindset, which is great for the operation of confident self-promotion but not so good for a more relationship-focused, collective mindset. As girls' self-esteem is more likely to rest as much on the quality of their relationships as on their personal achievements, then the self-inflation that fuels confidence can actually be a *threat* to their self-esteem rather than the booster it is to boys.

This means that boys and girls are essentially playing by different rules in a world in which projecting a self-enhancing view of one's abilities actually *works* in making you more successful in certain ways, for all the reasons outlined in Chapter 2. By definition, such self-promotion must be more stressful for girls than boys, because of the risk to their self-esteem that it entails. In what is essentially a boy's world of individual self-promotion, girls who try to compete according to the boys' rules will almost inevitably be more stressed and threatened in their self-regard – and this is precisely what the global data show.

This male–female gap in self-esteem in richer countries narrows as people get older – probably because the richer countries have better equality policies in place. Maternity leave and childcare provision, for example, help mitigate some of the disadvantages that plague women's status, but certainly don't eliminate it. Less easily tackled are the different rules governing confidence by which males and females play. Nowhere are these differences more apparent than when it comes to competition.

An appetite for competition

Paris's Ecole des Hautes Etudes Commerciales (HEC) is the leading business school in Europe, and is second in the world only to Harvard in producing chief executives of Fortune 500 companies. Each year, 3,400 eager candidates endure a gruelling set of entrance exams in mathematics, history, geography, French, two foreign languages, philosophy, general culture and current affairs, followed by interviews. They are vying for just 380 places.

The competition is intense, to say the least, with 46 per cent of women and 54 per cent of men making it through to the final cohort. But there is something odd in these figures, which appears when you look at how the 3,400 candidates perform in another exam, namely the French end-of-high-school assessment – the Baccalaureate, first introduced by Napoleon in 1808.

The HEC is enormously competitive because there is only a fixed number of places, no matter how many individuals apply, and so it is the *ranking* versus other candidates that makes you win or lose a place, not an *absolute* score on the exams. The Baccalaureate, on the other hand, gives as many passes as there are candidates able to make the grade, which in turn means automatic entry into university. As there is no limit on the number of university places in most subjects, this means that Baccalaureate candidates are not competing with each other; rather, they are in a contest against themselves and against the exam. This is precisely the opposite of the HEC assessment, where the fixed number of places makes all candidates compete fiercely against one another for one of these treasured places.

We've seen that the HEC process favours men by almost 10 per cent. The Baccalaureate exam shows the opposite pattern, with women HEC candidates outperforming men on their Bac grades by a comparable percentage. So why do women who outperform men on one exam end up underperforming on another? Maybe the HEC assessment is simply more rigorous and demanding? That argument doesn't work when you look at the end-of-year exam results for men and women who made it into the HEC. Here, the women again bested the men in most subjects, just as they had done on the Bac. So, what is going on?

The end-of-first-year exams at the HEC are tough, but less than 1 per cent of students fail, which is not surprising given how difficult the entrance exam is. This means that the end-of-year tests aren't competitive, unlike the admissions process. There isn't a fixed proportion of people who will fail – if you make the grade, you will pass, just like in the Bac, and so most students do. Women, then, aren't forced to compete with one another in a dog-eat-dog fashion in the HEC first-year exams – just as they didn't have to in the Bac. Only in the savagely competitive HEC entrance exam do they have to, and it is there that they underperform. All of which suggests that competition poses a greater challenge to women than to men . . . at least under certain circumstances.

In early June every year, sunny Santa Barbara in southern California hosts the State Street Mile, a set of mile-long road races that include a number of relatively non-competitive family (and other) runs. It also features an Elite Open Mile for competitive athletes to race against their own sex, for prizes of up to $5,000. Runners are encouraged to sign up for this elite competition if they think they will meet a qualifying time for the race, which is around four and a half minutes for men, and five and a half for women.

When economists from the University of California, Santa Barbara, looked closely at who chose which races to enter, they were taken aback: 88 per cent of younger men who predicted – and subsequently met – the qualifying time for the men's Elite Open Mile opted for that race. But for the women, only 64 per cent of those who could, and did, meet the qualifying time opted to compete against other women of a similar standard.

This apparent lack of appetite for competition was also apparent in the Cornell University science quiz study, where women underestimated their science abilities compared to men. In another part of this study, all those taking part were offered the chance to enter a science competition, where there would be prizes. Seventy-one per cent of the men signed up, but only 49 per cent of the women did – in spite of the fact that their science quiz scores were just as good as the men's.

So, women don't like competition? That seems to be the implication of this research. Some researchers have argued that this is because women don't like taking risks, but Muriel Niederle from Stanford University has reviewed the science and concluded that women aren't any more risk-averse than men. That's *not* why they seem to shy away from competition or perform more poorly than they should in competitive situations such as the admissions process to the HEC in Paris. Rather, she and her colleague Lise Vesterlund show that the reason is *confidence*. Women avoid competition because they have less confidence in their performance than men.

The more collective and *we*-thinking style of women means that in the battle of confidence they are once again playing by different rules from the more individualistic, *I*-focused men. Competition really shows up that difference. It's harder to be ruthlessly competitive in your desire to beat your friend when that person is part of your self-image and that friendship is at the core of your self-esteem. An appetite for hard-edged individual competitiveness is diminished not just because confidence is lacking, but also because of an ambivalence about *beating* someone else.

An appetite for competition and confidence are intertwined. Playing by different rules may be one reason why women are different from men in both competitiveness and confidence, but there is at least one other factor, which we discussed in the last chapter – the saboteur.

Saboteurs

Amidst the nerve-jangling mêlée of a thousand schoolchildren, two fifteen-year-old boys, Alan and Cormac, were eager to describe their research during the BT Young Scientist Competition in Dublin, at which I was a judge.

'Girls and boys start off the same, but by the time they are our age, the girls are turned off science and engineering. We wanted to know why,' Alan said.

So, they had gone off and gathered data from no less than 376 five- to seven-year-old children, and asked them, among many other things, to draw a picture of an engineer and give the person a first name so that there would be no doubt about the gender. Half the girls drew an engineer who was a man. The boys? Only 4 per cent of them drew a woman engineer.

'Girls had a more positive view of boys' abilities than vice versa' was Cormac's understated observation.

Potential solutions to female confidence are usually directed at girls and women themselves. Alan and Cormac discovered, however, that this may miss the real target – male attitudes, whether conscious or unconscious. This finding wouldn't have been a surprise to Jocelyn Bell Burnell. Nor would it have been a surprise to a former Cambridge colleague of mine. She was an acclaimed academic with an international reputation, and a fine intellect. She also had the capacity to terrorize people, like me, who were discovered using her lab space or otherwise causing her trouble.

One day I was taken aback after a lunchtime seminar in our

notoriously bear-pit-like institute, where speakers were subjected to merciless dissection of their talks. After a much less rancorous session than usual, I found myself standing with this woman – let's call her Jane – as well as the chair of the session and the presenter, both women. This was an unusual situation in an institute where a tiny percentage of the research principals were female.

'You know, usually I can't ask questions in these meetings, but it was so different today with two women up there,' Jane said suddenly, disorienting me with this new vulnerability that was emerging from her usual carapace of belligerence. She had indeed asked questions and made brilliant comments, in a way I had never noticed before in public meetings.

And then I suddenly got it. It is so easy for males to compete in male-dominated environments, but it is so much harder for even the most battle-hardened of women to do the same. Does the science support anecdote here? Let's do what Alan and Cormac did, and examine what is happening in younger children.

Some nine- and ten-year-olds had to run a 40-metre race. First, they ran as fast as they could on their own. Then they were matched with another child of similar running speed and ran a race against them. That child could be of the same sex or a different sex. When boys ran against boys, they ran faster. When girls ran against girls, they slowed a little. The really interesting question, though, is what happened when girls ran against boys?

Even a boy whose recorded time was slower than a girl's – on the first-time-only, no-competition run – had a 73 per cent chance of winning the next race with that girl when they ran against each other. And if his first time was slightly better than the girl's, his chance of winning the race was 83 per cent. In short, boys' chances of winning a race surge when they compete against girls, University of Chicago economists showed.

This is not to do with physical strength. A study of adults paid per item to solve puzzle mazes on computers in a group demonstrates this fact. Women solved roughly the same number of mazes as men. But that changed when the task altered to a winner-takes-all competition. Here, the best maze performer in the group was rewarded with a grand prize and no one else got anything. Now the men's competitive spirits took hold and they outperformed the women by an average of four mazes.

So, women can't hack competition, is that the conclusion? Not so fast. When the women were up against other women, they *did* perform better, just like the men did, and the competition gender gap disappeared, the Chicago economists found. This is similar to what happened to my colleague Jane in Cambridge. In a highly competitive academic environment, in which women were a small minority, her confidence was sapped and her performance as a discussant in seminars diminished. One can only marvel at Jocelyn Bell Burnell's persistence in the face of more blatant sabotage by men.

Women do not have the same access to the precious resource of confidence, largely because of disadvantages such as stereotype-threat, sabotage, and the fact that they play by different rules when competing. That raises the question – can you learn to be more confident?

CHAPTER 8

Learning to Be Confident

: :

T HE GOOD NEWS is that, yes, you can learn to be confident. Confidence is a belief, and beliefs can change. We have seen that confidence is a mental bridge to the future. Such a prospect is usually something tangible in the real world – that workout completed, a skill mastered, the presentation given, a phone call made, or a problem solved. But what if that bridge you are trying to build is to a place entirely inside your head? *I am not confident now – but I am confident that I can be confident in the future.* Tough call, but possible.

Kim

We met Kim in Chapter 5 – always overshadowed in her parents' eyes by her academically high-achieving brother. A vivacious and intelligent young woman, her adolescence and early adulthood had been blighted by a corrosive lack of confidence in her abilities and personal qualities. Kim was attractive and popular, but that's not how she saw it. She would accept an invitation to a Saturday-night party but then pull out at the last minute because of anxiety. The first encounter with difficult material in a university module and Kim would drop it – the words *I'm no good at this* would swirl through her mind and stop her from going to that class. Repeated over several courses, and she was out of college, looking for a job. *Can't do* was a default belief about her abilities.

No point in applying there – they'll have thousands of better-qualified applicants. These were her thoughts in response to an advert for a management training scheme with a leading company that perfectly suited her qualities. *Can't happen* was her baseline thought about potential opportunities.

Kim wasn't suffering from a physically based illness. Yes, she would feel down on the Saturday night after not turning up at a party. Yes, she would feel anxious, sitting at home in her parents' house with no job while her friends spread out across the globe, searching for careers, relationships and adventures. But no, she wasn't suffering from an 'illness' in the usual sense of the word. Kim was trapped on an island inside her head, with both spans of the only bridge off it – *can do* and *can happen* – broken.

Kim's father arranged for his daughter to have an interview with a friend's company for a solid job with potential for promotion. Reluctantly, Kim agreed to go, but insisted that she would make her own way there and not be driven by her parents. She missed the train and arrived for the interview half an hour late. She didn't get the job. Her tearful explanations of how she had misread the train timetable did not appease her furious parents. They believed that she had sabotaged her chances deliberately, which cut her to the bone. This belief was entirely unjustified. Kim's self-sabotage was unconscious, not deliberate. *Self-handicapping* is the term used to describe the mental gymnastics behind Kim's missed train. It is the mind's way of avoiding failure – *They'll never give me a job* – and so protecting self-esteem against failure-damage.

Kim was smart but an underachiever. A 2014 University of

Louisville study with similarly able but underachieving undergraduates at an elite university confirmed that people like Kim use self-handicapping to try to pre-empt the risk of failure. Based on their academic record, the students were told that they were gifted and then were asked to read one of two texts. Half read – and believed – that giftedness was a stable 'fixed' capacity. In contrast, the other group read, and again accepted, that giftedness was something that ebbed and flowed with motivation and effort. It was a 'changeable' ability, in other words.

With these two different mindsets established, the students then had to solve some problems. But half of them were given questions that had a solution, while the other half had questions that – psychologists can be tricky – were unsolvable. So, 50 per cent of these underachieving students had a success experience of solving some problems, and 50 per cent had the unpleasant failure experience of not being able to solve any. That gave the researchers four groups – fixed theory/success experience, fixed theory/ failure experience, change theory/success experience, and change theory/failure experience.

The students then went on to try to solve more problems of a different type. But before doing this, they had to complete a checklist of possible reasons why they might not perform at their best. The list included items such as test anxiety, fatigue and illness – all potential excuses to explain away feared failure. Sure enough, those who experienced failure first time around, and also believed that their giftedness was something fixed, made many more excuses than the others.

The researchers had one more trick up their sleeves. They told the students that brighter light boosted intellectual performance. They also showed them that they could adjust the level of light in the room from 0 (brightest) to 10 (pitch black) before working on the problems. The students who believed that their abilities were fixed, and who had the sour taste of failure in their mouths, chose a darker light on average for the second test. They were unconsciously preparing their excuse because of their terror of failure. This was self-handicapping equivalent to Kim's missed train.

Across the world, talented students like Kim self-handicap in ways that undercut their true academic potential. Kim had learned to self-handicap in school and university by not studying for exams, by handing in assignments late, or by leaving exams early. She did this to protect her self-esteem from failure. While it might have worked short-term to protect her ego, as she kept doing this again and again, it also began to undercut the success of which she was capable.

Kim's fixed mindset about her abilities – and, indeed, about her emotions and personality – came from her parents' doubts about her abilities in comparison to those of her brother. Every time she didn't get an A, wasn't invited to a party, or gave up another musical instrument, there would be a collective lurch in her parents' stomachs. Their terror of her 'failures' cemented Kim's fixed theory of herself. Rather than responding to a low test score by studying harder or asking the teacher for help, she mentally shied away from further evidence of the imperfect quality of her brain. She began to doubt most things about herself, including her ability to persevere at anything, her capacity to learn new things – and even her likeability as a person. Kim learned to mentally run away from 'failure', thus thwarting the development of her potential.

Many people live in challenging circumstances much less favourable than Kim's, where it is all too easy to have a fixed theory that cements your lowly achievement into its self-fulfilling place. IQ is widely taken as the reliable marker of the quality of one's brain, and is a strong predictor of how well children do in school and at university. IQ embodies a fixed theory of ability like nothing else, and this view shapes the thinking of policymakers, not least UK politician Boris Johnson. While Mayor of London, he made a speech arguing that tackling economic inequality is futile because some people's IQ is too low for them to compete.

A 2011 University of Pennsylvania study of over two thousand people showed that giving financial incentives to perform well on an IQ test increased participants' scores by an average of ten IQ points. The study found even more substantial increases in people in the lower IQ range. If you can boost a person's IQ by more than ten points by paying them for correct answers, then clearly this is far from a perfect marker of the quality of their brain. Nor does it fit with Boris Johnson's fixed mindset about IQ.

We can learn to be confident – but with one essential precondition. We have to *believe* that change is possible. If we think our mental qualities are fixed, then we won't try to change them. So, can such mindsets be altered? Most definitely yes, a remarkable 2019 paper in the world's leading science journal, *Nature*, showed.

Researchers from leading universities across the US enrolled 12,490 fourteen- to fifteen-year-olds from sixty-five US public schools. The teenagers participated in a web-based session on the evidence that intellectual abilities are changeable, not fixed. They learned that intellect can improve in response to effort, learning new strategies, or asking for help. The researchers compared this instruction with the effects of a similar session that explained about the brain, but did not specifically tackle fixed- versus growth-mindset beliefs. On average, the teenagers who simply had that one session about growth mindset performed significantly better in their school tests, and many more went on to sign up for an advanced mathematics course the following year.

A brief explanation that the brain is like a muscle that gets stronger with practice was enough to build the confidence of thousands of students. The effect was particularly strong for the low-achieving pupils – it both improved their school performance and increased their appetite for learning.

Kim could learn to be confident, but she had to dispel the

harmful assumption that her emotional and intellectual abilities were fixed and out of her control. First, she had to be told this, and second, she had to believe it. But then what?

'The road appears with the first step'

This quote by Rumi, a thirteenth-century Persian poet, captures another critical way of building confidence, first raised in Chapter 2 – *taking action.*

Lack of confidence makes you liable to feel anxious, and anxiety saps your self-belief – a classic chicken-and-egg situation. A study of over three thousand students from nineteen different countries discovered that the more generally anxious people are, the less they tend to do in life. This fact isn't surprising when you think about it. Anxiety comes from a feeling of being under threat, and retreat is the response – a withdrawal from engaging with a dangerous world. That's why Kim would cancel outings with friends at the last minute, give up going to the yoga class she had signed up for, or abandon job applications mid-way. Kim ended up doing much less stuff compared to her more confident, less anxious friends.

And the less stuff you do, the fewer opportunities you have for new experiences, surprise encounters, or little bursts of satisfaction at a challenge met. We saw earlier that there are repeated surges of reward-network activity in the confident brain. These rushes are equivalent to mini-infusions of a natural anti-anxiety drug dispensed with each small goal successfully achieved.

Former Facebook COO Sheryl Sandberg said that confidence is like a muscle that you can learn to use. Each time you force yourself to do something that you were once scared to do – such as speaking up at a meeting, for example – you strengthen the muscle, she claimed. And the science backs her up, as we saw in Chapter 1. Mastering difficult challenges is one of the best sources of confidence.

We've seen how the brain stores up memories of our bodily

sensations. When we manage to do something that scares us, a gut feeling is stored in body memory, which helps us to deal with the next challenge. Nothing quite builds our confidence like the gritting of teeth to get through the fear. It sounds easy – just do the scary stuff that stretches you a bit – to build confidence by taking action. But the trouble is, when people are anxious, this can be hard. The good news is that research has uncovered ways to make it a little easier.

'It is easier to act yourself into a new way of feeling than to feel yourself into a new way of acting'

This quote by the psychiatrist Harry Stack Sullivan expresses the power of *taking the first step*, as the poet Rumi would have us do. Because it isn't just the external road that opens up only once we start the journey, the same is also true for our internal, emotional pathway. Very often, once we take that first step, the emotions we actually have are different from those we anticipated.

Let's reiterate. Confidence is a bet we make on our future self, which creates a bridge to the future. The great American educationist John Dewey took this idea further, saying, 'The self is not something ready-made, but something in continuous formation through choice of action.' Confidence doesn't just take us to a new future state of the external world, but also to a novel future state of our inner world. This is a version of our self, sculpted by the actions we take and the choices we make. So, it becomes even more important to work out *how* to take the action that is crucial for building confidence.

Getting down to it

Kim's mind was a swirl of ruminations and doubts much of the time. She worried about what she might or might not do that evening, next month – or next year. She agonized about what others thought of her. She regretted cancelled meetings, abandoned lessons, jobs never applied for, and courses dropped halfway through. Her brain churned with ideas and fantasies about what she might do, but no sooner had an idea crystallized in her mind than the fear and the doubts swarmed like flies and quelled the hope. No sooner was there a glimmer of confidence than it disappeared under that fly-swarm.

In Chapter 6 I showed that women's confidence improves when they move from a deliberative mindset – thinking through the options of what to do – to an implemental mindset, where a specific course of action is planned. A 2014 University of Vienna study shed new light on this finding. The researchers coaxed volunteers into a deliberative frame of mind by asking them to think carefully about an unresolved personal decision and to reflect on their options for dealing with it. Others were put into an implemental frame of mind by being asked to name a project they had decided to do, and to plan how they were going to do it.

The researchers then studied the participants' eye movements as they looked at pictures. Each image had an object such as a boat, animal or plane in the foreground, set against a complex back-ground. True to the 'wide-ranging and open' idea, the people in the deliberative frame of mind were much more likely to notice details in the background of the picture. On the other hand, the implemental mindset participants focused more narrowly on the central object and didn't notice the background so much.

Knowing what you are aiming for narrows your attention, which has both good and bad implications. On the positive side, you don't have to agonize about what road to take. You have a clear sense of movement towards a goal and – perhaps most importantly of all – you free your mind from the distraction of what-ifs and other worries. On the negative side, however, your narrowly focused attention means that you might miss other possibilities, risks or relevant information. Your eyes feast on the central object of the picture. But you miss the intriguing object in the background that might lead you down an interesting path if only you had noticed it.

The open-mind benefits of deliberation are matched by potential costs. This is because they leave your conscious mind exposed to negative thoughts about the future and memories of the past. That is why the deliberative mindset makes people more cautious and realistic about their abilities and prospects – and hence less confident.

Kim spent much of her time in deliberation, and it dragged her down, depleting her confidence. Even once she had started on a course of action and was in the implemental frame of mind, she would switch back to deliberation. She would to and fro between should-I-shouldn't-I thoughts about continuing. Back in this open mindset, her confidence would collapse, and she would give up on the course, relationship, lessons or application process. She became even more anxious, which made it harder to think clearly and take decisive action.

We know that women's underconfidence is improved when they are in an action-oriented, implemental mindset. Kim's clinical psychologist used this fact when she extracted Kim from her isolated nest of tortured deliberation about her life. She coaxed her into *making a plan* – that is, listing in her mind, and on paper, a series of steps towards a goal. In the first instance, Kim narrowed her attention to the goal of finding a job. She wrote down each small step towards doing this, starting with getting up in the morning at a specific time, dressing for work, making the relevant phone call, and so on.

Kim's psychologist kept tabs on her as she implemented this plan. She coaxed her back into the implemental mindset when she showed signs of slipping back into deliberation. She then applied this same action-oriented, implementation-plan approach to other areas of Kim's life, including her social life, educational aspirations and leisure activities. Gradually, Kim's confidence grew because of the sense of momentum and achievement that taking action in the world produced. These achievements snowballed, and Kim redis-covered the potential she had always had in all these aspects of her life.

But having a plan doesn't guarantee you'll do it – as Kim found out to her cost. She lost heart one morning when she had arranged to meet a friend who had some ideas about a potential job for her. Ahead of the meeting, Kim's mind sank back into deliberation and rumination. Thoughts circled in her mind about how she couldn't stick at anything, and how maybe it would be better to go back to college. With this anxiety, it all felt too hopeless. Perhaps she'd be better off just staying at home. So the familiar text message pinged out to her friend – *Sorry, feeling terrible this morning, won't make the meeting. Sorry.* Rather than her confidence being boosted by taking a step forward, this further retreat from the world sapped it. Is there a way out of problems like this?

Research shows that, at best, people's intentions translate into concrete behaviour only 20–30 per cent of the time. This means that most people, most of the time, are deprived of the confidence-building benefits of taking action. That was certainly true for Kim – she had gone to bed fully intending to get up and meet her friend, but when it came to it, she had stayed put.

She took a different approach when she arranged a subsequent meeting, having planned with her clinical psychologist the *when*, *where* and *how* of her appointment. She backed up these concrete details with some *if-then* plans for what to do if certain things did or did not happen.

Kim mapped out precisely what time she would get up for the meeting, planned what she would wear, and laid out her clothes. Doing this meant that when the time came she wouldn't have to think – as thinking could open up a chink for confidence-sapping deliberation and rumination to find its way in. Not only did Kim plan how she would take the train to meet her friend but, after scanning the timetable, she also knew exactly which one to get.

Checking the route from the station to her friend's office in advance, and storing it in her phone, reduced the chance of last-minute cold feet.

If the train was late or cancelled, she would still have enough time either to get the next train or to phone a taxi – the taxi number was stored in preparation on her phone. *If* she woke up feeling bleak, self-doubting and anxious about the plan, *then* she would listen to her relaxation app on her phone for ten minutes. She would practise the slow breathing that she had learned could tamp down her anxiety. *If* Kim found herself losing her focus, she would take out the written plan and focus her attention on it. She would tell herself that now wasn't the time for mulling over *what* to do – now was the time to *do it*.

Hundreds of research studies have shown that planning out the detail of an implemental mindset like this boosts the intention–action link in many different domains of life. Just a few examples of this are taking physical exercise, stopping smoking, or eating more healthily. This approach also helps to overcome anxiety and many other mental health problems.

Kim met the friend. The job didn't materialize, but the small boost in confidence from carrying out her plan meant that she was able to make other plans. These were always detailed with *if-then* options and, eventually, she got a new job that she liked. She then applied the same strategy to her social and leisure life. The confidence-building effects of *doing stuff* meant that her *can do, can happen* beliefs strengthened. As a result, she did achieve a lot of what she wanted in life. She shook off the fixed mindset that had been like a concrete block tied around her feet for most of her life.

Harnessing fantasies

When Kim finally broke out of her mental prison, she had to decide which direction to take in life. It's fine to implement detailed plans, but if they don't take you where you want to go, their usefulness is limited. Kim had become more confident, not only in her work but also in her relationships and life in general. But sometimes she still felt a little trapped. She would fantasize about taking her life in another direction – anything from becoming a rock star, to travelling around the world, or going to medical school.

The trouble with daydreams like this is that they make it *less likely* that you will realize the fantasy. For example, people on a weight-loss course who fantasized about effortlessly becoming slim put on more weight than those who visualized the hard realities and temptations. Realists became more confident that they could do it, and they were more likely to lose weight. The same researchers went on to study hip replacement patients. People who spent their time fantasizing about the operation's outcome did more poorly than those focused on the post-operation steps they would have to take to recover.

Fantasies are like the *can happen* part of confidence occurring in a disconnected way from the tight planning of *can do*. In Kim's mind, the comforting daydream of being a world traveller or a successful doctor short-circuited the complicated and arduous steps to achieve these plans. They tricked Kim's brain into a state in which it didn't have to strive for the goals because *they had already been achieved* – in fantasy, at least.

So, should Kim have been discouraged from fantasizing about options in her life? Not exactly, the lead researcher at New York University, Gabriele Oettingen, discovered. She devised a new strategy for harnessing fantasy called *mental contrasting*.

The secret behind this method is to connect fantasy and current reality in the mind in such a way as to energize and motivate a person to choose which fantasies are feasible and which should be discarded. Kim took the idea of travelling the world and wrote out the main positives of doing this, visualizing these benefits in her mind's eye as she did so. Next, she had to focus on the current obstacles to this dream – money, effects on her career, parental disapproval – and she had to visualize these obstacles.

Kim went through this quite arduous mental exercise for each of her fantasy futures. She ended up discarding medical school and several others along the way, as this exercise brought fantasy and reality together in her mind. But what did emerge was a plan, namely to look for a job where she could travel and to perhaps spend some time in another country. Kim's world travel idea was now modified and crystallized into one that excited and motivated her. She could now switch into an implementation mindset and, with the help of *if-then* planning, execute her dream in reality. She ended up working for a global technology company and moving to their New York office for two years.

So how exactly did this work in her brain? It most certainly wasn't just a case of 'the power of positive thinking'. In fact, the opposite was true. To make this clear, let's consider what makes it *less* likely that Kim would have achieved what she did. Oettingen showed that simply indulging positive fantasies for the future without contrasting them with reality actually reduces your chances of realizing them. Second, people who reversed the order of the mental contrasting were also less likely to achieve their goals. Oettingen's research showed that had Kim thought about the obstacles first and the benefits second, she would not have been energized to achieve what she did.

The mental contrasting isn't, therefore, a general 'positive thinking' method. On the contrary, the wrong kinds of positive thinking, such as indulging (fantasy unshackled by obstacles) and reversal (obstacles first, fantasy second), have quite the opposite effect. Fantasies rubbed up against realities in Kim's mind to help her develop feasible goals that she could confidently strive for. This meant the fantasy was no longer unchained from reality, as fantasies tend to be. Instead, the fantasy and all its exciting, motivating qualities were active in Kim's brain but, crucially, so were the obstacles in present reality.

And this is where confidence comes into play. When Kim thought about studying medicine, she brought to mind the many barriers to doing that. She realized that she wasn't confident that she could do this, either financially or academically. And so, rather than wasting many hours – even days – fantasizing about being a doctor, as she had done for years, she could discard that goal as unrealizable. This mental exercise allowed her to focus on her other fantasy of travelling the world. She used mental contrasting first to summon mental pictures of elephants in India and beaches in Thailand, and then the dour images – the hurdles of bank account balances, career and family constraints.

Fortunately, through her work with the clinical psychologist, Kim had managed to become more confident – in the workplace and socially – and so could see some routes to overcoming these obstacles to achieving her travel fantasy. This mental embedding of hard reality in the nest of a fantasy future allowed Kim to adapt her dream to one that might be feasible. In this way she was able to harness the confidence-building qualities of the implemental mindset.

Fantasies on their own sap energy by giving the illusion of goals having been achieved. Mental contrasting, on the other hand, energizes and motivates people. This shows up in slight rises in their pulse rate and blood pressure to prepare them for action towards achieving goals. Indulging in fantasy without the mental contrasting lowers blood pressure and de-energizes. Fantasies on their own trick the brain into thinking that the goals have been achieved.

Kim's brain actually changed during the process of mental contrasting. In 2011, using a method called magnetoencephalography (MEG), researchers at the University of Konstanz saw that mental contrasting, compared to pure fantasizing, boosted activity in key brain regions. These areas included those involved in forming intentions, retrieving memories, juggling thoughts and memories, as well as visual imagery.

It wasn't just Kim's heart that was beating faster as she thought about her future. Her brain's activity ramped up as it made plans, pulling out past experiences from memory and juggling them with vivid images of what the future might look like.

Dealing with confidence underminers

Kim's confidence might have increased, but it still faced challenges, and one of these was her sex. As we saw earlier, women's performance and confidence are widely undermined by stereotypes about what women can and cannot do. Kim didn't have a long-term partner, but she did have a brother, and he – probably without knowing it – was a significant saboteur of her confidence.

In his eyes, he was protecting Kim when he cautioned her about moving away from their home city. To him, she was emotionally vulnerable, and he, like their parents, was focused on what he saw as her failure-proneness. This negative attitude to failure was a significant factor in Kim's fixed mindset about her abilities and emotions, and a mental concrete block that weighed her down for many years.

Kim and her brother had an emotionally close relationship, but their bond was complicated by his unconscious need for her to be weak and vulnerable. Her failures made his achievements feel more secure. He also had a fear of failure bred into him by his parents. He shed much of that by projecting his fear of failure on to his sister. This was not a confidence-building bond for Kim, and the siblings' closeness made it all the more difficult for her to see what was happening in the relationship. The mutually warm feelings also made it harder for Kim to free herself emotionally of her confidence-sapping brother.

In the end, Kim managed to escape this unconscious sabotage when she got a new job and moved to a different city. She was aware of the relationship with her brother cooling somewhat, because she no longer satisfied his emotional need for her to be weak and vulnerable. He found Kim's new, confident independence emotionally threatening.

Relationships at home – but also those at work or within friend-ship groups – can be empowering and confidence-building, but they can also sabotage confidence. Whether it is a parent, sibling, friend or partner who has chipped away at a person's confidence for years, or a colleague or boss, relationships shape self-belief and hence performance.

If someone needs you emotionally more than you need them, this puts you in a position of power, which in turn makes you feel more confident. It puts the other person in a position of relative powerless-ness and so reduces their confidence. But many relationships, such as that between Kim and her brother, are more complicated than that.

Kim's brother was less confident and more emotionally needy than his assured outward demeanour suggested, and his remedy for this was to undermine Kim's confidence. His sister's low confi-dence, and her consequent need for support and reassurance from him, helped him maintain his somewhat fragile self-confidence. But this is not a sound basis for any relationship.

An essential task for learning to be more self-confident is to audit who the confidence-enhancers and confidence-saboteurs are in one's life. What to do once these people have been identified is another matter. Families are often built around such relationships, and chan-ging their nature can have repercussions throughout the family.

Kim's parents imbued her with a fixed (and low) view of her abilities because of their attitudes to failure. Failure was a sign that something was not right about Kim, rather than something you can learn from and rise to the challenge of. This meant that, as success-ful people themselves, they were equally uncomfortable about their own up-and-down paths to adult success. Because of this, they 'hid the ladder' of past difficulties, failures and sheer luck that are inevitable in almost everyone's career.

'Hiding the ladder' is a phrase coined by clinical psychologist Fiona O'Doherty. It explains how some children grow up believing that their parents' success is an inherent feature of their talent;

something fixed and endowed. It doesn't occur to them that it came from persistence through failure, hard work and sheer luck. Such a mindset about parents' abilities means that there is no visible ladder for a child to climb to achieve equivalent success.

Kim felt like a failure because of her parents' reaction to her school performance. But they also had not helped Kim by hiding from her – possibly with the best of intentions – the uncertain snakes and ladders of their own progression in life. Instead, they portrayed themselves as effortless achievers endowed with natural talent. There wasn't any path for Kim between where she found herself and that level of success. For children to become confident, it helps for parents to be honest about the ladders they have climbed and to be role models for persisting through failure and anxiety.

It's not just in families that we find confidence-saboteurs. Every workplace has them – be it the jealous colleague sniping from the sidelines, or the patronizing boss damning a perceived upstart with faint praise. This is because undermining someone's confidence gives you power over them. Power has strong, mood-enhancing, drug-like effects in the brain's reward network. That's why it is essential to hook up with confidence-enhancing people and to try to avoid saboteurs. But this itself needs confidence. So is there any other way a person can develop it?

Self-affirmation

Below is an exercise in what is known as self-affirmation. Take a minute or two to do it, as it will make this confidence-building method more understandable.

Rank these in terms of their importance to you in life:

Your relationships with family and friends
Being creative
Having a sense of humour

Your independence
Business or work
Political commitment
Religious or moral values
Living life for the moment, being spontaneous

Which one is dearest to your heart? Take your top-ranked term –
let's suppose it was relationships, for example. Visualize in detail a
recent situation that captured why you value your relationships so
much. It could be a warm conversation, gratitude expressed by a
friend, or a heart-warming hug. The important thing is to recall the
details and to try to get as close as possible to that situation and the
heartfelt feelings about it. Now think about other relationships in
your life that are important to you, remembering enjoyable times
with friends and family. Imagine future encounters like these, too,
and what they will be like.

You have just completed an exercise in self-affirmation, which is
when you bring to mind the thoughts, memories and emotions
linked to your most cherished values. Brain imaging by University
of Pennsylvania researchers in 2016 showed a distinct pattern of
activity during self-affirmation. A network important when thinking about yourself – the medial frontal cortex and the posterior
cingulate cortex – becomes more active. The reward network
underpinning positive feelings and motivation – the ventral striatum and the ventral medial prefrontal cortex – is also involved.
This combined activity of thinking about yourself and raised mood
should make you feel more self-confident. And there are hundreds
of studies which have shown this to be the case.

Kim used the technique of self-affirmation when she lost confidence or felt belittled. For example, in one particularly ego-bruising
conversation, her brother mocked her aspirations to travel the
world. 'Forget it, you'd never cope,' he snapped dismissively. In the
past, Kim would have curled up inside and retreated to her room,

miserable and diminished. But now she mustered the energy to force herself to bring to mind her core values. She was a generous and much-loved friend with a great sense of humour who cared deeply about her family, despite all the challenges. This mental effort changed the state of her mind and brain. It was not easy to drag these positive thoughts and memories out from all the familiar negative ones and their attendant emotions, but she managed it.

Self-affirmation works when people feel their egos are under threat. That's one reason why it makes people more confident about changing their lifestyle to improve their health. Health messages can often threaten the ego – *If you smoke, you are likely to get lung cancer. Sedentary, overweight people are likely to die early*, and so on. People who smoke or don't take much exercise and are overweight often react defensively to messages such as these, mentally turning away from them and not changing their behaviours. But if people self-affirm before hearing one of these threatening health messages, their brains show a more positive response. Rather than mentally closing down when listening to the risks of not taking exercise, their thinking-about-self networks in the ventral medial prefrontal cortex activate. They then go on to exercise more.

Self-affirmation greatly eases the levels of the stress hormone cortisol in the blood. And perhaps even more importantly, research has shown that chronically stressed students who self-affirm are able to think more clearly and solve difficult problems better. Self-affirmation helped to switch Kim's brain into a less anxious, more action-oriented and less defensive mode.

Defending the ego takes a lot of mental energy, which leaves little to address the threatening problem. Self-affirmation broadens your attention beyond the immediate threat and allows your mind to access positive memories outside of the domain in which you feel threatened.

For example, Kim's feeling of academic failure focused her mind on memories of shame and disappointment. But after self-affirming, her attention opened up, and she was able to think about her strengths and values. This freed her to summon the confidence to take action. This confidence is more easily mustered with a self-affirmation-activated reward network and with a memory system focused on successes, not failures.

Our brains respond to mistakes with a burst of activity that can be picked up by electroencephalography (EEG), and this signal is called error-related negativity (ERN). It is a useful signal because it jolts us into paying attention and responding emotionally to a mistake. We are, therefore, more likely to learn from it and not repeat it. It can be tough for our egos to learn from mistakes because of our overwhelming need to see ourselves as better than average. The ERN can work as a 'failure signal' in a defensive person's brain, and therefore be psychologically unwelcome.

University of Toronto researchers gave students a test to respond quickly to one shape on a screen, but to avoid pressing another. Responding to the incorrect shape produced a glaring, ego-threatening 'WRONG!' message on the screen. Before the test, half of the participants self-affirmed. Remarkably, the students who felt less defensive because of the self-affirmation showed a much bigger ERN brain wave to their mistakes than the other group. Their brains embraced failure more and so were better able to learn from it.

One primary source of confidence is keeping going despite failure and setbacks. If we are too ego-defensive, then we shy away from failure and our confidence suffers. Self-affirmation makes it easier for us to tolerate setbacks, failures and mistakes, and so build confidence.

People who sabotage other people's confidence are usually trying to prop up their own egos. When this happens it is easy to descend into a spiral of mutual ego-attacks. John Gottman from the University of Washington is the leading expert on marital relationships, and discovered that defensiveness is one of the most significant predictors of discord in a marriage – and eventual divorce. A switch to affirmation can disrupt the downward, tit-for-tat spiral that is typical in such defensive relationships – with an unexpected compliment or an expression of respect, for example. The confidence saboteur may be disarmed by having the ego-protecting shield of affirmation turned on them.

Self-affirmation works best when the ego is under threat. As we saw earlier, women face the headwind of stereotype-threat when competing with men in subjects such as mathematics or physics. A 2010 study significantly reduced the male–female gap in physics performance through asking women to briefly carry out a self-affirming exercise twice during a fifteen-week physics course. The women who agreed most with the statement *According to my own personal beliefs, I expect men to generally do better in physics than women* benefited most from the affirmation. In articulating self-affirming words about themselves, they weren't affirming values about physics but rather about the things they cherished most, such as relationships. This lifted their confidence – and hence their physics performance – by reducing the mentally draining effects that negative stereotypes have on performance.

Elizabeth Warren, senior state senator and former US presidential candidate, confirmed this in a commencement speech in which she said that knowing what defines you irrespective of what others think is the critical compass for helping to uncover new opportunities and to cope with setbacks. Affirming these values to yourself, she argues, will steady you like the centreboard of a dinghy.

In a 2019 study, young American teenagers who affirmed their values also showed significant improvements in their school performance. The effect is greatest among children who are under threat because of their social or racial background – self-affirmation works best with those labouring against the headwind of prejudice. Suffering prejudice is stressful, and stress eats away at self-confidence. Affirming your values buffers you against that stress and makes you smarter.

Knowing who you are by grounding yourself in what's most

important to you in life is a big step in learning to be more confident. So too is how you set goals for yourself.

Setting goals and the comfort zone

Marissa Mayer, former CEO of Yahoo!, once said that part of the secret of her success was doing things that she didn't feel quite ready to do. She felt that she grew and learned a lot about herself by taking these small steps into uncertainty, and discovered that unexpectedly good things sometimes followed.

Mayer's experience captures a crucial route to learning to be confident – setting yourself goals that stretch you, that are neither too easy nor excessively hard. We know that confidence comes from success, and particularly the success of mastering a tough challenge. Mayer had learned this, and rather than only taking on situations when she felt fully ready, she stretched herself. But she knew how to judge her goals so that she had a good chance of meeting them.

Men find it easier than women to do things that – to use Mayer's words – they're 'a little not ready to do'. One apocryphal tale is of a job advert that lists six critical requirements of candidates. The woman applicant has only five of them, so doesn't apply, while the man who has three of them does – and gets the job. The difference is – of course – confidence.

Life throws up challenges for everyone. Research shows that those who have sailed through their young lives with little or no adversity end up more emotionally vulnerable and less confident than those who have had to cope with some moderately negative experiences. These no-adversity individuals are like people who catch measles because their parents didn't have them vaccinated. Vaccination teaches the body's immune system to recognize and fight a pathogen. Adversity-vaccination teaches us to recognize and mentally respond to anxiety.

To benefit from adversity, two things should be in place. First, you need to feel you have some control – that is, the belief that in spite of what you have been through, there are things you can do (in the external or internal world) to improve your current and future wellbeing. Second, you should be willing to learn from failure and not run away from it.

Control is really important for protecting disadvantaged people against depression and anxiety. Those who feel that sense of control have healthier hippocampus memory centres in their brains. A sense of control, and the confidence it gives, cushions the brain against stress by diminishing the repeated surges of the stress hormone cortisol that can impair the hippocampus.

Before Kim found her direction and confidence, she hadn't felt in control of her life for years. Feeling out of control makes you anxious, and if you see that anxiety as something medically wrong with you, and hence out of your control, then a vicious downward cycle can occur – which is what happened to Kim. What was hardest for her, however, was learning to worry less. Worry is a gruelling mental addiction that hooks people because it gives the illusion of control. Kim would ruminate about her fears for the future over and over again – *Will I ever manage to leave home?* – and her guilt about the past – *I shouldn't have let them down by cancelling that holiday at the last minute.* Though she wasn't conscious of this, worrying operated as a substitute for action. Somewhere at the back of her mind was the mistaken belief that if she fretted enough about something, that would magically prevent it from happening.

Kim learned to avoid this worry trap by separating what she could control from what she couldn't. When she worried about something she could control, such as finding a new job, she would link the concern to concrete action in the form of small, specific goals. Achieving these small goals was crucial in building her confidence and feeling more in control of her anxiety.

While Kim found dealing with failure difficult because of her fixed mindset, her brother was, in his own way, just as haunted by this, which is why it suited him for her to be the lightning rod of failure in their family.

In his late twenties, Kim's brother went through emotionally turbulent times as he faced the hard realities of working life, where success is not guaranteed. Anxiety was a new – and frightening – experience for him. Because he had never been vaccinated against it, it shocked him and sent him to the doctor for 'treatment', as he could only approach it with a fixed mindset. Paradoxically, as each sibling entered their early thirties, Kim was the more confident and emotionally secure of the two.

Setting goals and achieving them is critical for becoming more confident. Setting trivially easy goals doesn't deliver a success 'buzz', and doesn't build confidence. But goals that are too distant or difficult doom a person to experiencing failure and demotivation. This is why perfectionists have a hard time becoming confident. A parental voice in the head of the perfectionist often dismisses modest achievements as worthless, and so demotivates. For confidence to grow, imperfection, like failure, must be embraced and learned from, not feared and avoided.

One other crucial fact about confidence that Kim learned was that goals have to be authentically *yours*. Kim was burdened by achievement goals set by her parents and based on her brother's path. But with the help of the mental contrasting technique, she was able to sort out what her own goals were and which ones were feasible to achieve. Before that, she was haunted by not being first in her class in school or a straight-A student in college, like her brother had been. But these weren't authentic goals because they were about comparison with others. The trouble with needing to beat others is that there will always be someone who is better than you. This type of comparative goal is a recipe for anxiety and fear of failure.

A 2014 study from Korea University in Seoul looked at what happened in the brains of students who, like the younger Kim, set comparative goals for themselves. They contrasted them with 'mastery-oriented' students who were motivated mainly by understanding better what they were learning, not by competing with others. The first group agreed with statements such as *It is important for me to do well compared to others in this task*, while the second group endorsed statements such as *It is important for me to understand the content of this task as thoroughly as possible.*

Lying in an fMRI scanner, the students had to solve problems of different levels of difficulty, and were told after each answer whether they were right or wrong. When they gave the wrong answer, the brains of mastery-oriented students recorded a surge in activity in the prefrontal cortex. This showed they were trying to process the error and work out where they had gone wrong. For those motivated to compare themselves with others, the prefrontal cortex activity declined substantially, showing that they shut down and retreated mentally rather than making sense of their mistake. The first group would learn from their errors and grow in confidence as they corrected them in the future, while the second group would not.

Kim had found herself in the second group, but after many years of fear and a sense of failure, she learned to set goals for herself that were uniquely hers. She didn't care about her ranking compared to others – she set her own goals against *her* metrics. As a result, Kim experienced confidence-building success in meeting the goals that she defined. Like the mastery-oriented Korean students, she now learned from her setbacks, and this helped her to grow more confident. She then applied this to her social life. She learned not to care how popular some other people were, but rather to focus her mind on the small circle of good friends that she had.

Fake it till you make it?

'Just believe in yourself. Even if you don't, pretend that you do and, at some point, you will.'

This was Venus Williams speaking on ABC News in 2013. It's something successful people often say, but what is the scientific evidence for it? And what does that pretence look like? For a while it was thought to be physical. A study of 'power posing' by Columbia and Harvard University researchers claimed that an expansive, confident-looking power pose – legs spread wide, arms intentionally out at your side, or on your hips – made people feel more confident because it raised testosterone levels in the body, but the findings weren't replicated in further studies.

This was not before various politicians and business leaders were seen legs akimbo and shoulders thrown back like strutting medieval sentries as they gave their speeches. On his first day in his new post as the UK's Chancellor of the Exchequer in 2018, Sajid Javid adopted this extreme stance and was largely ridiculed for it.

So, is there any truth in Venus Williams's claim? We saw earlier that it is often easier to *act* yourself into a new way of feeling than to *feel* yourself into a new way of acting. If leaving a comfort zone without the certainty of success is a form of 'faking', then yes, you can fake it till you make it. A 2020 review of all the studies on posture showed that expanding your body in space with a wide stance or spread-out shoulders and arms doesn't raise confidence much at all. However, it did conclude that shrinking your posture – with folded arms, bowed head, hunched posture and crossed legs – diminished people's confidence quite significantly.

A power pose won't necessarily increase your confidence, but standing tall in a stressful situation and avoiding hunching and making yourself small *will* help you keep confident. In addition, people tend to think more abstractly when they wear formal versus casual clothing because wearing it makes them feel more powerful. Just putting on a white lab coat improves your ability to focus your attention and concentrate, a 2012 study by Northwestern University researchers showed.

So 'faking' the externals of confidence can have some effect, but not on their own. Kim gradually learned to be confident by changing her thinking and taking action in the world. Dressing sharply also helped, as did smiling more confidently than she felt inside, holding someone's gaze and resisting the temptation to make herself small, but no amount of attention to fashion or bold eye contact could have substituted for the change in her thinking.

Asking for reassurance

Kim was always looking for reassurance, and it had become an ingrained habit in almost every interaction. *I hope I didn't come across as too aggressive . . . Did I make any sense? . . . Please tell me if I'm talking rubbish . . . I hope you weren't too bored listening to me . . .* On the surface, these may appear to be healthy feedback-seeking queries that make someone a good friend or colleague who gets on well with others. While that may be partly true, there is a much higher cost to the individual of continually seeking reassurance. It constitutes a haemorrhage of confidence because it perpetuates anxiety.

Reassurance-seeking reduces anxiety in the short term but worsens it in the long run. Kim's chronic self-doubt meant that after every conversation she would chew over every word in her head. She would worry about stupid things she might have said. These ruminations made her anxious, so to stem the anxiety, she would ask for reassurance. It might be from the person she had spoken to, or more likely from a friend – *Do you think I was terrible to say that to her? I think she might not like me.*

Usually, the friend would reassure her – *No, of course not, she really likes you* – and Kim would feel less anxious, but only for a while. Then the doubts would creep back in, and she would look for more reassurance, which she would get. Again, the anxiety would decline, but then it would come back with a vengeance. Reassurance had become a habit. Each time she got it, her brain would get a little burst of reward, a lessening of the ugly feeling of anxiety. But this would be temporary, and soon she would need to seek out further assurances to get the same 'hit'. As with many habits, the reward is reduced each time.

Too much reassurance-seeking can become a dominant mental stance in the unconfident person that makes them more and more anxious and less and less confident. The mere act of seeking reassurance can sabotage confidence by increasing anxiety and lowering mood.

Looking for too much reassurance can bleed into relationships – *If she has such doubt about herself, maybe she's right?* Confidence, we have seen throughout the book, is contagious – but so is self-doubt. If confidence is a source of persuasion, then self-doubt can have the opposite effect and dissuade people from believing in you.

Learning to bite her tongue and not ask for reassurance was one of the hardest things Kim had to learn in her journey towards being more confident. Over time she realized that as well as the assurance-seeking habit, she had many others that signalled self-doubt to others and hence perpetuated it. Here are just some of the patterns she gradually became aware of:

> Apologizing too much – *Sorry, I'm such a mess . . . Sorry,*
> *I should have phoned sooner.*
> Brushing off compliments – *Oh goodness, that was just*
> *luck.*
> Upspeaking at the end of a sentence so that it sounds
> like a question.
> Putting off even small decisions because she wasn't sure
> if she had chosen correctly.
> Self-deprecating jokes – *I'm such an idiot . . . I'm just so*
> *disorganized.*

Kim had to unlearn each of these habits. She forced herself to put up with the short-term anxiety she felt when she didn't apologize for some non-existent transgression. She learned to smile and say thanks when she received a compliment. She stopped speaking as though every sentence was a question. She learned to love her decision – *It's right because I made it*. And she stopped warding off imagined criticism by making fewer self-deprecating jokes.

Most of these habits were forms of reassurance-seeking that she'd relied on for too long. If you use a crutch too much, your leg muscles waste, and mental crutches have a comparable effect on the confidence muscles. Kim learned to shoulder the doubt that is inherent in every decision we make or action we take. Confidence is what allowed her to do this.

CHAPTER 9

Overconfidence

∶∶

O N 25 MAY 1978, thirty thousand football fans swarmed excit-edly around the gates of Hampden Stadium in Glasgow. They had come to see their national football squad, pricey tickets clutched in sweaty hands. The famous Hampden roar went up as their team came on to the pitch. But not to play. No, the fans were there first to watch the team coach – Ally MacLeod – then his players, enter the stadium one by one through two lines of majorettes, to delirious applause. Coach and team then boarded an open-top bus, which drove around the stadium once and then exited, en route to the World Cup Finals in Argentina.

'I want to prove I am the best manager in the world,' MacLeod had boasted a year earlier.

Asked by a journalist what he planned to do after Scotland won the World Cup, he replied, 'Retain it.'

The results in Argentina tell a somewhat different story. Scotland lost to Peru in the first round and then drew against Iran. Then, despite winning heroically against Holland, they were out of the competition and homeward bound in ignominy. It wasn't that Scotland had a bad team – the fact that they managed to defeat the great Dutch side testifies to that. Nor was a lack of confidence a problem. Patently, their manager had whipped his team into a froth of hyper-confidence.

Ally MacLeod was what is colloquially known as a bullshitter – a familiar personality type that has generated its own academic research. Take one international survey of educational achievement in which adolescents were asked whether they were familiar with a list of sixteen mathematical concepts, such as *arithmetic mean*, *cosine* and *linear equation*. So far so good for most budding mathematicians. But the researchers also smuggled three non-existent terms into the survey – *declarative fraction*, *subjunctive scaling* and *proper number*. The teenagers had to say how familiar they were with each of these terms, and how much they understood them, ranging from *never heard of it* at one end of the scale, to *know it well* and *understand it completely* at the other. Their answers give a measure of bullshitting – how confidently someone declares that they understand a concept that they cannot ever have heard of because it doesn't exist.

Unsurprisingly, male students bullshitted much more than females, across all nine English-speaking countries in the survey. Wealthier children also bullshitted more than poorer children. And adolescents from North America bullshitted much more than teenagers from Scotland and Ireland, with England, New Zealand and Australia in the middle.

This finding highlights the ambiguity of confidence. It transpired that bullshit-prone teenagers were more confident about solving practical problems. As well as exaggerating their own maths knowledge, they also believed they were more popular in school than the non-bullshitters, and that they would persevere more with difficult problems. In other words, they were more self-confident than non-bullshitters, and, as we have seen, self-confidence has a potent self-fulfilling quality to it.

But if you are a surgeon, a financial trader or a truck driver, you have to know the limits of your abilities. You must try to avoid the overreach caused by overconfidence. Here is the sobering truth revealed by Cornell University researchers in 1999: the lower your ability, the more you tend to overestimate your skill. Poor surgeons think that they are better than they are, while good ones overestimate their skill much less. The less intelligent people are, the more they tend to overestimate how bright they are. Most of us share the conceit that we are above-average drivers. And if you have glanced in alarm at your languishing pension pot recently, consider this sad fact: 74 per cent of fund managers think that they are above-average investment performers.

There's a paradox at the heart of this thing we call confidence. Our faith in the future and our motivation to keep going requires that we are over-optimistic about both the probabilities of what can happen as well as our own *can do* capacities. Mildly depressed people make more realistic predictions about uncertain future events than those who aren't depressed. 'Healthy' normality, in other words, demands a degree of self-delusion about the future and our abilities. In other words – confidence. Higher levels of depression tilt predictions unrealistically in the opposite direction, towards pessimism. In a normal, relatively healthy life, this optimistic bias we call confidence tricks us into doing stuff that we wouldn't otherwise try. And often it works, because these common delusions make things happen.

But overconfidence has costs as well as benefits.

The amputated leg

The surgeon swept into the room, his white coat flaring in his slipstream. Nurses bustled nervously around the patient, and junior doctors shuffled and mumbled in response to barked queries as he speed-skimmed copious notes. He yanked back the sheet to expose his patient's legs, which he prodded and peered at briefly before finally addressing the man on the bed with a beneficent beam.

'And how are we today?'

The man's startled look at being spoken to dissolved into one of puzzled meekness.

'F-fine . . . Th . . . thank you . . .'

'Pain?'

That startled look again. 'S-sorry?'

'The leg – painful?'

'Oh, y-yes.'

'So you understand that it has to come off?'

A cloud passed across the care-worn face. 'I think that was what the other doctor . . . said, but . . .'

'Good – I'll sort that. I'll operate tomorrow.'

The surgeon's coat ballooned as he whirled around and away, his juniors scrambling to keep up.

Early the next morning, the master of the operating theatre swept into his demesne and removed the leg. But it was the wrong leg – the healthy one. The surgeon had to amputate the other leg a month later.

The above story is a composite story based on fact. It is also a portrayal of a rather old-fashioned style of medical practice that many countries have managed to change by reforming medical training and the way hospitals are run. But a 2016 study concluded that medical error is the third leading cause of death in the US, after heart disease and cancer. Studies in other countries have come to similar conclusions. Mistakes include one Rhode Island hospital operating on the wrong side of patients' brains no fewer than three times in one year. Of course, doctors make mistakes – we all do – but their mistakes have graver consequences than most. And one of the main reasons for this is overconfidence.

Overconfidence in political leaders has even graver consequences, however, because it causes wars. For example, in 1980,

Saddam Hussein led Iraq into a disastrous eight-year conflict with Iran. He overestimated his military strength and underestimated Iran's. Up to two million people died, with millions more maimed. An early negotiated peace would have benefited both countries, which is true in almost all wars. But overconfident political leaders are also too optimistic about the likely consequences of conflict. They defy the hard facts of reality and probability with an illusion of superiority.

But here's the rub: overconfidence is a bluff, and bluffs sometimes work.

On 16 November 1532, the Spanish conquistador Francisco Pizarro and 168 Spanish soldiers faced an army of eighty thousand Inca soldiers, as described in the book *Overconfidence and War* by historian Dominic Johnson. A Spanish eyewitness wrote that having arrived, 'they could not turn back or show fear, as it would have made them seem uncertain of victory'. Pizarro had attempted to boost his soldiers' morale by telling them there were 'only' forty thousand Inca soldiers. It seems as though the Spaniards were determined to maintain the illusion that they expected to win.

Pizarro's forces did win, but not primarily because of their horses and cannon, rather because of a massive bluff that demoralized the spear-, club- and bow-and-arrow-armed Incas, shattering their confidence. Johnson's extensive analysis of hundreds of historical battles, mainly from the Second World War and the Arab–Israeli wars, suggests that comparable bluffs underpin success in many battles.

Johnson uncovered numerous examples of military leaders beating the odds, as Pizarro did, with overconfidence that defied the reality of opposing military strengths. He concluded that overconfidence didn't work by somehow supercharging the weaker combatant. Instead, it deceived the enemy into overestimating their opponent's real strength.

Overconfidence is effectively a public relations strategy that works because it persuades your opponent that you are more formidable than you actually are. But for every Pizarro-like victory, there are disasters caused by overconfidence. Gallipoli in the First World War is one example, as is Napoleon's invasion of Russia. The latter was an overconfident folly that Hitler could not resist emulating a century later.

A 2007 University of Toronto study asked 527 petroleum geologists to find oil in a simulation exercise. The researchers drip-fed them increasingly negative evidence that their – what in the real world would be very expensive – efforts were unlikely to yield results. But the most self-confident geologists of the group escalated the exploration after this negative feedback. Instead of abandoning the false trail and accepting sunk costs, they burned up virtual millions of their companies' money in vain. Those who were less overconfident abandoned the fruitless and expensive search much earlier.

Overconfidence can trigger dangerous certainties about the world. It nurtures simplistic analyses and solutions to super-complex realities. Researchers have shown that over-simple thinking is a characteristic of both left- and right-wing political extremists. Such radicals are even overconfident in their answers when they estimate how many grains of sand there are in a glass.

Of course, we would all prefer that our surgeon exudes confidence – and who are we to know whether it is overconfidence or not? And there's the dilemma. Confidence has the power in the right dose to make us more persuasive and effective, but in overdose it tips us into a folly of wrongly amputated limbs and gruesome wars. It lies at the heart of many tragic and expensive mistakes, and is so common and familiar that it has spawned its very own curse.

The winner's curse

The entrepreneur's meteoric rise had made him an international celebrity sought out by world leaders because of his inspiring plans for the future of humanity. His company's size and scale could solve the world's biggest problems, he told the *New York* magazine, and he needed the largest possible valuation of his company so that he could provide help with issues of global warfare: 'There are 150 million orphans in the world. We want to solve this problem and give them a new family.'

His company's mission, he further claimed, was to *elevate the world's consciousness.*

At 7.07 a.m. on Wednesday, 14 August 2019, Adam Neumann's WeWork company issued documents about its first public offering of shares at a valuation of $47 billion. By mid-October, this collapsed to less than $8 billion, 2,400 employees were laid off, and Neumann was forced to stand down as CEO as a condition of a bailout that sweetened his exit with a $1.5 billion payout.

Overconfidence is the overestimation of your abilities and likely success. Adam Neumann was surely overconfident. In the space of nine years he had grown his start-up from a single office to one of the largest private workspace tenants in New York and London, with locations in over twenty-three countries. But ultimately, he couldn't find families for 150 million orphans, stop global conflict, nor elevate the world's consciousness. Nor, unfortunately, could he prevent an unprecedented $39 billion collapse in his company's valuation.

Yet this buccaneering ambition had equally contributed to his investors – including SoftBank CEO Masayoshi Son – ploughing billions into WeWork. Confidence, as we have seen already, makes people more persuasive, and overconfidence makes them super-persuasive. It can also make them more risk-friendly. According to the US business magazine *Fast Company*, Neumann called executives who tried to convince him to take fewer risks 'B players'. He allegedly barred such pessimists from meetings or otherwise ignored them.

The winner's curse is the tendency in a competitive auction for the winning bid to be higher than the actual value of the auction's target. Three engineers first coined this term in 1971 when they noticed that the winning companies bidding for oil exploration rights paid more than the eventual real value of the fields. Overconfidence makes people over-optimistic.

And this is apparently what happened to WeWork in the hands of Adam Neumann, who, for all his visionary idealism, eventually had to answer to his investors' doubts over the company's annual losses and inflated valuation. Except, of course, he walked away personally uncursed and reportedly very, very rich – which is more than can be said for many of his employees. Here, the paradox of overconfidence is encapsulated – it can work up to a point, before the winner's curse kicks in. Some, like Neumann, are adept at harnessing it up to that moment, before exiting, which can leave others cursed, and not them.

Overconfidence can be either an asset or a curse, depending on circumstances. If 74 per cent of the fund managers who control our pensions and investments believe that they are, on average, better than other fund managers, that fact should give us pause. If they are capable of such skewed self-assessments, how safe is our money?

In 2008, a University of Haifa study subtly 'primed' either risk-seeking or risk-avoidant states of mind in senior professional financial advisers, and also in a group of undergraduate economics students, by giving them an ostensible word memory test into which they had smuggled risk-seeking or risk-averse words. The risk-seeking words included *enterprising, daring* and *adventurous*. The risk-averse ones included *conscientious, responsible, careful* and *well-considered*. The participants didn't know that these words were subtly biasing their thinking.

Unconsciously primed for either risk or caution, the financial professionals and the students then made investment decisions concerning stocks, about which they were given detailed information. Simply having read the risk-positive words in the so-called memory test increased everyone's appetite for risky choices about the stock. Disturbingly for our pensions, however, the senior financial professionals were much more affected by the unconscious priming of risk-prone attitudes than the economics students.

Far from being more rationally analytical, as you would expect from professionals, these senior people shot from the hip. Cognitively speaking, they relied on hunch and intuition more than cool-headed decision-making. And it *wasn't* the case that well-honed intuition leads to better decisions. On the contrary, experienced professional traders made poorer financial choices than students, because of their overconfidence in their hunches. With his work-hard-play-hard lifestyle, and management decisions seen by many as unpredictable, Adam Neumann's cognitive style seems to have been one of shooting from the hip. It is overconfidence, more than anything, which can create this mentality.

Senior people have power, and power can make you overconfident and therefore prone to the mental shortcuts that blind you to risk. One example of this was the dotcom technology bubble – an investment-fuelled rapid rise in the stock market valuation of technology companies – that peaked in March 2000, only to lose 80 per cent of its value within two years. In 1999, the *Wall Street Journal* noted that adding the domain suffix '.com' to a company's name caused its share price to surge.

The financial wizards trading these shares were sucked into a tornado of overconfident thinking that spat them out when the cold reality of a share-price collapse dawned, just as happened with WeWork. And the problem is made worse because as global financial markets expand, it becomes expensive for smaller institutions to do the due diligence on investment risks. So, as research shows, they tend to follow the lead of bigger investors. But, as we have seen, many of these financial leaders are even more prone to irrational hunches and emotion in their decision-making than untrained students. If you need more evidence, consider this fact: between 1982 and 1997, across twenty-six countries, the amount of morning sunshine was found to strongly correlate with a city's stock exchange returns that day. Even the transient happiness of a sunny morning can irrationally boost confidence in the financial future.

But it's not just big financial traders who experience the winner's curse of overconfidence.

Finland, like other Scandinavian countries, has remarkable data on its citizens. A 2009 study by UCLA and the Helsinki School of Economics looked at stock trading by many thousands of its male citizens. They were able to study citizens' trades in relation to how overconfident they were about their intellects, compared to their actual abilities, which had been assessed for military service. Intellectually overconfident men traded much more often – and, incidentally, got many more speeding tickets – the Finnish state records showed.

However, the thing about amateur trading by individuals in their living rooms is that the more you trade, the higher your losses on average. Using data from thirty-five thousand US households, a 2001 study discovered that between 1991 and 1997, men traded 45 per cent more than women. And because of this, their annual losses were 50 per cent greater.

Something similar happens in start-up businesses. Economists have discovered that for 75 per cent of entrepreneurial start-ups, staying in a waged job would be much more financially rewarding than going out on one's own. So what spurs people into becoming entrepreneurs, when reality dictates that most start-ups fail? Overconfidence. The bright-eyed, risk-ignoring optimists that we call entrepreneurs wouldn't do what they do without a healthy dose of that most potent of rocket fuels – overconfidence. Most will fail, but a minority will succeed tremendously. The gambler's dream of the big prize trumps their rational calculations of risk.

The poet T. S. Eliot famously noted that humankind cannot bear very much reality, which seems to be true for much of business and finance. Overconfident bravado may seed disasters like Napoleon's invasion of Russia, Adam Neumann's grandiose expansion of WeWork, and Ally MacLeod's Argentinian humiliation. But it also launches human beings into the future, blinkered by optimism and hubristic about their competences. And sometimes, just sometimes, it pays off, and they manage to evade the winner's curse.

In 1957, the Danish architect Jørn Utzon won a competition to design a public building on the edge of Sydney Harbour at a projected cost of $65 million at today's value. Sixteen years and a billion dollars later, the Sydney Opera House opened on 20 October 1973. According to Danish economist Bent Flyvbjerg, it was the most expensive cost overrun in the history of world megaprojects. The Opera House is a prime example of the planning fallacy – a bugbear of big projects around the world, and one to which overconfident people and organizations are particularly vulnerable. Confidence makes you feel more in control, and overconfidence magnifies that feeling to the point that you underestimate the project pitfalls that you can't control.

An exaggerated sense of control also makes you over-optimistic about timelines. Furthermore, researchers at London Business School showed in 2008 that the brains of overconfident people suffer less 'loss aversion' – the preference for avoiding losses more than acquiring gains.

Big projects need big teams, so how can an overconfident leader override the realism and caution of his team? We know that overconfidence makes you super-persuasive, and that is one reason. But the other is known as the MUM effect – where more junior people in an organization stay silent – mum – about warning signs because of the power and dominance of their bosses.

Researchers in a 2015 study randomly allocated volunteers to work together on a problem in pairs. One person in each pair was given the role of supervisor, and the other of employee. The supervisor was also given the power to rate the employee and hand out rewards. The researchers coached half the supervisors to have a very confident demeanour, with much direct eye contact, upright posture, a fluent speaking voice, and broad, confident gestures. The remaining supervisors were coached to have low eye contact, non-upright posture and other low-confidence-related behaviours.

What might surprise you is that the teams with the confident-seeming boss found it harder to solve problems than those with a less confident-appearing supervisor. The employees in these pairs felt inhibited by the boss's confidence and were unable to make suggestions and give opinions. This was true even when the 'employee' had unique information about the problem that their boss didn't have – they stayed mum.

Smart teams have their own group intelligence, separate from the averaged IQ of each individual member. Clever teams are talented at solving problems because of how members interact with each other, much more than how intelligent each individual member is. The whole, in other words, is much smarter than the sum of its parts.

Researchers at Carnegie Mellon randomly assigned volunteers to forty small groups to work on a range of intellectually demanding problems for several hours. They found that the smartest groups were not those with the highest IQ members. Instead, the individuals in the clever groups were adept at reading other people's facial expressions and took turns in discussions without one person dominating. The proportion of women in the group also predicted its smarts, but that was because women tend to be better than men at reading other people's emotions.

Overconfident people with power are more likely to dominate discussions. If they don't read emotional expressions, then they don't pick up signals that others might be annoyed, bored, excited, thoughtful, angry or anxious. So, they don't bring them into problem-solving discussions. This depletes the group intelligence because its members are inhibited from contributing by the over-dominant, overconfident member of the team. In this way, the overconfident person of either sex weakens group intelligence. However, men's higher average levels of confidence, power and dominance make them behave like this much more often than women.

But staying mum and not contributing to the discussion is the least of the confidence-sapping effects of our relationships in a group. In 2012, Virginia Tech researchers allocated students into different problem-solving groups, having measured their individual IQs first. They then told the people in one group where they ranked on IQ within their group. The other group, which had the same average IQ as the first, weren't told their personal ranking.

The ranked group became less smart, solving fewer problems than the others, who were not burdened by knowing their rank. In the ranked students' brains, there was lower activity on the left outer surface of the frontal lobe, plus boosted activity in the amygdala – the anxiety centre. So, not only do confidence-sapping relationships prevent us from contributing to problem-solving within teams, they also deplete our brain function.

We have seen the consequences of overconfidence, but where does it come from?

What makes people overconfident?

In 2020, as the Covid-19 crisis grew in the US, President Donald Trump paid a visit to the scientists and doctors working to develop a vaccine at the Centers for Disease Control and Prevention in Atlanta. He told them about a great 'super-genius uncle' who had taught at MIT, and professed that this talent must run in the family.

'People are really surprised I understand this stuff,' he said. 'Every one of these doctors said, "How do you know so much about this?" Maybe I have a natural ability.'

President Trump also tweeted this in 2019: 'I'm great looking and smart, a true Stable Genius', one of many such expressions of super-confidence about his abilities and attributes. Trump's over-confidence is his calling card. It is part of his brand and it has served him very well in politics and business. But where does overconfidence in general come from?

In an attempt to answer that question, University of Minnesota researchers approached a thousand trainee, largely male, truck drivers at a Saturday training camp as part of a 2013 study. They paid the trainees to conduct intelligence and personality tests. They then asked them to estimate their ranking on the IQ test compared to the other drivers. As you would expect by now, many more thought they were in the top 20 per cent of rankings than was statistically possible. Personality played a big part in how big this illusion was. High scorers on one personality dimension called social potency rated themselves more highly on items such as these: *forceful and decisive; persuasive and liking to influence others; enjoying or would enjoy leadership roles; enjoying being noticed, being the centre of attention. Enjoys visibility, dominance, likes to be in charge, persuasive, strong – a leader.*

Even the truck drivers who scored as below average on social potency were overconfident about their intelligence – 33 per cent of them judged that they were in the top 20 per cent. But of the forceful and dominant influencers – the guys who slap you on the back and put cream in your coffee without asking – 55 per cent of them judged they were in the top 20 per cent in smarts.

A different set of personality characteristics made people less overconfident about how intelligent they were. These included sensitivity to other people's criticisms, nervousness, proneness to guilty feelings, or sensitive and worry-prone vulnerability.

Where do such personality patterns come from? As with most behaviours, it is a combination of nature and nurture. Identical twins are more alike in overconfidence than non-identical twins are, researchers at MIT showed. This is true even if they grow up apart, though life experience also makes a significant contribution. But these genetically transmitted differences needn't be substantial at the beginning of life in order to accumulate over time into large effects. For example, some neonates have more placid temperaments than others who are a little more prone to crying, having disturbed sleep, and so on. A negative parental response to a child's emotionality could worsen the behaviour over time, leading to a growing negativity of the parent in a tit-for-tat escalation over the years.

What begins as a very small inherited difference in temperament may end up as a very large difference in adult emotionality. It might look as if this adult emotionality is mainly genetically determined, but in fact, what is happening is similar to the confidence-as-compound-interest analogy from Chapter 4. Small initial differences – in the present case genetic – are steadily amplified by how the world responds to them and by the gradually accumulating advantages – or disadvantages – that result.

As we saw with the confidence-as-compound-interest analogy, a small initial difference can become magnified over years and turn into a yawning gap, because the initial advantage creates benefits that lead to further advantage, and so on, in an accumulating cycle that greatly magnifies the original small difference. Small initial boy–girl differences in inherited early confidence-linked temperament may undergo a similar compound-interest development because of the accumulating advantages – or disadvantages – that these behaviours produce. The very early stereotype, expectation and perception differences of females versus males that we saw in Chapter 7 systematically exaggerate any small, initial, inherited differences over time.

One source of overconfidence, then, is personality, and, in particular, the motivation to dominate others. But such personalities only fully manifest themselves if they acquire the status that they crave.

Status seeking

Why do people bother with the effort of being overconfident? You might think that life would be so much easier if we were all just honest and accurate about our abilities. Why invest all this energy into over-selling?

Well, overconfidence seems to work – up to a point. It makes people listen and do what the overconfident person wants. But why should people listen to a bullshitter? One persuasive reason emerged in an experiment in which university students took a test about US geography, but weren't told their grade. They then had to estimate how well they'd performed on the test compared to their fellow students, revealing how over- or underconfident each student was. They then answered more geography questions, but this time in teams of two. After the pairs had agreed their answers, each privately rated their partner as to how good they were at US geography. They also rated how much status and respect they thought the partner was due, in terms of their leadership, influence and contribution to the task.

How did overconfident people do in these influence ratings? They aced it, and duped their partners into buying into their overconfidence. Not only that, but their partners afforded them a higher status rating as a result.

In a second study by the same researchers, MBA students working on projects in groups of five or six over the course of seven weeks were studied to see whether overconfidence also had these effects in the real world.

The 243 MBA students were asked to fill out the 'over-claiming questionnaire' – a measure of a person's propensity to bullshit. They read words or names from literature, history and science, and rated how confident they were that they knew each term on a zero-to-six scale. But, as with the adolescents and their maths test, there were a few fictional items smuggled into each category. For example, in science, *cholarine*, *ultra-lipid* and *plates of parallax* were included alongside genuine terms such as *Manhattan Project*, *nebula* and *plate tectonics*.

At the beginning of the seven-week project, and again at the end, each member of the group secretly rated one another in terms of how much they influenced group decisions. This score had real-life implications because the other members' ratings were used in the person's actual course grades. And sure enough, the overconfident bullshitters were ranked higher in influence and status than the non-bullshitters.

How do overconfident people dupe others into giving them higher status? The researchers delved into this question by comparing the behaviour of the students perceived by their peers to be highly confident with that of the others. What they found wasn't surprising. Their peers saw them as more competent if they talked more and used a factual, confident tone of voice. The impression strengthened if they sat with an expansive, open posture, offered more answers, and expressed certainty about their opinions.

How many people have been chosen for jobs because selection panels overestimated competence due to the overconfidence of a candidate? And how many more – women much more than men – have been rejected because they didn't bullshit at the interview? Men, as we have seen, are more overconfident than women, on average. They have the advantage of accumulating benefits of this achievement fuel additive over many years. Status, power and wealth tend to accrue to the overconfident.

Could better assessment and monitoring processes detect the bullshitter and make it easier for the modest and accurate self-appraiser to gain influence? A 2013 study suggests that it is going to be very difficult.

University of Pennsylvania researchers confirmed that in problem-solving groups, fellow members tended to see overconfident participants as more competent and accord them higher status. But what if they were to reveal the true performance scores of these overconfident people to the groups? Would that destroy the illusion of competence and bring their status down?

No, it would not. Even when the real abilities of the overconfident were exposed to the group, it didn't change their status, and they remained respected as high-status influencers.

The resonance with what we see in the present political world is formidable. Fact matters less than presentation. Appearance yields status and power, much more than mere competence and achievement, it seems. Why does this happen?

The research suggests that overconfidence is a signal of high status more than it is information about someone's actual competence. If you can portray a veneer of overconfidence, that will elevate you and accord you the privileges of higher status, including respect, influence and power. In the real world, these valuable resources can be cashed in and create a self-fulfilling cycle of success. Once a person has banked the booty of overconfidence, the gap between real abilities and pretensions is obscured. He (and it is, of course, mainly he) will have secured respect, influence and power through exaggerating – bullshitting – his abilities. His overconfidence has paid off.

There is a period of time when the gap between reality and pretension is visible before overconfidence turns into a self-fulfilling prophecy. Here, overconfidence often – but not always – pays dividends, as it did for Neumann, for example. If it works, it can create its own reality – again, as it did for Neumann, even if only for a time. If people gain status, power and wealth because of their capacity to bullshit, then once they have it, it becomes a reality and not an aspiration.

The University of Pennsylvania study shows why this works. It seems that people care more about appearance than reality. It doesn't matter to them if the bullshitting is unmasked – the mere capacity to appear bullishly confident garners status and the illusion of competence. One reason for this is that the trappings of overconfidence – strong voice, eye contact, open posture, strong statements – are primitive signals of dominance that bypass more rational circuits in our brains. And when you start working with strangers in a group, these rational circuits are fully occupied with two main tasks. The first is doing the group activity. The second, much more importantly, is trying to work out what others in the group are thinking about you.

With your limited-capacity, rational, conscious mental processes fully occupied, the more primitive dominance relationships establish themselves through the signals that overconfident people emit. This dominance gives a status that takes precedence over any actual information about the performance of the bullshitter. That status is the currency both for the bullshitter but also, crucially, for those linked to him.

Merely having status, irrespective of how the overconfident person gets it, becomes the source of social reward that he can now dispense to the group. People like to be associated with status, and as they also judge it by seeing others deferring to the high-status person, then their perception is strengthened.

This is the dynamic behind social climbing and status-seeking. Merely being in contact with a high-status person makes it feel like some of that standing will rub off on you. Crowds flock to celebrities for this reason. They don't clamour for contact with the famous because they think they will get anything tangible from them; it is status that they think might rub off a little on them. And this is why overconfidence is a lucrative pattern of behaviour. It pays off in spades because it tricks people into giving you status. Once you have it, it is near-indelible, even when your incompetence becomes evident.

Overconfidence can give you status in the eyes of others. And with that position comes power.

Power

In late September 2017, the CEO of American Airlines, Doug Parker, met with Wall Street analysts to discuss his industry's future. Here is what he said: 'I don't think we're ever going to lose money again . . . We have an industry that's going to be profitable in good and bad times.'

Roll forward thirty months. The Covid-19 pandemic has grounded much of Parker's fleet, and he is lobbying the US government for emergency aid. This effort results in a $5.8 billion bailout.

You might assume that this titan of the airways had never seen crises like this before and was unprepared. But no, only four years previously his twice-bankrupt former employer, US Airways, bought American Airlines out of Chapter 11 bankruptcy, a process which allows companies to reorganize their debts. The airlines merged to form the new carrier. His own America West Airlines had spent three years in bankruptcy in the 1990s. So Doug Parker had a very up-close experience of the vulnerability of the aviation industry. How on earth could he make a statement like 'I don't think we're ever going to lose money again'?

Forbes journalist Dan Reed responded with restrained incredulity in an article the week after Doug Parker made that jaw-dropping statement. He said that there will always be events that can disrupt the airline industry, whether that be a volcano erupting, a nuclear power plant meltdown, a major terrorist incident, a war . . . or any one of the myriad threats that have always existed for Doug Parker's industry. Something will *always* happen, Reed asserted.

What happened was Covid-19.

How a modestly salaried journalist was able to engage in a more realistic scenario assessment than an executive with an eight-figure salary is perplexing. How could Parker be so mistakenly overconfident?

There are at least two answers. One is that this is what Parker's board paid him to do. He pitched to Wall Street analysts hoping they would invest in his shares. And as we know, overconfidence makes you persuasive and buys you respect, influence and status. A second reason is power.

Power is one of the most potent brain-changing agents in the world, and the more power someone has, the bigger these effects are. Power means having control over what others want, need or fear, and being a highly salaried CEO of a major company offers that. The effects of power include focusing your attention and memory on rewards, while powerlessness orients your attention and memory towards potential punishments. Power increases dopamine-related activity in the brain's reward network, making people feel good about themselves, optimistic and motivated.

Powerlessness lowers mood and demotivates. Power narrows your attention towards your current goals. In contrast, lack of power widens your focus as you scan the horizon for threat. High levels of power make you less self-aware, less empathetic and less anxious. In contrast, low power makes you very self-aware, more empathetic and more anxious.

Like many of the brain's neurotransmitter systems, dopamine has a bell-shaped curve, meaning too little and too much distort your brain function. Power in some people – and extreme power in many – supercharges dopamine-related reward activity in the brain. It can do so to levels that distort judgement and can even exaggerate personality characteristics to make people more narcissistic. Narcissistic thinking causes people to overvalue their own opinions and judgements, prioritize their own interests and – because of the over-optimistic, tunnel-visioned focus on goals and rewards – neglect risk.

All the above are features of overconfidence, and power is one of the biggest causes of it. I don't know whether Doug Parker showed any of these behaviours, except for one. He made a startling misjudgement of risk in saying about the airline business that 'I don't think we're ever going to lose money again.' His attention was blinker-focused on success, and it would seem he couldn't easily remember examples of things going badly wrong in the world. Such memories were dormant and not readily accessible in his bullish frame of mind.

This distortion of his judgement, which we call overconfidence, was the source of his charismatic and leaderly ability to inspire and persuade. It is what got him where he was.

For Parker, and for his company, it worked – until it didn't.

Some might argue that we can't live as if a disaster could strike at any moment. We mustn't hamstring ourselves with the fear of rare events such as Covid-19. We should be optimistic and chipper as we ride our overconfident wave. But a pandemic had been widely predicted. For example, Microsoft founder Bill Gates gave a prescient warning at the World Economic Forum in Davos three years before Covid-19 hit. The vast unpreparedness of the world to deal with a much-predicted risk was a consequence of the sort of bullish overconfidence that political and business leaders like Doug Parker have repeatedly shown.

Ordinary confidence is a valuable asset that inevitably entails some unrealistic overconfidence. But it is hard to avoid the conclusion that high levels of overconfidence do an awful lot of damage in the world. Confidence is a double-edged sword. But it is central to life – and, in particular, to economic life.

CHAPTER 10

The Confident Economy

❧

A TOP A PLINTH on London's Highgate Hill perches a stone cat – poised, alert, as if she has suddenly sensed a mouse. This feline was indeed a prodigious mouser who became part of a legend about the economics of confidence.

The cat's owner, the Dick Whittington of English folklore, was lured from rural poverty by the rumour that the streets of London were paved with gold. Instead, he found cruelty and servitude in verminous servants' quarters in the city. So bad was his lot that one day he decided to return home, only to be lured back to his garret by the seductive sound of the bells of Bow Church.

The stone cat now sits at the side of the road where Dick reputedly turned round. His was a lucky decision because, in the meantime, his wealthy boss had dispatched the cat as chief mouser on a valuable cargo ship. She was so good at her job that a Moorish king bought her for more than the cargo's value. Delighted with the fortune the cat brought, the merchant generously shared it with Dick, who went on to become Lord Mayor of London.

It turns out that Dick Whittington was right about the

capital – the streets are indeed paved with gold, at least metaphorically speaking. This adage is true not just of London, but of most large cities, with the amount of gold scaling up with size. The bigger a city, the wealthier and more creative – measured, for example, by the number of patents filed there – it tends to be. And this is an exponential rise, with the benefits mushrooming disproportionately with size.

Today, 55 per cent of the world's population lives in cities. People flood to them in ever-increasing numbers so that by 2050, two-thirds of human beings will live in a metropolis. What exactly is it that makes the modern-day Dick Whittingtons across the globe decide to swap small-town tranquillity for the chaotic roar of a big city? After all, it's not only wealth and creativity that thrive there, but also crime and poverty.

When I first visited the US in the 1970s, I was struck by the number of U-Haul rental trailers on the roads. The mini-wagons sway along freeways towed behind cars packed with chairs, lampshades and toys. Families head west, or east, or south, or north, to a future they peer into over their steering wheels. They sweep past the vast, windowless storage buildings where they have lodged their less transportable belongings until they set up in their new city.

While Europeans baulk at moving fifty miles away from their hometown, many Americans will shift a thousand miles for a better job, zig-zagging back and forth across the continent, setting up home after home among strangers. Economists have a term for this – labour mobility – and it is part of what has made the US economy so strong. Yet the majority – 56 per cent – of forty-year-old Americans still live in the same city they lived in when they were fourteen. And even for those with college degrees, that figure is 40 per cent. So, who are these Dick Whittingtons, and what is the source of this brave and bewildering mobility?

Youth and education seem likely drivers. In one study of migration to major cities within the US, that was the case – the young moved more than the old, and those with college degrees were also more mobile than those without. But even more significant factors, one might think, are ability and, in particular, intelligence.

Intellect predicts so many things in our lives – from jobs to health to how long we live. But it turns out not to be a factor in mobility, according to the work of researchers who trawled through a large US study called the National Longitudinal Study of Youth. This survey measured the cognitive ability of six thousand young men and women at the age of nineteen, and followed up with them as they built their lives in their hometowns or fanned out across the country to further their careers. It wasn't always the smartest who moved to the big cities. There was another ingredient that the researchers identified – self-confidence.

The more confident young men and women, irrespective of their intelligence levels, tended to move to big cities, and, on average, they became wealthier and more successful than those who stayed home. Smart people with low self-confidence tend to stay put while their less able but more self-confident friends uproot themselves and move. In the metropolis, they plunge into a vortex of new ideas, networks, opportunities, experiences and relationships. These factors accelerate their wealth and expertise beyond that of their often cleverer, stay-at-home friends, brothers and sisters.

Naturally, some suffer the familiar big-city problems along the way – isolation, addiction, family breakdown and crime included. But the Dick Whittingtons of this world are, by definition, optimists, and we know that optimism is a sister to self-confidence. Their minds are tuned to expect success rather than to anticipate failure.

This super-additive has to be taken up early, though. If the more talented left-at-homes pluck up the courage and follow others to the big cities a few years later, they don't catch up. The early movers have already benefited from the compound interest of success and exponential growth that big cities provide. This works in a similar way to childhood confidence, where the more confident schoolchild will pull away and open up a growing and irrecoverable gap ahead of her equally able but less confident schoolmate.

This interest compounds internally (in their heads) and externally (in their skills, experiences, contacts, resources, networks and finances). These untried but self-confident migrants see their confidence pay off: success creates success. In turn, this breeds confidence, and confidence seeds yet more confidence. As a career fuel additive, this is a resource of unparalleled value, yielding a lifetime of compound interest.

Confident people – whether they are customers in a shopping centre or purchasing managers in a company – focus their attention more on the potential upsides of a decision than its downsides. This makes them more likely to pay attention to positive, optimism-inspiring indicators in a complex world. They are less inclined to attend to negative, pessimism-inducing ones. The confident person will invest because she focuses on the *can happen* dimension of confidence in a never-quite-certain future. The unconfident person's attention will be more focused on the potential risk, and will be more likely to save his money than spend it.

In other words, the *can happen* confidence of individual people in an economy *should* make that economy grow and create a virtuous cycle in which that confidence leads to economic success, which, in turn, feeds back to higher confidence. And there is evidence to support this. Between 2000 and 2014, for example, across thirteen EU countries including the UK, Germany, France and Spain, the confidence of individual consumers and company executives strongly predicted the unemployment rate in each member state. The relationship was in one direction – the confidence of individual people predicted eventual unemployment levels. Other indicators, such as consumer spending and industrial production, had a two-way causal relationship with confidence, each shaping the other.

We know that more confident people are more likely to start

businesses. Inventors with patents will more readily find a company to commercialize them if they are more confident. And, as Arizona State University researchers showed in 2011, companies that manage to make their employees feel more confident boost their productivity.

So, if confidence is so important, how does it work in the minds of hundreds, thousands, or millions of people in national economies?

Are you thriving or struggling?

Imagine a ladder with zero at the bottom and ten at the top.

Think of these number-steps like this: ten is the 'best possible life for you' and zero is the 'worst possible life for you'.

Picture your life right now. Which rung of this ladder would you say you are on?

Have you done that? Consider this: which rung of the ladder would you say you will be on roughly five years from now?

These questions are based on the so-called Cantril Scale, which is used by the Gallup organization to monitor human happiness and satisfaction in over 160 countries across the world.

What were your two numbers? If you chose seven or more for the present, and eight or more for five years hence, then you are *thriving*.

If you scored yourself five or six for life now, *or* five, six or seven on life in five years' time, then you may be *struggling*.

And if you scored yourself as little as four or less now, and four or less for five years in the future, you are *suffering*, according to the Gallup researchers.

If you are *thriving*, you will tend to be healthier, wealthier, less worried, stressed or sad. You will also be less angry, happier and more respected. You will have fewer sick days and enjoy life more than people who Gallup do not classify as thriving.

If you are *struggling*, you will be more stressed, will worry about money, and be off sick more than twice as often. You will more likely be a smoker and also an unhealthy eater.

If you scored as *suffering*, you will be short of the basics of food or shelter, suffering from pain and high levels of stress, worry, sadness and anger. You will more likely be chronically sick and depressed.

As we discussed in Chapter 3, in 2016, Brexit shocked the world. Few global experts saw it coming, and in their defence, most economic indicators didn't point to a political upheaval. The UK gross domestic product (GDP) was growing at 2 per cent, and unemployment had fallen to 4.9 per cent. Things seemed fine – except, that is, to Gallup. It had captured the mood of the British people in its annual survey, just as it had done for 160 or so other countries around the world.

The organization's researchers traced the steadily rising economic indicators on their screens. In 2013, the mean per capita UK GDP was $38,873, and, by 2015, it had grown by almost 7 per cent to $41,478. Happy days for an economist. But then, as the researchers traced another graph, their eyes widened. Britain was one of the wealthiest and most developed countries in the world, with near full employment and a growing economy. But the Gallup staff watched in amazement at a line that plunged between 2013 and 2015, in the biggest two-year drop ever observed in any nation by the organization – the thriving–struggling–suffering graph.

In 2013, the majority of British citizens – 55 per cent – felt that their lives were thriving. This figure was slightly below the United States at 59 per cent, but well above Russia, only 25 per cent of whose citizens felt as if they were thriving.

In the light of what we have seen about 'happy Latins' in Chapter 4, it shouldn't be a surprise that Colombia, despite its lack of wealth, saw 59 per cent of its citizens thriving in 2013. In China, this was true for only 21 per cent, and India, 13 per cent.

But that it should fall from 55 per cent to 40 per cent in the space of just two years in the UK meant that roughly seven million people suddenly felt the carpet of confidence yanked from beneath their feet. This fall was a remarkable event for one of the world's wealthiest countries, and there is little doubt that it was a warning sign for the momentous 2016 Brexit referendum decision.

Why was there such a sudden drop in how so many people felt about their lives? Immigration is often cited as a spur to Brexit voting, but there was no change in inward migration between 2013 and 2015 sufficiently large enough to account for such a dramatic shift in feelings of wellbeing and confidence in the future. Globalization is also often blamed for the Brexit vote, but there was no sudden tilt in its effects during those two years. Quite the contrary – GDP was rising and unemployment falling.

However, one thing did change – very significantly – in precisely that short period. That was the *austerity* public spending of the UK's Conservative government. Back in 2010 David Cameron's legislature started to slash public spending. The depths of these cuts in education, welfare and social protection reached their nadir between 2013 and 2015 when seven million people's confidence collapsed.

In the smaller cities and towns of northern England and the Midlands, local economies are very dependent on local government and state jobs. Therefore, despite the national economy performing very well, the draconian cuts in local public expenditure ate away at these communities' sense of confidence in the future. For example, police community support officers, who patrol the streets and offer a sense of security to people, saw their numbers slashed by 40 per cent after 2010. The number of police officers nationally dropped by over twenty thousand – a 15 per cent fall.

When these seven million psychologically shaken individuals

then faced a referendum, they saw an opportunity to give their government a bloody nose. Even though Brexit had previously hardly figured in the public mind as a political issue, they voted for it. They voted even though the EU had played no role in the austerity cuts that had undermined their confidence.

Across the Atlantic, another momentous political event took place the same year – the election of President Donald Trump. Like Brexit, the pollsters didn't predict this. Nor was it explicable by sudden economic reversals – per capita GDP rose in the US from $52,742 in 2013 to $57,436 in 2016. But, as in the UK, there was a sudden drop of around thirty million individuals who felt they were thriving – from 59 per cent in 2014 to 50 per cent in 2016. What's more, the most significant shift towards voting for Donald Trump happened in US states that had experienced the largest drop in wellbeing and confidence in the preceding four years.

During that same two-year period – from 2014 to 2016 – the US saw life expectancy fall – an almost unprecedented event for a rich country in recent history. One reason for this was the soaring rates of deaths by drug overdose from opiate addiction – the forty-seven thousand lives lost to this in 2014 had risen to sixty-three thousand in these two years.

What was happening to explain these changes in the UK and the US?

The Easterlin paradox

Economists have long assumed that wealth and happiness go hand in hand, but in 1972, Richard Easterlin dropped a cat among the economic pigeons, with his now-famous paradox. He noted that there were countries in which wealth and happiness were disconnected. Take the US, for example – while wealth more than doubled between 1972 and 2016, average happiness dropped slightly. This disconnect is what we saw in the UK and the US in the periods leading up to their political earthquakes – greater wealth but lower levels of wellbeing. The shrunken confidence in the future of seven million English had its political outlet in June 2016. Against predictions, the UK voted to leave the EU by a narrow national margin of 51.9 per cent to 48.1 per cent.

Apart from a weakened social fabric caused by public spending cuts, what made people vote for Brexit against their economic interests, as most economists confirmed happened? UK researchers discovered two critical psychological factors that predicted whether people voted for Brexit. The first was that they felt under threat from beyond their country's borders, a perception carefully nurtured by populist leaders such as Nigel Farage. As an example of this, one of many related statements Farage made was this: 'Tuberculosis is costing the National Health Service a great deal of money, and much of that [disease] is coming from Southern and Eastern Europe.'

You might think that such an attitude would go hand in hand with a particularly strong commitment to a nationalist British or English identity. But that wasn't the case – the strength of such nationalism didn't predict a Brexit vote. But what did presage a vote to leave was a rejection of European identity. People who voted for Brexit hated the idea of being European much more than they loved the idea of being English, University of Lincoln researchers showed in 2017.

Does this go any way to helping to explain what makes people unhappy and lack confidence despite economic growth? Can this question of identity thrown up by the Brexit research shed any light on the Easterlin paradox?

One remarkable feature of the US collapse in health, wellbeing, confidence, and even life expectancy, was that it was mainly confined to one demographic – white Americans without a college degree. Between 1999 and 2013, people in this category began to die younger than expected. Researcher Angus Deaton received the Nobel Prize in Economics for his work in the area, estimating that half a million people died in these fourteen years because of this reversal in life expectancy. What was striking about this discovery – an Easterlin paradox on steroids – was that it didn't happen to other groups in the US whose objective economic conditions were even worse. Hispanic and black Americans showed the usual rise in life expectancy seen across most of the world. Their sense of wellbeing, happiness and confidence also increased in lockstep with their swelling life expectancy.

White Americans with lower levels of education *feel* under more financial strain than Hispanic communities. They believe this even though they are wealthier on average – the silver-medallist effect discussed in Chapter 4. It is who we compare ourselves with that determines how happy we are.

Deciding how rich or poor you are is also up for grabs, depending on who you choose to compare yourself with. White Americans without a college degree tend to compare themselves with their parents and grandparents. That generation fared well in a strong, blue-collar, manufacturing-industry-based economy compared to other ethnic groups. Then came globalization, technological change and the shrinking of traditional heavy industry. Together with several other factors, this eroded the relatively privileged economic status of white blue-collar workers and made them feel poor in comparison to their parents and grandparents. Hispanic and black Americans also tend to compare themselves with their parents and grandparents, who tended to have been objectively poorer than their children. Relatively speaking, then, and compared with the fallen-from-economic-grace white Americans, they felt less poor. *Feeling* rich or poor is as vital as *being* rich or poor.

A parallel set of circumstances played out in England and Wales for the Brexit vote. The collapse of heavy industry and the weakening of the blue-collar economy through less secure jobs led to some people feeling poorer than their parents. This mindset was supercharged by those government cuts in local services. And, as in the US elections, it was more often the less educated who defied the pollsters by voting against the establishment when given the opportunity.

A racial narrative also played out in both votes. There was a common theme of 'take our country back' from what was perceived to be a loss of the dominant status of white people in society. An unfavourable comparison with an imagined past status fractured wellbeing and confidence in both nations. In England, in particular, fantasies of the world dominance of a former empire figured in the popular mind and tabloid press.

Your feelings about your life are based on a mental social thermometer. The reading on this instrument only has meaning by comparing yourself with others. Non-college-educated whites in the US, and many Brexit-voting English people, felt poorer – and hence less happy and confident – because of who they compared themselves with.

It's possible to see negative comparisons like this in the human brain. If you feel unfairly treated, your brain's reward network will respond with reduced activity, corresponding to feelings of low mood and unhappiness. That is what happened to many Brexit and Trump voters.

Small fish in big ponds

A globalized world means that we are all smaller fish in a much bigger pond, and this is one source of the epidemic of anxiety affecting the Western world. More educated people can thrive more readily in bigger ponds. But no one – not even the privileged and well educated – is exempt from the pressures of competitive social comparison. Researchers from the University of Tübingen discovered this in 2018, using data from a fascinating fifty-year study of US high school students.

In 1960, a representative selection of US high schools enrolled in 'Project Talent'. A cross-section of almost four hundred thousand American teenagers from over a thousand schools were followed up for periods of between eleven and fifty years. A true, randomly selected cross-section of schools, it included teenagers from both the poorest and wealthiest neighbourhoods, and from all types of schools – public and private. The researchers were interested in how well students from different schools fared in life, in terms of academic achievement, income and job prestige.

Children from poor areas of any country tend to fare worse on average on these indices than those from higher socioeconomic backgrounds. Socioeconomic status is a major source of confidence, and this is one reason why economic advantage and achievement go together.

What was remarkable about the Project Talent study, however, was that the researchers could compare the effects of socioeconomic background on students' success in life with one other crucial factor. This was the size of their high school's academic pond – the average academic achievement, as opposed to the average social class, of each school. Factors such as neighbourhood and school academic culture affect a school's average academic performance. These, in turn, shape the size of the academic pond in terms of the level of academic competition that any student would face.

The question posed by the researchers, then, was a simple one. How did the average socioeconomic background of a school compare with the academic-pond size in shaping the life success of hundreds of thousands of American teenagers?

One other crucial measure was used in this study – the teenagers' educational expectations for themselves while they were in school. In other words, the researchers gauged students' *confidence* in themselves, educationally speaking, based on questions about how far they expected to progress in education (undergraduate, master's, doctoral), such as *What is the greatest amount of college you expect to attend?* The most striking finding was that confidence – the expectations students had of themselves – was the driver of the success measures. These included job prestige, income and highest educational attainment.

So yes, confidence is key to achievement and success – but how does your social class versus the academic pond shape this confidence? Not surprisingly, the higher the average socioeconomic background of the school, the greater the students' educational expectations. But what were the effects on confidence of going to a 'big pond' school where the average achievement level was high?

The results were surprising. The effects of the school's average achievement level were the opposite of the impact of social class. The higher the level of average achievement in the school, the lower the average confidence. And because educational expectation is the driver of success, this was lower among students of the big-pond schools decades later, once they had eliminated social-class effects.

Because the researchers included well over a thousand schools and almost four hundred thousand students, it meant that, statistically, they could disentangle the effects of school socioeconomic profile and school academic-pond size. This is important because the socioeconomic background and school achievement levels are tightly linked. Only when you statistically strip out social class from the data can you look at academic-pond-size effects under the impartial spotlight of statistical analysis.

The average child from a middle-class background in a high-academic-performance school ended up less confident than the equivalent middle-class kid from a more run-of-the-mill-achieving school. And so they ended up less successful in life than teenagers from the same background who had been immersed in a less competitive, academically 'smaller' pond. Conversely, teenagers from less privileged backgrounds who entered these smaller ponds became more confident and hence more successful in life, on average.

There is only one plausible reason for this finding – and it is the same reason underlying the political revolutions in the UK and the US: *Who do I compare myself with?* In a small academic pond, it is easier to feel confident about my academic abilities because I see many people doing the same or worse than me. In the big pond where the average achievement levels are high, it is easy to lose confidence in my academic abilities.

The teenage years are critical not only for brain growth but also for the development of a sense of self, and central to that self is confidence. It turns out that the whole course of our lives can be shaped enormously by the comparisons we make of ourselves with others at this crucial time.

As we saw recently in the UK and the US, it is not just in the teenage years that these comparisons have such profound effects – they affect us throughout life. We all, like it or not, live in a much bigger, globalized pond, and so the challenges of maintaining our confidence are getting progressively bigger. The very poorest in the world can now compare themselves with the richest in ways that were not possible before near-universal technology was available. The challenges for our economies are now as much psychological as they are physical, which brings us to the concept of egonomics.

Egonomics

A random group of people takes an IQ test. They then judge whether they have performed above or below the average of the group. Each receives feedback on a computer screen telling them whether they are truly above or below average – but only with 75 per cent accuracy. They then have to decide again whether they are above or below average IQ for the group. They repeat this process four times, getting feedback from the computer – but noisy feedback, not 100 per cent reliable – about their IQ level within this group. And each time they say whether they are above or below average. This is like most feedback in real life – it's almost never 100 per cent clear and reliable.

So what happens to the volunteers' estimates of their ability after these four rounds of noisy feedback? If the brain were entirely rational, it would obey what is known as Bayesian statistics. It would revise each self-estimate up or down, taking into account the fact that the feedback is only 75 per cent accurate. By the end, a purely rational brain would end up with a self-estimate that was accurate. Let's call that judgement *intellectual self-confidence*. Is it accurate after this feedback? No, it most certainly is not.

As we saw in Chapter 2, our brains update good news more quickly and more strongly than bad news. That's exactly what happened here – people were more likely to change their estimate about their IQ after positive feedback than after negative feedback. They were also conservative. When they received positive news about their IQ, they updated their estimate only 35 per cent as much as they statistically should. After bad news about their IQ, they downgraded their self-assessment only 15 per cent as much as they should.

Our intellectual self-confidence is sticky. It doesn't change easily and is biased more towards good news than bad. And a significant minority of people – more often in the below-average group – didn't want any negative feedback.

But we knew this already, so what's different here? The answer lies in what happens when these same people do the same test – not for themselves this time, but on behalf of a notional intelligent robot. On this occasion, they behaved like almost perfect Bayesian statistics. They updated to the positive and negative feedback equally, and weren't over-conservative. Instead, they changed their original estimates of above- and below-average IQ appropriately and rationally in line with the feedback.

This is what happens when you take the ego out of confidence. Without the self to protect, confidence as a bridge to the future becomes a rational statistical exercise. Confidence is an act of trust in my future self. It believes *I can do it* – acting as a sort of internal coach. It is like a benevolent mentor who *believes* in me and energizes me to live up to that belief. But here's the challenge for this coach's belief in me. For this magic to work, *I* have to believe in my coach – who exists only inside my head. And the coach's name? *Ego*.

A critical element of economics, therefore, is *egonomics*. How poor or rich we feel, whether we feel as if we are thriving or struggling, depends on who we compare ourselves with. It also depends on the success or failure of our attempts to protect our positive view of ourselves. But our feelings of how rich or poor we are – and remember, it is our *perception* as much as reality that determines this – are ever more vulnerable to something that makes most people anxious: change.

Change

The world is changing very fast, with the rate of economic, social and technological shifts accelerating exponentially. In 2018, the University of Toulouse economist Roberta Dessi proposed that the confidence that propels us forward with rose-tinted spectacles is a necessary psychological strategy for dealing with change. Using a method known as game theory mathematical modelling, which attempts to predict how humans behave together in large groups, she predicted that being somewhat overconfident about one's abilities and chances creates a harmonious equilibrium in an economic system. Healthy overconfidence propels individuals to take risks and start new projects rather than sticking with old ones, which, in a changing world, can pay off.

But this is not so in stable environments. There, predictability and lack of change penalize overconfidence. In such low-change conditions, overconfidence can be a potential liability. It can make people more reluctant to identify and address problems with existing projects, and to seek and invest in improvements to the status quo.

Dessi and her co-author Xiaojian Zhao measured overconfidence in over three thousand Chinese citizens by giving them a puzzle to solve and then asking them to rate how confident they were that their answer was correct. They then asked them how much change they envisaged that they would experience in their lives. Their findings confirmed that the more change people expected in their lives, the more inaccurately overconfident they were in their answer to the puzzle.

They went on to compare average self-confidence measures across thirty-eight countries with indices of social and economic stability in each nation. Their focus was on measures of stability that intuitively would be expected to correlate positively, if at all, with confidence: low average unemployment rates over a twenty-eight-year period, low levels of internal and external conflict. The model instead predicted, counterintuitively, that more stable countries, even using such measures, should have *lower* average self-confidence. This is indeed what Dessi and Zhao found. The US, for example, scored 17.2 for self-confidence, compared to 13.3 for Japan. Switzerland, a very economically and socially stable country, scored 14.3, compared to the much more dynamically changing UK at 16.4.

Extreme overconfidence causes significant problems. However, moderate levels of 'normal' overconfidence are a useful response to a rapidly changing world. They may even be economically and psychologically necessary. Given that change in the world is universal and accelerating, this makes confidence an even more precious commodity if the world is to prosper.

But economics cannot exist outside of politics, and confidence plays just as important a role in political life.

CHAPTER 11

The Politics of Confidence

So, I want to speak to you first tonight about a subject even more serious than energy or inflation. I want to talk to you right now about a fundamental threat to American democracy.

I do not mean our political and civil liberties. They will endure. And I do not refer to the outward strength of America, a nation that is at peace tonight everywhere in the world, with unmatched economic power and military might.

The threat is nearly invisible in ordinary ways.

It is a crisis of confidence.

The erosion of our confidence in the future is threatening to destroy the social and the political fabric of America.

Confidence has defined our course and has served as a link between generations. We've always believed in something called progress. We've always had a faith that the days of our children would be better than our own.

On 15 July 1979, US president Jimmy Carter spoke these words during a televised address to the nation, which became famous as the 'Crisis of Confidence' speech. Carter's advisers had told him that the American people's beliefs about the future of the country were in crisis. These advisers blamed this collective feeling on the cumulative effect of the assassinations of John F. Kennedy, Robert F. Kennedy and Martin Luther King; the failure of the Vietnam War; the scandal of Watergate; and the 1970s energy crisis. This fuel shortage saw cars on freeways forced to drive at 55 mph, even on empty Midwest roads, mile after featureless mile in a gloomy slowdown that matched the sepulchral tone of Carter's address.

The President's speech is fascinating because, of all the economic, social and military challenges facing the country at the time, he fingered one core problem – a psychological one. For a US president to turn psychologist and diagnose the state of mind of hundreds of millions of people was unprecedented. This presidential doctor's prescription turned out not to be very popular because he went on to call for self-sacrifice, frugality and a rejection of materialism. This message did not activate the brain reward networks – and hence confidence – of a critical segment of the American people.

In the election year 1980, one presidential-contender-also-turned-psychologist sensed the mood of the nation and recognized that Carter's prescription was not going down well. Former movie actor Ronald Reagan declared that there was nothing wrong with the American people. He made optimism and confidence the core of his political message, revving up the reward networks of tens of millions of supporters and so winning the election.

Like Carter, Reagan played the psychologist to dig beneath the economics and the policies to diagnose a deeper cause of the nation's woes. But his verdict was different – the crisis in confidence was caused precisely by President Carter's inability to inspire confidence in Americans, he asserted. And his prescription was rather different – elect a charismatic leader who could revive the self-belief of a large segment of the population. The fact that he did so at the expense of public programmes that sustained the confidence of another segment of the population ended up creating a set of political and economic ramifications that still resonate today.

The thirty-seven-year-old Soviet officer nervously eyed the angry crowd as it swelled against the gates of Dresden's KGB headquarters. It was 5 December 1989, and his call for armed back-up had elicited, down a crackly line, the curt response 'Moscow is silent.' Lieutenant Colonel Vladimir Putin marched to the gate and told the heaving mass of East Germans they would be shot – by nonexistent armed soldiers inside the building – if they tried to enter. The bluff worked, and the crowd shuffled back and turned away to find other offices of the Stasi state to ransack.

The loyal Soviet Russia KGB officer felt as if his world and identity were collapsing around him. 'I had the feeling that the country was no more. It had disappeared,' he later revealed. He believed, as a speech to the Federal Assembly of the Russian Federation on 25 April 2005 shows, 'Above all, we should acknowledge that the collapse of the Soviet Union was a major geopolitical disaster of the century. Tens of millions of our co-citizens and compatriots found themselves outside Russian territory.'

Putin's major preoccupation was not with the economic or political tribulations of his country. Instead, he was concerned with the *psychological* effects on his beloved Russia. This intensely personal, national humiliation was at the core of his reaction, and the same seemed to be the case for millions of Russians.

Russians have the lowest level of trust in their public institutions in the world. The quality of life of the average citizen has declined to a level below that experienced in China. Yet Vladimir Putin retains, at the time of writing, a remarkable 70 per cent approval rating because of his success as a national psychologist. He rebuilt collective confidence and self-esteem by harnessing a national narrative of his predecessors' courage, endurance and victory during the Second World War – or the Great Patriotic War, as it is known there.

'For the first time in the past 200–300 years, Russia faces the real danger that it could be relegated to the second, or even the third tier of global powers,' Putin warned in 1999. He called on Russians to unite in order to make sure that the country remained what he called a *first-tier* nation. He built on the wartime notion of material self-sacrifice for the cause of national pride. The aim was to create a highly nationalist and belligerent stance towards the Western world – a stance which rebuilt a sense of self-worth and confidence in tens of millions of people who had experienced a national humiliation as a very personal one.

It is hard to exaggerate the importance that such national collective emotions have played in human affairs throughout history. Millions have died over the millennia because of perceived slights to the *amour-propre* of kings, princes and warlords. The concept of *honour*, or *face*, has been responsible for much carnage, and that continues today. The US government continued the Vietnam War for many years after they explicitly and secretly concluded that they could never win it. And they did so for one simple reason – to save national face, namely, the self-esteem of a government and nation. Similarly, the overwhelming support for Hitler in 1930s Germany was a response to what millions of Germans felt as both a personal and a national humiliation after the punitive Versailles peace agreement.

The protection of collective egos is one of the turbines of human destiny. It triggers overconfidence that propels people not only to murder and war, but also to feats of creativity, innovation and civic duty. But is there really such a thing as *collective confidence*?

Collective confidence

Any football, hockey, rugby or team player will tell you that there is such a thing as team confidence. There's even a simple, scientifically validated way of assessing collective confidence with this question:

> Assess the confidence of your team in how they estimate their ability to perform at a high level so as to be successful in their next competitive match. 0 (not at all confident) . . . . 100 (completely confident)

You can measure the collective confidence of a team by taking the average of the individual members' scores on this simple scale. And research shows that collective confidence plays out for groups in much the same way that personal self-belief works with individuals. Athletes who have more confidence in their team set more challenging goals for themselves, put in more effort, demonstrate greater physical endurance, show more resilience to setbacks and adversities, and persist more despite failure.

And because of this, teams with this collective confidence achieve better results in competitions – as any sports fan will acknowledge, and as a review by University of Roehampton researchers showed in 2016. Sports fans will also tell you that team managers or coaches are crucial to building a team's confidence and, therefore, their success: the science backs them up. Leaders can transmit their level of confidence to the team's collective *can do* spirit, even if they are just temporary bosses in newly formed teams.

In one study, a hundred Belgian basketball players took part in a basket-shooting competition, after being randomly allocated to several small teams. Each team appointed a leader who was not only a basketball player of a similar skill level, but who was also working with the researchers. Half the leaders adopted a high-team-confidence approach, expressing belief in the team's ability, reacting enthusiastically when the team scored, and showing confident body language. The other leaders were scripted to respond with annoyance when the team missed a basket, to make critical comments, and to show a discouraged, unconfident body posture.

The confidently led teams became more sure of their team's ability and developed a stronger sense of *us* – that is, a collective team identity to match the collective team confidence. As they began the shooting match, the two sets of teams had similar levels of accuracy. But by the end, those with leaders expressing high collective confidence were netting 30 per cent more of their shots than the others.

And you can see collective confidence at work in the individual brain. When people are working collaboratively together in a group, their brains track their performance as well as that of others in the group. This happens in a region called Brodmann area 9, at the front of the brain. It is as if each individual brain is keeping a tally of group performance, and so builds a neural signal of collective confidence.

When people compete with each other rather than collaborating in a team, the opposite pattern occurs in the brain. Activity for the self and the other person diverge completely. The last thing you want in a competition is for your brain to confuse *your* performance with that of a rival.

If we are confident in *us*, that will make me more confident in *me* – with all the positive effects on brain performance, attention, emotion and behaviour that follow from this. But the collective confidence has an additional impact, because it helps to make people work together better as a team, with many resulting benefits. And this doesn't just happen in sport. CEOs who convey confidence in their organizations end up with better company performance. Deprived areas of big cities have lower crime rates when locals have higher collective confidence about exercising informal controls over their communities.

But it is in politics that collective confidence has come into its own as an energizer of action across the world – from Chile to Hong Kong, and from Iraq to North Africa. Individuals' ability to network using social media has led to massive and unpredicted demonstrations, uprisings and unrest across the world.

Research from Chile and the US in 2017 showed that the more people are engaged politically on social media, the more confident they feel about taking further political action. They assessed political confidence through responses to statements such as *If enough citizens got organized and demanded change, politicians would take steps to end their problems.*

Interestingly, two leading social media platforms, Twitter and Facebook, work in different ways to generate this confidence and subsequent action, the research showed. Twitter has an individual-orientation, with a focus on disseminating information to followers rather than on shared or reciprocal social interactions. Facebook, on the other hand, is more oriented to social connectedness and mutual exchange of opinions. But despite this difference, people who share political information on either platform are more likely to engage in political action outside of social media, though for different reasons. While Twitter political-sharing boosts individual confidence in taking political action, Facebook political-sharing boosts *collective* confidence, the research showed.

So, confidence is contagious, spreading vertically downwards from leaders and horizontally across groups. And the more cohesive a group, the higher the contagion of confidence. Confidence evolved in human beings as a way of us networking our brains together, and helping people to work together effectively. One way of assisting this networking is the *confidence heuristic* we encountered in Chapter 3 – the rule-of-thumb mental shortcut for judging who we'll team up with, based on how confident they appear to be.

Confidence, then, is not just a property of one person's mind – it can take hold in, or leach out of, millions of minds. And when it does, history is made.

'The bomb is a currency of self-esteem'

On 11 May 1998, the desert of Rajasthan shuddered as India deto-
nated a thermonuclear bomb. Two more explosions erupted under
the stony soil that day – fission bombs, this time. India had become
the sixth member of that exclusive club of nuclear-armed nations.
A prominent Indian politician, editor and journalist, Chandran
Mitra, commented on India's achievement: 'I think it is a reality
that the bomb is a currency of self-esteem.' By saying this, he
grounded this extreme military-political act firmly within the psychology of national confidence.

Just seventeen days later, at 3.15 p.m. on 28 May 1998, a similar
shudder rippled the arid soil of Balochistan, across the border in Paki-
stan. India's bitter rival had responded in kind with an underground
nuclear test, also declaring itself as a member of that exclusive club.

There are practical consequences of becoming a nuclear state,
including leveraging political negotiating power. North Korea's
Kim Jong-un demonstrated this forcefully by using nuclear activity
and threat to achieve his strategic goal of presidential-level engagement with the US in 2019. Being nuclear-armed can also be a
deterrent against military aggression by another country. But, as
Chandran Mitra correctly pointed out, there is also a psychological
function of possessing this daunting weapon – that of boosting the
self-esteem and self-confidence of a nation.

How can a whole country experience such personal mental states?

This question is more easily answered by citizens from former
colonies than by those from more affluent, privileged countries
without a history of colonization.

Chandran Mitra expanded on his nuclear self-esteem argument:

> And when you are looking towards the end of the twenti-
> eth century towards [the] twenty-first century as to how

you can instil national pride, overcome the feeling of infer-
iority which had been ingrained in your mind for 200 years,
something like the bomb would seem could deal [sic] with
the world better. So that you feel more completely
yourself.

These words read like the case notes of a psychotherapy patient
talking about personal anxieties and humiliations. Yet this is a
leader talking about his country in almost precisely the same terms
as if his country were an individual. This distinguished political
figure and editor of a national newspaper is exploring the psychological journey of hundreds of millions of people whose views he
represents. He continued:

Certainly when we go abroad, when we have to prove ourselves in international forum we have to shout out louder
and also there is a very strong element of patronizing about
an ex-colonial doing so well . . . Nonetheless we have this
problem of either being treated as inferiors or being
patronized.

Nations with a history of being colonizers (most of Europe and
Japan, for example) tend to take their national self-esteem and self-
confidence for granted. So it is too for those holding great economic,
political or military power over other countries (the US, for example). This happens because power alters our brains to make us
more focused on our own goals and less inclined to notice or care
about the thoughts or feelings of those over whom we have power.
Power also makes us more egocentric and less self-aware.

Powerful nations or groups don't engage in soul-searching about
how others see them in the way that less powerful ones do. They
don't brood about their inferiority/superiority vis-à-vis other groups
in the way that Chandran Mitra was compelled to. They don't have

to. If you hold power, you call the shots, so it is less important to try to put yourself in the shoes of the less powerful. The powerless, on the other hand, have to expend a considerable part of their mental energies on trying to read the minds and intentions of the powerful, and self-reflecting upon their collective status – and confidence – in relation to these.

But if a nation or group loses power, then the blithe assumption of self-evident, confident superiority crumbles. Suddenly, the painful process of self-questioning and self-awareness erupts with all the consequent threats to the no-longer-dominant egos of the once-powerful group. So what happens in the individual brains of the group mind?

The group mind

Volunteers for a research study enter a room with other strangers. The researchers show slides of abstract paintings by two artists – Paul Klee and Wassily Kandinsky – and ask each person to decide which artist's slides they prefer. They are then assigned to be a member of a group – supposedly based on their preferred painter, but, in fact, randomly. There are now two random groups, one notionally based on liking Klee paintings, and the other preferring Kandinsky's.

These are called 'minimal groups' – meaning ones that have no purpose, past or future. They are just arbitrary, transient groups to which a person temporarily belongs. These groups are different from most of the other ones we belong to in life. Our real groups have a purpose – family protection, football-team victory, religious dominance or national prestige, for example. Such groups have long histories – sometimes lasting hundreds of years – and rationales that usually involve trying to achieve a competitive advantage over other groups.

They also have a strong sense of continuity into the future – our legacy as a political party, our nation's glorious future, the eternal light of our faith, the future of our family, and so on. The world is racked by the consequences of competition between groups that have purpose, pasts and futures. Hindu versus Muslim in India, Catholic against Protestant in Ireland, or Republican versus Democrat in the US are just a few examples. One could even say that the history of humanity is the story of such groups and their conflicts.

But suddenly, in this experiment, people find themselves in a completely arbitrary group with no history or common values or purpose or future. Surely that makes the group irrelevant and unimportant? Not so, a series of research studies have shown since the 'minimal group' effect was first discovered in 1971 by a brilliant social psychologist at the University of Bristol called Henri Tajfel.

Tajfel and his colleagues found that merely belonging to a random group brought out a whole series of behaviours and attitudes that are eerily familiar throughout the human race. These are *ingroup favouritism* and *outgroup discrimination*. And here's a remarkable fact from this research. People allocate rewards to their ingroup and impose sanctions on the outgroup, even when the overall costs and benefits of their group-favouring choices are to everyone's detriment! In other words, the group mind inclines us to cut off our noses to spite our faces.

This daunting fact arises from a situation in which there is no competition between the Klees and Kandinskys. There is no zero-sum game – that is, if I win, you lose, and vice versa – in play here, because the two groups are entirely without purpose or future. But there nevertheless appears to be a primitive drive in the human mind to instantly define oneself in a group and then automatically favour that ingroup at the expense of an outgroup. Why on earth does this happen – and can it help us to understand how confidence operates in groups and nations?

A clue comes from a 2003 German study that used the Klee–Kandinsky minimal group method. Researchers observed how much people favoured their ingroup when allocating money to other individuals – in their ingroup and also in the outgroup. Cleverly, the researchers manipulated each person's individual confidence by telling them that they had performed poorly or well on a problem-solving test given previously. Those told they had done badly became much more prejudiced *against* the outgroup and *for* their ingroup. Feeling bad about themselves, in other words, made people more *tribal*. The false feedback about their intelligence threatened their egos, and so, as if in compensation, the collective ego of the ingroup offered some protection.

This research begins to make further sense of the dramatic political changes of 2016 in the UK and the US. The loss of confidence of millions of people made these individuals immediately more vulnerable to the ego-boosting comfort of ingroup favouritism and its sinister twin, outgroup prejudice. That is why populists could harness the ego-threatening post-2008-recession collapse in confidence of millions of people who then flocked to their causes. Donald Trump in the US, Nigel Farage in the UK, Marine Le Pen in France, and Matteo Salvini in Italy are all examples of this phenomenon. People mobilized by populists embraced ingroup bias and outgroup prejudice because their confidence had been eroded by feelings of having lost out.

The fuel for these political movements, however, wasn't just their ingroup mindset. There was also a much more visceral, emotionally laden consequence of ramped-up tribalism for these confidence-challenged millions. Research from 2008 shows that simply being made to feel part of an arbitrary ingroup has a profound mood-enhancing effect on the brain's reward network. This, for the populist, is the equivalent of dispensing free anti-depressants to millions of his followers. And supporters of extreme ideologies are in greater need of such anti-depressants, 2019 research from Amsterdam's Free University showed.

Supporters of extreme right or left ideologies are more psychologically distressed than other people. The black-and-white thinking of extremist belief systems offers simple solutions to complex problems. This is attractive to people whose confidence and self-esteem are low. It also makes them more intolerant of other groups and overconfident about their own judgements. Strong ingroup feelings and overconfidence both activate the brain's reward network. This helps to alleviate the psychological distress of those captivated by the simple and over-optimistic solutions dangled in front of them by extremists.

Confidence from the group mind can make us individually more confident and hence less anxious. But is there something more fundamental lurking beneath the anxiety that drives people into the consolation of the group?

Managing our terror

On 11 April 2020, at the height of the Covid-19 crisis, a video was tweeted from a McDonald's restaurant in Guangzhou, China, showing black people not being allowed to enter the restaurant. A few weeks earlier, on 24 February in London's Oxford Street, a twenty-three-year-old student from Singapore – Jonathan Mok – was attacked by a group of men. One of them said, 'I don't want your coronavirus in my country,' before smashing his fist into Mok's nose. These are just two examples from thousands across the world of how fears of Covid-19 infection during the 2020 pandemic prompted xenophobic aggression against people perceived to be from an outgroup – and hence a threat.

In 2014, rates of another highly infectious disease, Ebola, mushroomed in West Africa. The blanket worldwide publicity kindled a fear that it would spread to other countries such as the US. Even though the chances of contracting Ebola in the US were infinitesimally small, millions of people expressed fear of the disease. When researchers at the University of California, Santa Barbara, surveyed a thousand Americans, they discovered that the more vulnerable

people *felt* to Ebola, the more xenophobic they were in their attitudes to immigrants in general, and West Africans in particular.

When people are frightened, they assuage their fear through the
anxiety-reducing comfort of the ingroup, with its inevitable outgroup prejudice. And this fear extends well beyond pandemics.

It is 7 a.m. on a Monday, and you are putting on your shoes. I'm
going to ask you some questions and take the liberty of imagining
your answers:

> *What are you doing?*
> Putting on my shoes.
> *Why are you putting on shoes?*
> So I can go outside.
> *Why are you going outside?*
> To go to work.
> *Why are you going to work?*
> Because my boss expects me to be there.
> *Why do you care about what your boss expects?*
> I want to do well in my work and be successful in my career.
> *Why do you want to be successful?*
> So that I can provide a good life for my family.
> *Why do you want to do that?*
> So that I can feel like a good parent.
> *Why do you want to feel like that?*
> Because I am a good person.
> *Why do you want to be a good person?*
> Ah, for God's sake, no more questions – I'm late for work!

And with that imaginary exchange, we come to the question 'Why?'
It is an existential demand about what all this busy-ness and effort
is *for*. And it is a question that we shy away from most of the time,
with the help of another handy defender of our egos – *denial*.

Everything we do has multiple purposes, embedded within a hierarchy. This fact is best captured by the following story, beloved of motivational speakers.

Some workers are laying bricks, and the inquisitor asks the first what he's doing. The worker looks up and answers, 'I'm laying bricks.' The inquisitor asks the second man, who answers, 'I'm building a wall.' Then he comes to the third, who replies, 'I'm creating a cathedral.' All three are correct, with each of their goals embedded like Russian dolls within what the scientific jargon calls a *goal hierarchy*.

However, if you continue up that hierarchy, as we did with the putting-on-my-shoes interview above, we ultimately bump into an existential ceiling of our mortality. Most of the time, we manage to avoid thinking about this, with the help of a bit of healthy denial. It is quite normal for us to keep our attention away from the higher levels of our goal hierarchies. We tend to focus on achieving mid-level, mood-lifting goals such as getting a pay rise, buying a new house, establishing a relationship, or finally planning that long-dreamed-of trip. Denial keeps my mind away from the more dizzying questions of what, ultimately, I am doing this for, particularly given that I will be no more in a few decades.

Validated over many continents and countries, one theory to explain this goes by the rather forbidding name of *terror management theory*.

It can be upsetting and saddening if we are exposed to thoughts of death, but from time to time we do come across reminders of it. For example, people take part in an experiment where the researchers make them more aware of their mortality by asking questions such as *Please describe your emotions when thinking about your own death* or *What do you think happens to you when you are physically dead?*

According to terror management theory, being reminded of your mortality – for instance, in a pandemic – triggers a set of responses in you that are mostly unconscious attempts to protect your ego (and with it your self-esteem) from a frightening awareness of its future extinction. Being edged up to the top of your life-goal hier-archy has a similar effect. Mulling over the ultimate purpose of your daily routine inevitably leads to the reminder that you are mortal.

Hundreds of research studies over many scores of countries have confirmed that being reminded of death leads us to think, feel and behave in very particular ways. Above all, it makes us rush to shore up our self-esteem by committing ourselves more to our ingroup and its worldview. The purpose of this self-esteem, the theory goes, is to shield us from the terror of our individual insignificance within the void of eternity. Reminded of our mortality, we strive, mostly unconsciously, to see ourselves as worthy vehicles for the ingroup values of our cultural or political affiliation. This makes us feel some sort of continuity of the self as part of a broader virtue that we fer-vently desire to be part of. That sense of moral value gives our death-threatened self-esteem some symbolic immortality.

Most religions promise a real, not a symbolic, immortality to pro-tect the ego against the terror of extinction. When thoughts of death tug at the edges of our consciousness, even the brains of the most devout show the typical response, and this psychological reaction has enormous political ramifications.

Take this 2007 University of Alberta study of Canadian students, for example. A group were selected for their strong pro-Canadian views, answering *strongly agree* to statements such as *Being Canadian is an important part of my self-worth* or *I am proud to be a Canadian*. They were then split into two groups and given an article to read. Half read an anti-Canadian article by an American, which mocked and criticized all things Canadian, such as its health system and the politeness of its citizens. The other half read a similarly negative article about Australia.

The students then played a word game in which they had to fill in the letters of incomplete words on a page. Most only had one solution, such as W _ _ D O W (window) or P _ P _ R (paper). Clev-erly, six of the words had at least two possible solutions, one of which was death-related and the other not. The word fragments were B U R _ _ D (buried or burned), D E _ _ (dead or deal), G R A _ _ (grave or grape), K I _ _ E D (killed or kissed), S K _ _ L (skull or skill) and C O F F _ _ (coffin or coffee).

The patriotic young Canadians who read the article demeaning their culture and national identity chose the death-related words more often than those reading the Australian text. This supported the idea that our self-esteem – including our collective, national self-worth – operates as a sort of anti-anxiety drug soothing our fear of death.

Does it work the other way round? Does boosting our self-esteem offer any protection against these disturbing thoughts of death? To find out if this was the case, volunteers in a 1992 University of Arizona study took a phony personality test. They were given fake feedback about their personality. This could be neutral – *Some of your aspirations may be a little unrealistic.* Or it could be positive – *Most of your aspirations tend to be pretty realistic,* or *Your personality is fundamentally strong.*

Half of each group then watched a video called *Faces of Death,* a documentary about the many different ways in which a person can die, and which included footage of an actual autopsy. The remaining half of each group was shown a neutral video with no death-related content.

That yielded four groups: high self-esteem/watched death video; neutral self-esteem/watched death video; high self-esteem/watched neutral video; neutral self-esteem/watched neutral video.

The question was, did the boosted self-esteem quell the anxiety aroused by thoughts of death? Neither of the groups that had watched the neutral video became more anxious – on average, each scored a normal forty-four out of eighty on an anxiety questionnaire. But those with un-boosted self-esteem who watched the death film saw their anxiety spike to fifty-four.

What about the death-video watchers with bolstered self-esteem? They were untouched by the upsetting video, and their anxiety levels stayed low at forty-four, thus supporting the core idea of terror management theory. We work hard to gain self-esteem and support for our worldview in order to ward off existential anxiety. And it works.

Such inklings of death at the fringes of consciousness also provoked more worrying reactions. Iranian university students were made more aware of their mortality by being asked to 'describe the emotions that thinking about their death aroused'. They then read questionnaire responses supposedly written by fellow young Iranians on the subject of political martyrdom. Some of the answers supported suicide bombing (for example, *Deaths in the name of Allah will bring an end to the imperialism practised in the West*). Others did not (for example, *Human life is too valuable to be used as a means of producing change*).

The students then rated how much they agreed with and liked the people who had answered the questionnaires. Respondents primed by thinking of their death rated the pro-suicide-bombing respondents more favourably. They also agreed with them more than students who hadn't been made to think about their death did.

The researchers then conducted a similar study with US students, who, after thoughts of their personal death were kindled, became more likely to support extreme military violence that could kill thousands of civilians.

We have all seen distressing images of destroyed cities in Syria and other wars. Merely viewing these images makes us more aware of our mortality. And because of this, we become more dogmatic about our worldview and more inclined to support military aggression or terrorism against the other. It's a sobering and vicious cycle – deadly conflict changes our brains to make that conflict worse. Our fear of death inclines us to defend our worldview to protect our self-esteem. Canadian journalist Jessica Stern interviewed religious terrorists from different religions, including Hindus, Jews, Muslims and Christians. In her 2003 book, she concluded that they were motivated by damaged self-esteem caused by feelings of personal and communal humiliation.

It can be hard for millions of people to feel part of a group, but one sure-fire way of making that happen is to remind them of their mortality through fear and threat. Just as one person can feel humiliated and their self-esteem damaged by a slight, so too can the collective self-esteem of an entire population be diminished. And when this happens, it breaches an essential mental defence against the Grim Reaper – we are reminded of our mortality. It makes people cleave to their tribe and dehumanize outsiders more virulently.

There are high costs associated with these strategies to cope with our fear of death. Paradoxically, they can sap our confidence directed in collective action towards solving big problems by side-tracking us into energy-sapping efforts at protecting our egos. Self-esteem is not an action-focused bridge to the future in the way that confidence is.

Political drugs

The most valuable asset a politician can have is a population that feels confident about its collective future. President Jimmy Carter's diagnosis was an accurate one, but his remedy failed because it demanded a level of self-denial and moral self-scrutiny that didn't appeal to a critical majority of his citizens. Ronald Reagan seized Carter's diagnosis but prescribed an altogether (for some, at least) better-tasting medicine: deregulation, optimism and economic expansion in the US that flourished until it hit the financial crash of 2008 and then the Covid-19 pandemic of 2020. Reagan's deregulation of the financial sector played a major role in triggering this crash, and while the economic policies yielded economic benefits for many of his supporters, they also vastly increased the inequalities in US society and impoverished millions.

Fear replaced avarice as the dominant emotion in 2020, and

nothing erodes confidence quite like anxiety, as we have seen. Politicians' loss of this precious resource means that they have had to resort to more risky methods to lift their citizens' mood. That strategy entails bolstering their self-esteem by opening the pharmacy of the group mind.

Its medicines are powerful. They knit people together with a sense of synthetic superiority over an outgroup. This approach lifts their mood, lowers their anxiety, and soothes them with the togetherness of the ingroup's social bonding hormones. Such nationalist, racial or religious pharmacies have been opened up across the world – by Prime Minister Modi in India, President Erdogan in Turkey, President Putin in Russia, President Trump in the US, Prime Minister Orban of Hungary, and many other political leaders.

The problem with these self-esteem-enhancing drugs is the same as for all feel-good agents. Eventually, they lose their effectiveness, and side-effects appear. The percentage of people in India who feel confidently *thriving* – the same measure that fell dramatically in the UK before the Brexit referendum – dropped from 14 per cent in 2014, when Narendra Modi became prime minister, to a mere 3 per cent in 2017. Harnessing the group mind to bolster self-esteem is, like all mood-lifting drugs, ultimately self-destructive to national self-confidence. It distracts people from confidence-building *action* and instead focuses on ego-protecting mental gymnastics to maintain a sense of ingroup superiority over the outgroup. Protecting the ego is not a rational business. So it sucks mental resources from the confidence-inspired, problem-solving creativity that has driven civilization.

The global population was at 7,779,263,050 as I began writing this sentence, and had risen to 7,779,263,300 as I finished. We will not cope with pandemics, global warming and other challenges to humanity if we focus on protecting self-esteem rather than building collective confidence. We need to work out how to harness confidence for our individual and collective good.

CHAPTER 12

How to Harness Confidence

∶ ⊱

IN THE WINTRY afternoon gloom of 29 December 2019, a man left his Tokyo house and walked eight hundred metres to a local hotel. There, he met two men, and the trio then boarded a bullet train for Osaka. The two men left a hotel near Osaka's Kansai airport wheeling two large containers, before boarding a private jet for Istanbul. On New Year's Eve, two days later, Carlos Ghosn was reunited with his wife in his home city of Beirut, Lebanon.

Since his detention in Japan more than a year earlier, the auto-industry magnate had been in prison, followed by house arrest. He had escaped prosecution, justifying his illegal flight by claiming political motivation for the prosecution and a biased judicial system. Back in a country with no extradition agreement with Japan, he was now a free man.

Ghosn's dramatic escape from Japan attracted global attention that was even more intense than that which he received for his extraordinary corporate achievements. His confidence was on vivid display. He had had the self-belief not only to shape the future of the global motor industry but also to determine his fate in the face of criminal prosecution.

Highly confident people are often rule-breakers rather than rule-takers, and the story of Carlos Ghosn is an excellent example of the double-edged sword of confidence at work. Confidence may build a bridge to a future you can see, but breaking rules, whether formal or informal, creates conflict and bad feeling. Sacha Romanovitch and Cathy Engelbert, both pioneering woman leaders of major financial institutions, learned this in their companies' response to their initiatives. Congolese surgeon Denis Mukwege was made altogether more violently aware of this fact. And Nadia Murad, the Yazidi women's rights advocate, had no illusions about the conservative pressures pushing against her campaign.

Creating change in the world demands confidence that allows you to keep going despite the opposition it generates. Even Kim, the underconfident young woman who struggled for years, felt her brother's resistance when trying to change how their family viewed her. Confidence's anti-anxiety and mood-elevating effects on the brain make it possible for people to cope with such resistance, as does the optimism – sometimes too much – that high confidence can inspire. Ghosn, Romanovitch, Engelbert, Mukwege and Murad all needed this anxiety-reducing mood-enhancer to break the mould in their respective domains.

Confidence creates success, and success gives power. Power and confidence are self-reinforcing siblings that change brains in ways that foster several healthy and unhealthy appetites. High tolerance for risk matches the hunger for success. A laser goal-focus goes hand in hand with a narrowed attention that can blinker. Intense self-belief can diminish empathy for others, and the impulse to change something in the external world can lessen one's self-awareness. Carlos Ghosn's obliviousness to how his Japanese colleagues at Nissan were reacting to his plans and actions was likely a result of these power-induced brain changes. Or, as the title of a *Bloomberg* article about his arrest put it: 'He never saw it coming.'

The world needs confidence and begs for confident leaders who can enhance the self-belief of millions of people. But many leaders have found ways of making people feel confident that are destructive and damaging, such as by fostering tribalism. So, how do we develop leaders whose confidence is less double-edged?

Narcissism and leadership

'No, I don't want to think about it,' he said when Mr D'Antonio asked him to contemplate the meaning of his life. 'I don't like to analyze myself because I might not like what I see.'

Donald Trump spoke to his biographer in 2014, two years before he was elected president of the US. The quote shows that there isn't one single Donald Trump but at least two versions – the one avoided, and the other doing the avoiding. As we have seen, Trump is an outlier of overconfidence, so we have to ask whether this 'watcher' and 'watched' division is something that overconfident people do more than others.

A 2010 study by MIT researchers suggests that this is indeed true. They proposed that people routinely deceive themselves when their claims about themselves diverge from their beliefs. In the above quote, Trump revealed doubts about himself that in most situations he shies away from, replacing any doubt with exaggerated assertions of competence. One video compilation shows him claiming that 'nobody knows more than I do' about scores of topics – from drones to banks, infrastructure to nuclear weapons, and ISIS to environmental impact.

Overconfidence, the MIT researchers argue, is a form of bluster to persuade and dominate others, like a dog's threatening growl. But to pull it off, you have first to persuade yourself, hence the self-deception.

If you *don't* self-deceive about your true abilities, that doubt will leak out in your facial expression, posture and way of speaking, and so sabotage your ability to sell yourself as a superman.

Such inflated views or claims about oneself are examples of what psychologists at the University of York called *defensive zeal* in a 2003 study. Characterized by hyper-certainty and ardent proclamations of belief, defensive zeal often shades into 'rants'. The researchers showed that people whose fragile self-confidence is shielded from their conscious minds are much more inclined to express defensive zeal than others. This is particularly true when they think about situations that make them feel anxious and uncertain. This can work, because the loud proclamation of their certainties helps to quell underlying anxieties, albeit imperfectly.

Confidence is seldom a guaranteed bridge to the future, and always involves some overconfidence because of that lack of certainty. But extreme overconfidence is another matter, a bluff of enormous proportions that demands self-deception far beyond the needs of ordinary life. Being very overconfident demands a big ego, and such egos often veer into narcissism. Overconfidence is a critical ingredient in the narcissistic personality, of which there are seven key signs for which every potential leader should be scrutinized.

> **Authority:** *I am very good at influencing people and being recognized as a leader – I like being boss.*
> **Self-sufficiency:** *I seldom depend on others to get things done because I'm better at doing them myself and I like to make decisions.*
> **Superiority:** *I'm good because people tell me that, so I know I'm special and I like it when I get compliments. At some point, someone will write my biography, I hope.*
> **Exhibitionism:** *I'm a show-off and like attention – modesty isn't for me.*

Exploitativeness: *I can get others to believe what I want because I don't find it hard to manipulate them. If there's a problem, I find I can talk my way out of most situations.*

Vanity: *I look good in the mirror and like to look at myself, just like I enjoy showing off my body.*

Entitlement: *I'll not be content until I get all the things I deserve, so my expectations of others are very high. And if only I could run things, the world would be better.*

Extreme overconfidence almost always causes problems, from wrongly amputated limbs to failed companies. Extreme narcissists can wreak havoc when they are in charge, because they both overestimate their abilities and fail to see a difference between their interests and those of the organization they lead.

Research from 2015 on narcissism among leaders has also yielded a more nuanced conclusion, finding that the more narcissistic a person is, the more likely he is to be promoted into a leadership position – mainly because of his more extrovert personality. Once in the job, however, they didn't find any relationship between the degree of narcissism and his performance as measured by supervisor, peer and subordinate ratings. Narcissism got him the boss's job but didn't make him good at it. (We don't know to what extent this applies to women leaders.)

There was, however, a wrinkle in this neat conclusion. The investigators at the University of Illinois saw evidence of a bell curve relating narcissism to leader performance: some narcissism, in other words, *was* associated with being a better boss, while too much made you very much worse.

Can a bit of narcissism be positive in a leader? Sigmund Freud thought so – 'the leader himself need love no one else, he may be of a masterful nature, absolutely narcissistic, self-confident and independent', he wrote in *On Narcissism*.

Following up on this observation, a 1997 study extracted

personality descriptions of US presidents from standard sources, stripped them of all identifying details, and had student psychologists rate the presidents for narcissism against rigorous criteria. They went on to compare these with expert historians' ratings of each president's performance or 'greatness' and charisma. Charismatic leaders have a way of speaking and carrying themselves, generating a personal magnetism that inspires and influences their followers. This was true in the corporate world of Carlos Ghosn. It was also true for Sacha Romanovitch and Cathy Engelbert's financial world, and it's possible to speculate as to whether their female brand of charisma was not to the taste of a male-dominated industry.

The research discovered that presidential narcissism was indeed correlated with both charisma and performance. The most narcissistic president of the twentieth century was, according to the researchers, Franklin D. Roosevelt, who was both famously charismatic and widely admired for his stewardship of the US during the Great Depression and the Second World War.

It may mean that there are circumstances in which narcissistic overconfidence is a virtue, but it is probably not a coincidence that Roosevelt was the last president to serve more than two terms in office – he was elected to power no fewer than four times. Power grows, the longer it is held. This swells the chances of the power-holders' overconfident narcissism increasing to the wrong side of that narcissism bell curve.

This is the double-edged sword of narcissistic overconfidence – it can inspire and energize millions of people with empowering confidence that creates positive change. But, equally, it can drag down millions because of the self-centred, self-interested decisions and over-optimistic misjudgements of the narcissistic leader. Narcissism's purpose is to shore up the ego, and as grandiosity grows with increasing power and success, so the ego becomes more vulnerable to slight and humiliation. The prime motivation of the highly narcissistic leader is seldom the greater good alone – protecting a large and fragile ego is always a priority in his preoccupations.

But sometimes the leader's view of himself as a statesman allows his energies to flow behind *both* the greater good *and* the big task of protecting his ego. In that case, the narcissistic overconfidence can be a powerful force for the inspiration of millions of people, as happened with Roosevelt. It is a risky strategy, and few leaders manage successfully to harness power in this way. Behind the inspiring grandiosity of the narcissistic leader, there always lurks the vulnerability – the anxious watcher, wary that *he might not like what he sees*. Vast amounts of mental and emotional energy are needed to sustain that never-ending vigil, and to fight off the enemies of the inflated ego that exist both inside and outside the skull. So how do we find leaders who can inspire confidence without abusing it?

Women's leadership

Nothing tests a leader quite like a pandemic, governments around the world discovered in 2020. Some countries performed very well during the first wave, as measured by death rates. These included Taiwan, Germany, Finland, Denmark, Iceland and New Zealand. Other countries performed badly – for example, the US, Brazil, Russia and the UK.

What is striking about this league table is that the leaders of these high-performing countries with the fewest deaths were all women. In contrast, the four worst-performing countries had male leaders with strong narcissistic, overconfident and populist tendencies. This is an observation and not conclusive evidence for many reasons, including population size. Nevertheless, the question arises whether women's leadership is one way of harnessing the positives of confidence while minimizing the negatives.

Leaders have power, and women leaders *can* fall victim to these narcissistic personality changes. Former UK prime minister Margaret

Thatcher, for example, did succumb, according to a study by the neurologist and former UK foreign secretary David Owen. But women are less vulnerable to the addictive and personality-distorting effects that power can have on the brain. There are a couple of reasons why.

We saw that only men benefit from the hot hand effect. Women don't experience the same hormonal surge after beating another person – in other words, dominating them – as men do. These hormone changes boost testosterone and dopamine activity in the brain's reward network. When these surges are repeated and substantial, this can lead to a quasi-addictive process similar to that experienced with cocaine and other addictions. Women are relatively protected against this.

Another feature of the hormonal surges that come when competing with others is *choking*. If your desire to win is too high, your brain can generate excessive dopamine, which interferes with performance. Economists found that in high-stake professional tennis games, for example, players are more likely to choke at crucial points and squander their lead, compared to lower-stake games. However, in analysis of professional tennis games, women are much less likely to choke under pressure. They may not benefit from the hot hand effect, but nor do they succumb to its ugly sister, choking.

Disliking losing more than you enjoy gaining – *loss aversion* – also puts a brake on taking risks. Women show more loss aversion than men, meaning that, on average, they have a healthier appreciation of risk than men do. This cautious approach paid off among the amateur financial traders we saw in Chapter 9. More frequent trading means greater losses, and men traded much more than women and so ended up with 50 per cent greater losses. Sacha Romanovitch was very aware of the reputational and other risks to her company of taking on ethically unsavoury clients and took action to reduce it. The fact that she was ousted reflected a clash of values with her colleagues rather than an unwillingness on her part to take business risks.

A global pandemic demands that leaders have a keen appreciation of risk and take the appropriate steps to reduce it. Presidents Bolsonaro, Trump and Putin all played down the threat from Covid-19 when the pandemic could have been forestalled. And UK Prime Minister Boris Johnson was filmed boasting on 3 March 2020, at the height of a surging pandemic, that 'I'm shaking hands continually . . . I was at a hospital the other night where I think there were actually a few coronavirus patients and I shook hands with *everybody*.'

A month later, Johnson was admitted to intensive care in a London hospital, where he was described as 'fighting for his life'. His Covid-19 risk awareness increased after this experience. But what was remarkable was that an intelligent man – a world leader – needed such brutal personal experience of risk for it to impinge on his consciousness and behaviour. Had Johnson been more willing to consider risk based on overwhelming evidence from across the world, even ordering a UK lockdown just one week sooner could have saved twenty thousand lives, a UK government scientific adviser stated. Many tens of thousands more people in the US, Brazil and Russia died because their leaders were similarly over-confident and insouciant about risk.

Male overconfidence is dangerous. It might have worked for Carlos Ghosn, but his surprise at being arrested in Tokyo that morning perhaps reveals a risk-blindness on his part. He did not pay enough attention to the opposition to his plans and practices in Japan, and paid the price.

Leaders must take risks. Without them, the bridge to the future would be a short one. But harnessing confidence demands a balance between striving for the goal on the one hand, and anticipating danger on the other. On average, women may be better able to achieve that balance compared to men, because of their brains' responses to competition and power. They neither get the same rush by defeating the other person nor choke under pressure to the same degree when the stakes are high. They aren't invulnerable to overconfident narcissism, but it affects them less than men.

Of course, many men in powerful positions have maintained the reward–risk balance – it is an average difference between the sexes here, with a significant overlap in response to power. But as we saw in Chapter 6, women's capacity to benefit from confidence, and balance reward and risk, is systematically diminished by their interactions with men. They can compete fiercely, but tend to avoid doing so when men are in the game. This reduces their ability to benefit from the elixir of confidence.

Another reason why female characteristics allow leaders to handle power with fewer side-effects is that women in Western cultures tend to have a self that is more embedded in relationships, while men's self-concept tends to be more that of the isolated sole-trader. This is one reason why women experience challenges with competition, because beating or dominating other people can threaten their relationship-entwined egos.

As University of Michigan researchers showed in 2005, women's more social self-concept allows them to accept power with fewer distortions of their brains and behaviour. People of either sex whose power motivation is more communally driven – on behalf of a family, group, cause or organization, for example – than ego-driven show less of a potentially addictive hormonal surge in response to exercising power. These sex differences explain why the sort of risk-blind braggadocio of leaders such as Bolsonaro, Trump, Putin and Johnson is such a feature of male leadership – much more than of leadership by women.

Women make just as good leaders as men, two separate reviews of hundreds of studies of leadership effectiveness have concluded. In fact, the later of these reviews, in 2014, found that when leader competence was based entirely on colleagues' ratings, women were, on average, better leaders than men. Women can be just as competitive too – though competing is harder for them when men are in the race. And they can be just as aggressive as men if you provoke them, as we saw in Chapter 7. In general, women are not more risk-averse either.

It seems clear that one crucial way to avoid the downsides of overconfidence while benefiting from the upsides is to increase the number of women leaders across the world significantly.

Collectivism versus individualism

> If we were to rethink ourselves as social creatures who are fundamentally dependent upon one another – and there's no shame, no humiliation, no 'feminization' in that – I think that we would treat each other differently, because our very conception of self would not be defined by individual self-interest.

These words by the writer and academic Judith Butler capture the idea of a *connected self*, addressed in Chapter 7. Because it is embedded in its relationships, this intertwined ego is less vulnerable to the distortions of power, overconfidence and narcissism. Power, on average, is safer in women's hands because of this.

Hundreds of millions of men across the world also have more connected self-concepts because of their cultures. They live in *collectivist-minded* countries, not highly individualist Western ones, such as the US.

Wheat is weird and rice is nice

Collectively minded people show profound differences in thinking and outlook compared to those who are more individualist in orientation. Let's look at one way of picking apart these differences.

Try this short test. Below are five sets of three words. From each set, pick the two words that you think go together best:

Train	*Bus*	*Tracks*	. . . .	. . . .
Panda	*Banana*	*Monkey*	. . . .	. . . .
Shampoo	*Conditioner*	*Hair*	. . . .	. . . .
Chair	*Cushion*	*Table*	. . . .	. . . .
Wallet	*Purse*	*Banknote*	. . . .	. . . .

Before we look at your answers, do this. Get a piece of paper and a pen or pencil. Now draw a diagram of your group of friends. Use one circle for you, and a circle for each of your friends. Draw straight lines between the rings to show where there is a relationship between two of the people, but no lines between your circle and the others, as you are linked to all of them.

Let's look at your answers to the word quiz now. Did you answer *train, bus*; *panda, monkey*; *shampoo, conditioner*; *chair, table*; *wallet, purse*?

If so, you are probably WEIRD – not *weird*, let me hasten to add – but WEIRD. Namely, Western, Educated, Industrialized, Rich and Democratic in background. And, if you live in China, you are more likely to have come from a wheat-growing region in the north of the country rather than from the rice-growing south. If, on the other hand, your answers were something like *train, tracks*; *banana, monkey*; *shampoo, hair*; *chair, cushion*; *wallet, banknote*, then you are more likely to come from an East Asian country and, if you are Chinese, from a rice-growing region of that country.

Confused? Let me explain in a moment, but first, look at the circles in your social network. Find a ruler and measure the size of the circle representing you and compare it with the circles representing your friends. If you are from the US, then your self-circle will be, on average, 6 millimetres bigger than the circles portraying your friends. On the other hand, Europeans draw themselves, on average, 3.5 millimetres bigger than their friends. And Japanese? Their self-circles are slightly smaller than those they draw of their friends.

So, what's going on here? Cultures vary in how individualistic or collective-minded they are. Western cultures such as the US, Europe and Australia are individually focused societies while East Asian countries like Japan and Korea are more communally oriented. And to reassure us that this is not due to racial or economic factors, wheat- and rice-farming regions of China also divide in this way.

Rice farming is exceptionally labour intensive – at least twice as much as wheat farming – and the building and continual maintenance of irrigation systems, the time-sensitive bursts of activity for planting and transplanting, and many other activities mean that the only way a community can feed itself is by working together collectively. Wheat farming, on the other hand, is much less demanding of collective effort.

Most people in the wheat- and rice-growing areas of China no longer work as farmers. However, their culture has developed out of a history in which the majority of people were socialized into either individualistic or collective mindsets. These then become part of the culture, transmitted parent to child.

Practically speaking, all this means that individualistic *I* societies tend to be WEIRD, and their thinking is analytic in contrast to the more holistic thinking style of collective *we* cultures. Analytical thinking is shown in the abstract relationship found between words (monkey and panda, for example), which is extracted independently of the strong everyday association between the other two words – monkey and banana. Analytical thinkers rise above the specifics or the particulars to extract more abstract features.

Another example of analytical thinking is when you compare the length of a line inside a small square with a line of the same length inside a bigger square. Analytical thinkers are much better at ignoring the context of the frame, whose effect is to make the line in the small box appear *relatively* longer, and the other relatively smaller. Analytical thinkers tend to correctly judge that the two lines are the same length, by ignoring the context. Holistic thinkers find this much more challenging to do. They tend to be influenced by the context and judge the two lines as being different in length.

This difference applies to emotions too. Analytical thinkers are more prone to experiencing emotions that are focused on them as individuals achieving or failing to achieve personal goals – namely pride, anger and frustration. Holistic thinkers from collective cultures, on the other hand, emphasize more strongly social emotions such as guilt, shame and friendly feelings towards others – the feelings of social harmony, in other words.

This prioritizing of relationships leads to more nepotism among holistic thinkers – the Chinese from the rice-growing areas were more likely to show favouritism to their friends than those from the northern wheat-growing cultures. They were much less likely to punish bad behaviour by their friends than by strangers. On the other hand, analytical thinkers were much more likely to punish their friends if they misbehaved, because they were applying the abstract concept of fairness and impartiality, as befits this mindset.

These north–south Chinese differences mirrored those between Western and East Asian cultures – and there are many other countries in the world where holistic thinking is prevalent. It's interesting that WEIRD cultures also have higher rates of innovation in the form of patents for inventions – presumably because the analytic mode of thinking can generate novel ideas more readily. But divorce rates are also higher because of the individualism. These comparisons are not merely features of Western capitalist societies. Patents and divorce rates are also higher in the former wheat-growing areas of China than in the old rice-growing regions, irrespective of wealth or urbanization.

Western liberals tend to show more WEIRD thinking than

moderates or conservatives, wherever they live. Liberals show the analytical pattern of thinking more typical of China's wheat-growing areas – namely, concern for fairness and reciprocity. In contrast, conservatives espouse a set of values that incline them more to the holistic rice-type of thinking. The first of these is *loyalty* to the group or tribe. The second is a respect for and deference to *authority* because leaders and institutions are essential to social order. Finally, there is a *sanctity* of some people, objects and ideas that have to be respected and protected from desecration – for example, flags, leaders, or core beliefs that bind people together.

We can view the Brexit and Trump political upheavals more clearly in this light. In both episodes, there was a strong trend for older, more conservative, less educated and poorer people to vote for the option that so outraged the more analytically inclined WEIRD-thinking political establishment of both the UK and US.

The European Union is the apotheosis of WEIRD thinking. It is a system of rational, rule-based, trans-national government dominated by fairness, reciprocity and a desire to develop the poorest countries and regions. Donald Trump's presidential opponent Hillary Clinton was also a paragon of WEIRD thinking – cool and rational, with no resort to the emotional attraction of tribal outgrouping.

Wheat- versus rice-thinkers represent not just different styles of thought, they represent two cultures with entirely different values. The analytical wheat-thinkers value fairness to all and care of the vulnerable, while the holistic rice-thinkers value loyalty, authority and sanctity. Rice-thinkers are more comfortable with hostility and discrimination against the outgroup, whereas wheat-thinkers are against this.

The bitter enmity between pro- and anti-Brexit people, and between pro- and anti-Trump citizens, can be understood in these terms. This is not about rational political debate, this is *tribal* conflict based on a fundamental clash of values between two warring groups. Such inter-group conflict is a universal of human group behaviour.

In regions such as Japan and southern China, there is more 'we' mixed among the 'I'. In highly individualistic countries like the US, the *I* is pure I. People in countries like Japan give less priority to individual self-esteem and self-confidence – hence, perhaps, Carlos Ghosn's downfall in that country. As a result, they have lower average self-esteem and self-confidence levels than in Western countries. But we know it's not racial factors explaining these national differences, because of a 2004 University of British Columbia study that showed Canadians who move to live in Japan become *less* self-confident, while Japanese who move to Canada become *more* individually self-confident.

Having an individually focused versus a collectively focused ego biases your memory too. US and Japanese volunteers recalled situations in which they had either *influenced* or *adjusted to* other people. An example of influence would be when *I talked my sister out of dating a guy I knew was a jerk*. On the other hand, *I had to adjust last school year when one of my roommate's boyfriends moved into our house* would be an example of adjusting. Americans remembered many more occasions when they wielded influence, and the Japanese recalled more situations when they adjusted to other people. And the influence made Americans much more personally confident than it did the Japanese. In contrast, the adjustment made the Japanese feel much more closely connected to other people, which was not the case for Americans.

We know that one way in which confidence works is by the distorting lens, where our brains respond more readily to feedback that boosts our ego than to information that threatens it. This results, for example, in a statistically impossible number of us believing ourselves to be *above average* in domains such as driving ability. This self-enhancement effect is much higher in individualistic cultures such as the US and Western Europe than in collective cultures like

Japan and Korea. *We* people feel less of a need to big up their egos than *I* individuals, and so are more realistic about their abilities.

These variations in ego lead to quite different responses to success and failure. For example, Canadian students will persist much more with a task which they believe they have done well on, while Japanese students persevere much more on one where they think they have done badly.

We saw in Chapter 3 that parents' attitudes to their children's failures are crucial in shaping their offspring's theories about their abilities. Parents who see their children's failures as learning opportunities rather than as a problem in their inherent abilities kindle a change mindset in them. It turns out that the reason the Japanese persisted more after apparent failure was because their more collective egos were less threatened by individual failure. Hence, it was easier for them to use it as a teaching signal to allow them to practise and improve. Because their theory of self was not a fixed one, but rather a more fluid interconnected one, they could benefit from failure as a means of self-improvement.

The more isolated, individual egos of the Canadian students, on the other hand, were threatened by failure. So, they shied away from it, concentrating instead on improving on tasks they believed they were good at, thus affording some protection to their more isolated egos.

In the context of all this, it's interesting to view the different responses of Carlos Ghosn, as then chairman of Nissan, and its recently appointed CEO, Hiroto Saikawa, to a 2017 crisis. Nissan had to recall 1.2 million cars because of inadequate inspections, and the company had to shut down its Japanese factories for two weeks. Saikawa had been in the job for only a few months, and the problems had happened when Ghosn had been in charge as CEO. Nevertheless, it was Saikawa who gave the ritual public apology required of dishonoured Japanese bosses, and who took a voluntary pay cut in a compensation package that was already a small fraction of Ghosn's.

According to media reports, Ghosn allegedly had Nissan pay his sister $100,000 per year for non-existent advisory services, for private family trips, and also for his five luxurious houses in Paris, Tokyo, Amsterdam, Beirut and Rio de Janeiro. A 2018 comment piece in *The Japan Times* by the president of Japan's Foreign Policy Institute illustrates the clash of mindsets we have been discussing above. He wrote that Ghosn was welcome in Japan, even with his vast compensation, so long as he espoused 'values of hard work, an ascetic life, saving for the future and service to the community'. He went on to say that '[. . .] what was revealed so far about Ghosn's public and private life irritated many of Nissan's Japanese employees'. Ghosn has denied all allegations of wrongdoing, claiming there was a conspiracy to oust him from the firm.

Ghosn was the ultimate individualist and super-confident magnate whose perspective clashed with collectivist Japanese culture to the extent that he ended up in prison. Of course, there were many other political and corporate factors at play in these events as well. But there is no doubt that the driving self-confidence that produced his undoubted achievements also led to Ghosn's corporate downfall. He illustrates the positives and negatives of supercharged confidence, but also presents a fascinating case study in how individual confidence may play out in a collectivist culture. Which immediately raises the question: is it possible to harness collective self-belief and become more confident – *together*?

Learning collective confidence

Kim spent a lot of her teenage years and early twenties on social media, and that worsened her feelings of being a 'loser' (her choice of word). She could see the parties that she hadn't been invited to, the trips not made, and the missing achievements. There is no hiding from other people's successes on Facebook or Instagram, and so for people like Kim, plagued with a lack of confidence and anxiety, evidence for being a failure and loser is all too easy to gather.

On social media, teenage girls follow men more than women celebrities, a 2019 study by data science company Starcount and University of Cambridge researchers showed. When teenage girls were encouraged by 'The Female Lead' campaign to follow confidence-inspiring, high-achieving women, that picture changed. Interactions with social media were enhanced by offering teen girls a diverse range of female role models to follow, aligning with their personal interests and career aspirations. Their social media posts began to use words linked to confidence, such as *aspire*, *dream* and *enthusiast*.

This happened both because of the new women they were following, and also because the algorithms responded by changing their feed. A more confidence-positive set of further examples and articles began to flow into their devices. This changed the online community for these girls to one with a greater sense of collective confidence in achievement. Groups of people, even where millions of people are involved, can have a sense of collective confidence. Leaders play a major role in building this. So, can collective confidence be learned? A 2014 study from an impoverished, food-insecure region of Ethiopia suggests that it can. Poverty in an area shapes the *can do* and *can happen* expectations of whole communities. When everyone around you is struggling, it is understandable that expectations become tailored to what seems to be an unchangeable reality.

The researchers at the Centre for Economic Policy Research asked local development agents to find stories of people who had improved their wellbeing despite adversity. They chose ten people and made short documentaries about their lives. They told the stories of their achievements, which ranged from starting a small business to diversifying their sources of income. Their spouses and mentors gave testimony to their personal qualities such as perseverance, determination and reliability. The fact that they succeeded through their efforts, albeit with some outside help, was emphasized.

In other words, the films tried to build confidence – both its *can do* and *can happen* elements. A one-hour screening of these ten short documentaries was then shown to groups of people in their villages. Compared to placebo control groups who watched entertaining movies, the confidence-building film groups showed significant changes in their behaviour six months later.

First, their aspirations – their *can happen* expectations – were raised, and they began to save more and become financially more stable. They sent more children to school, and the people in these communities showed a boosted sense of control over their lives – something that we have seen already is crucial for confidence.

Confidence can be learned – and that includes the collective confidence of large groups of people, including whole nations. Denis Mukwege and Nadia Murad both harnessed collective confidence within their conservative societies in a bid to change attitudes to women.

Is there a way to combine the positives of individualistic and collective cultures to better harness both individual *and* collective confidence?

Empowered by thought

Education makes individual people, and hence the countries in which they live, wealthier and healthier. A country with an educated population can attract the sort of high-skill, high-value industries that build economies. But there is another, much less obvious reason.

First, take a moment to consider these two snippets of dialogue about health.

Dialogue 1

How might you become healthier?
I could exercise regularly.

How could you exercise more regularly?
I could go running.
How could you set about going running?
I could set a time in the morning before work.

Dialogue 2

Why might you want to become healthier?
So I could lose weight and look better.
Why would you want to lose weight?
Because being overweight is bad for your body.
Why are you concerned about it being bad for your body?
Because I want to enjoy life, which is hard when you are sick.

The difference between these two types of conversation is that the first narrows down to a couple of concrete specifics, driven by the 'how' questions, while the second, prompted by the 'why' questions, is more general and abstract. The 'how' questions focus the mind on to specifics and actions. The 'why' questions force you to think in broader, more abstract terms.

Merely using abstract language, as in Dialogue 2, makes you feel more powerful – and therefore confident. Abstract words and ideas are umbrella categories that gather different specific instances of the more general concept – *furniture* versus *chair*, *emotion* versus *anger*, or *goal* versus *I want to stop smoking*. When you think using these terms, it tends to unfetter you from the immediate and so open to your mind a whole range of possibilities offered by the specific instances of the category. This frees up your mind to many more options, making you feel more in control – and hence more powerful and confident.

Abstract thinking also helps project yourself into the future, because you are liberated from the specifics of a particular situation and so widened into a much broader time horizon. This inclines you to consider opportunities in the future – including quite distant possibilities and far-off threats, including health. This is one reason education is one of the strongest predictors of healthy lifestyle actions – such as not smoking and eating well – and how long you live.

Abstract thinking also connects you to people outside your immediate circle or community. It binds you together through concepts such as human rights, common humanity, or European citizenship.

The type of thinking a good education fosters makes you feel more powerful, but it also changes how you behave. In one experiment, a group of people were asked to plan a new organization and then to allocate roles in that set-up to each of the participants. Half of the participants engaged in concrete thinking, as in Dialogue 1 above, while the other half had to think abstractly. Irrespective of their education, those randomly assigned to abstract thinking allocated themselves more senior, responsible and powerful roles in the organizations they were planning.

When you think concretely, you focus on the details of a situation – the language pulls you into the specifics. For example, if people are concerned about immigration levels to their country, a concrete response is to physically strengthen borders to reduce the numbers coming in – *build the wall*, in Donald Trump's terms. Abstract language frees you from the detail of the situation and so helps you imagine a range of possibilities not tied to the specifics of the perceived problem. Examples of these would be helping to develop the economies of the home countries of immigrants or introducing a national identity card system that would make illegal immigration harder.

In turn, this freeing from the immediate, concrete detail of the problem you are considering gives you a greater sense of control, and therefore confidence and power. And because of this sense of possibility, power and confidence, abstract thinking puts you in a more eager, hopeful state of mind focused on possibility. Concrete thinking, on the other hand, makes you think more about specific implementation and potential obstacles. That said, it's key to remember that concrete, practical thinking has its place in the implementation phase of any enterprise.

Values

Company CEOs with a robust moral and ethical code make better bosses, a 2008 study of seventy-three Dutch companies showed. Assessed by their direct reports, the morally driven managers were rated as having more effective management teams. Their employees were more optimistic about their company's future.

This is perhaps not surprising in the light of the discussion about self-affirmation. Bringing your deepest values to mind buffers the ego against threat and humiliation. It also makes a person less tribal and prejudiced against the outgroup. And because the ego is less under threat because of the self-affirmation, the person in power doesn't have to use a lot of mental energy to defend it. This is true for all of us, not just for dominant leaders. Values and a moral code embed the self in a more secure base than is the case for the sole-practitioner ego that has to be on guard night and day against threat. They also act as an antidote to the effects of power on the brain and hence help to reduce the downsides of overconfidence.

Ethical values tame the ego by making it feel like part of something bigger. This both constrains the ego and liberates it. Values constrain by clipping the ego's wings. They liberate it because the ego is less exposed to threat and humiliation because it feels part of something larger than itself.

Wealthy people have more power and confidence than more impoverished people, and also behave less ethically and more selfishly than poorer people, University of California, Berkeley, research has shown. This is true, however, only if materialism – that is, money and possessions – dominates their values.

People across 132 countries were asked this question by Gallup

in 2007: *Do you feel your life has an important purpose or meaning?*
Remarkably, the richer the country, the fewer people answered yes
to this question. Top of the list for feeling their lives had meaning
were citizens of countries such as Sierra Leone, Ecuador, Angola,
Chad and Laos. At the very bottom of the league table were Japan,
Spain, France, Belgium and Hong Kong.

What explained this difference was religiosity. If you answered
yes to the question *Is religion an important part of your daily life?*
then you were most likely to say that your life had an important
purpose or meaning. Values are the *raison d'être* of most religions,
and having a sense of purpose in life makes people live longer and
healthier lives than those without a sense of meaning. Values tem-
per the risk of narcissistic overconfidence in powerful people, and
also reduce the corrosive effects of low status on the confidence of
poorer, lower status individuals.

So, how to combine the advantages of the individualist and collectivist mind-states to build healthy confidence? One answer is by
fostering ethical values in leaders, which influence the values of the
people they lead. Values-based leaders are, in effect, collectivist
leaders, psychologically speaking. The leader's ego is embedded –
and therefore constrained – within a framework that is bigger than
his or her ego. Such leaders are less prone to tribal thinking because
their 'tribe' is a set of values, and not a group of people striving for
ingroup advantage and domination of the outgroup. They can allow
education to empower them by developing abstract thinking. They
can also self-affirm to strengthen their psychological resistance to
feeling demeaned, hence avoiding the pitfalls of tit-for-tat retribu-
tion to which this feeling so often leads. And they can take all the
advantages that individual confidence offers in creativity and
innovation.

Carlos Ghosn, like almost all Western corporate leaders, earned
eye-watering sums of money. It is very hard to hold ethical values
against the drug-like effects of such wealth. If we are to keep

overconfidence in check but still benefit from it, then we have to find ways to protect corporate and political leaders from the corrupting, brain-changing effects of dangerous doses of money.

The confidence to change

The one thing we can be certain will happen in our lives over the next decades is change. It will happen ever faster because of exponential developments in technology, climate change and accelerating pandemics. Artificial intelligence, robotics and communications will disrupt our lives like nothing we have seen. Along with global heating, these changes will make people migrate in their tens of millions, and will sweep away whole industries. It will, if unchecked, magnify inequalities to unsustainable levels.

Change can lead to both good and bad outcomes, so while the risks multiply, so do the opportunities. Accelerating advances in science have eliminated smallpox and wild polio from the globe, diminished hunger and extended life expectancy enormously, even in the poorest countries. But harnessing the good out of these exponential changes requires one essential and fundamental quality of every human being on the planet, and that is confidence. Without the bridge to the future that confidence offers, we risk being overwhelmed by the tsunami of oncoming change.

Change makes us anxious, as is evidenced by the epidemic of anxiety across the developed world. This emotion saps confidence, and the best antidote to it is confidence. Embracing change means that we have to prioritize – we have to make our children feel confident so that they can navigate the changes facing them in their century-long lives. Some countries, such as the US, spent decades trying to build up their children's self-esteem, which was the wrong target. Confidence empowers people to act in a way that self-esteem does not.

Confidence is less valuable as a commodity in highly stable

societies, but exponential technological change will make stable communities a rarity. We have to find ways of making people and populations more change-ready. To do that, people must become confident – both individually and collectively.

Anna is a fourteen-year-old girl who lives in a big city somewhere in the world. What does she need in order to be confident in facing up to immense change?

Above all, Anna needs a family that makes her feel as if she is held in someone's mind. She needs to believe that they prioritize her interests and future at least as much as their own. Next, she should have some confidence-building success experiences in sport, music, drama, dance or some other domain. Her family and teachers should tell her that her abilities and personality are not fixed and can be changed. She should also learn that anxiety and low mood are normal, healthy emotions that can be harnessed and learned from. Her family shouldn't pay attention to her school class-ranking. Instead, they should focus on what she's achieving against her own personal standards.

Anna finds out early how stereotype works in people's brains, including hers, to sabotage female performance. There is no science, mathematics, computing, engineering or related subject that she cannot master and excel at as well as any boy. Her visuospatial abilities are excellent, so long as prejudice doesn't sabotage them.

Anna should be clear about the values she learns from her family and school. She should learn that affirming these values is one of the best ways of stopping criticism, humiliation or bullying from eating into her soul. Anna's education makes her more confident because thinking abstractly makes people feel more powerful and confident. Strong women role models shape her social media feed through empowering platforms such as 'The Female Lead'.

Anna realizes that to help influence the way in which the world is changing, she needs to band together with others and grow collective confidence to foster change. She is inspired by countries and organizations that have broken the mould by electing women leaders, and understands that individuals can achieve massive amounts when they unite.

But she is super-aware of the risk that groups can be hijacked by populists peddling too-easy solutions. She understands that these men – for they are usually men – know how to snare basic tribal impulses that exist in all of us. They use ingroup–outgroup prejudices to make disempowered people feel more powerful and confident. But she realizes this is a synthetic, false sort of confidence.

As she grows up, she also understands that the bigger the rich–poor gap in a country, the more she will find that left-behind, low-confidence people will look for a strong leader willing to harness their tribal instincts. She realizes that females and like-minded males should come together to support leaders who are less likely to become overconfident, risk-blind and power-addicted. And she understands that the wealth generated by technological advances and the clean, cheap energy of the future must be more equally distributed for this to happen.

She understands that WEIRD approaches to life have their upsides and their downsides. Loneliness and a potential lack of purpose can come from an over-analytical approach to life. She has read how some poorer countries have a stronger sense of meaning than people from her own country. Anna senses a sterile, unspiritual type of materialism where she lives, and she can see that it makes her friends restless, unhappy, and some want to experiment with drugs. But she knows that the anti-analytic, tribal approach to life has a whole other set of problems. So Anna seeks out values-based leaders who articulate a sense of meaning for humanity as a whole, with a sense of connectedness and purpose against common enemies such as climate change and pandemics. Anna is acutely aware of the ego-trap of leadership and knows that authentic values are crucial in protecting against this pitfall.

We are asking an awful lot of Anna, wherever she lives on the globe. But the Annas of this world and her friends – male and female – have no choice but to rise to the challenge. Anna and her friends need confidence like they need nothing else. With it they will build their *can do* and *can happen* bridges to the future. To harness it, they need to understand not only the outside world but also the internal worlds of themselves and other people. Only when they are aware of the threats and opportunities of confidence can they harness it.

Source Notes

1 **The future champion replied matter-of-factly:** Reed S., 'Cheer on 14-year-old Venus Williams's dad as he defends her from a pushy reporter'. *InStyle*, 30 August 2018.

1 **. . . the *New York Times*:** Williams V., 'Venus Williams: Confidence can be learned'. *New York Times*, 6 December 2018.

3 **. . . believe less strongly that they can get ahead by their hard work:** Giuliano P., Spilimbergo A., 'Growing up in a recession'. *Review of Economic Studies*, 2014; 81(2):787–817.

3 **In a UK study of two thousand sixteen- to twenty-five-year-olds . . .** 'never succeed in life': Prince's Trust, 'The aspiration gap: The lost hopes and ambitions of a generation'. September 2020. [Available from https://www.princes-trust.org.uk/about-the-trust/news-views/aspiration-gap-research] Accessed 2 November 2020.

4 **. . . easier for young people to have the confidence to aspire and achieve:** Lyubomirsky S., King L., Diener E., 'The benefits of frequent positive affect: Does happiness lead to success?' *Psychological Bulletin*, 2005; 131(6):803–55.

4 **. . . if your partner feels confident about your condition:** Rohrbaugh M. J., Shoham V., Coyne J. C., Cranford J. A., Sonnega J. S., Nicklas J. M., 'Beyond the self in self-efficacy: Spouse confidence predicts patient survival following heart failure'. *Journal of Family Psychology*, 2004; 18(1):184–93.

4 . . . As confidence waxes and wanes, we see profound changes in the physiology of the brain and the rest of the body: Cortese A., Amano K., Koizumi A., Lau H., Kawato M., 'Decoded fMRI neurofeedback can induce bidirectional confidence changes within single participants'. *NeuroImage*, 2017; 149:323–37.

4 . . . boosts your immune system, despite the fear you feel: Wiedenfeld S. A., O'Leary A., Bandura A., Brown S., Levine S., Raska K., 'Impact of perceived self-efficacy in coping with stressors on components of the immune system'. *Journal of Personality and Social Psychology*, 1990; 59(5):1082–94.

8 . . . car companies would not be the ones to manufacture electric cars: Khalaf R., 'Le cost killer: The relentless drive of Carlos Ghosn'. *Financial Times*, 15 June 2018.

8 '. . . Nissan's future on the line by going for the electric car and the Leaf': *Revenge of the Electric Car* [film]. Paine C., dir. (USA, 2011).

8 'We have an analysis . . . we think it's going to bring a lot of benefit': 'Nissan's Carlos Ghosn seeks revenge for the electric car'. *Yale Environment 360*, 4 May 2011. [Available from: https://e360.yale.edu/features/nissans_carlos_ghosn_seeks_revenge_for_the_electric_car] Accessed 5 November 2020.

9 . . . in 2018, 45 per cent of all new cars in Norway were electric: Lambert F., Electrek, 2018. [Available from: https://electrek.co/2018/10/01/electric-vehicle-sales-new-record-norway-tesla] Accessed 5 November 2020.

9 . . . Toyota Land Cruisers that roared into her Yazidi village of Kocho in northern Iraq: Murad N., Krajeski J., *The Last Girl: My story of captivity and my fight against the Islamic State* (New York: Tim Duggan Books, 2018).

11 Years later, she told a reporter from *Forbes* magazine that she lacked confidence: Valet V., ' "Your career is not linear": Deloitte CEO Cathy Engelbert on her rise to the top'. *Forbes*, 3 April 2018.

12 She told a reporter from the *Financial Times* . . . did not like the short-term reduction in profits caused by her policies: Marriage M., 'Grant Thornton chief executive faces partner dissent'. *Financial Times*, 21 September 2018.

14   ... a ramping-down of your motivation in a part of the cortex called the anterior cingulate: Bonnelle V., Manohar S., Behrens T., Husain M., 'Individual differences in premotor brain systems underlie behavioral apathy'. *Cerebral Cortex*, 2015; 26(2):807–19.

15   Your brain's self-appraisal system in the middle of the frontal lobes whirls with thoughts of failure and self-doubt: Ochsner K. N., Bunge S. A., Gross J. J., Gabrieli J. D. E., 'Rethinking feelings: An fMRI study of the cognitive regulation of emotion'. *Journal of Cognitive Neuroscience*, 2002; 14(8):1215–29.

15   In this half-bridge version of confidence ... angry and anxious: Mahon N. E., Yarcheski A., Yarcheski T. J., Hanks M. M., 'Relations of low frustration tolerance beliefs with stress, depression, and anxiety in young adolescents'. *Psychological Reports*, 2007; 100(1): 98–100.

15   In its primed-for-action state, your brain's reward network signals pain: Sokol-Hessner P., Rutledge R. B., 'The psychological and neural basis of loss aversion'. *Current Directions in Psychological Science*, 2019; 28(1):20–7.

15   Your brain anticipates reward with a surge of dopamine activity: Hamid A. A., Pettibone J. R., Mabrouk O. S., Hetrick V. L., Schmidt R., Vander Weele C. M., et al., 'Mesolimbic dopamine signals the value of work'. *Nature Neuroscience*, 2016; 19(1):117–26.

17   Self-esteem is assessed ... *I have high self-esteem*: Robins R. W., Hendin H. M., Trzesniewski K. H., 'Measuring global self-esteem: Construct validation of a single-item measure and the Rosenberg Self-Esteem Scale'. *Personality and Social Psychology Bulletin*, 2001; 27(2):151–61.

17   The more you agree with them ... satisfied you are likely to be with your job: Kuster F., Orth U., Meier L. L., 'High self-esteem prospectively predicts better work conditions and outcomes'. *Social Psychological and Personality Science*, 2013; 4(6):668–75.

17   ... and also with your partner, among many other benefits: Erol R. Y., Orth U., 'Development of self-esteem and relationship satisfaction in couples: Two longitudinal studies'. *Developmental Psychology*, 2014; 50(9):2291–303.

17   **Confidence *is* that prediction . . . more strongly than her level of self-esteem:** Diseth Å., Meland E., Breidablik H. J., 'Self-beliefs among students: Grade level and gender differences in self-esteem, self-efficacy and implicit theories of intelligence'. *Learning and Individual Differences*, 2014; 35:1–8.

17   **Confidence also predicts . . . if your company goes through a re-organization:** Jimmieson N. L., Terry D. J., Callan V. J., 'A longitudinal study of employee adaptation to organizational change: The role of change-related information and change-related self-efficacy'. *Journal of Occupational Health Psychology*, 2004; 9(1):11–27.

17   **Confidence . . . presages how many interviews and job offers you'll receive on a job search:** Moynihan L. M., Roehling M. V., LePine M. A., Boswell W. R., 'A longitudinal study of the relationships among job search self-efficacy, job interviews, and employment outcomes'. *Journal of Business and Psychology*, 2003; 18(2):207–33.

17   **It also has many other benefits . . . how quickly you'll return to work after a car crash:** Murgatroyd D. F., Harris I. A., Tran Y., Cameron I. D., 'Predictors of return to work following motor vehicle related orthopaedic trauma'. *BMC Musculoskeletal Disorders*, 2016; 17(1):171.

17   **It also has many other benefits . . . your performance in sport:** Woodman T., Hardy L., 'The relative impact of cognitive anxiety and self-confidence upon sport performance: A meta-analysis'. *Journal of Sports Sciences*, 2003; 21(6):443–57.

17   **But self-esteem did *not* predict confidence as the years went on:** Erol R. Y., Orth U., 'Self-esteem development from age 14 to 30 years: A longitudinal study'. *Journal of Personality and Social Psychology*, 2011; 101(3):607–19.

18   **The mental energy it takes to protect self-esteem . . . barely scraped a dollar at $1.07:** Sachdeva S., Iliev R., Medin D. L., 'Sinning saints and saintly sinners: The paradox of moral self-regulation'. *Psychological Science*, 2009; 20(4):523–8.

20–2 **'I was six under par . . . hitting a great shot and giving them something to cheer about':** Neville S., 'My caddie won me The Open: Padraig Harrington relives his 2007 glory'. *Irish Examiner*, 19 July 2018.

24 To the brain . . . the prospect of punishment makes us fearful: Wagner
A. R., 'Frustrative nonreward: A variety of punishment' in Campbell
B. A. and Church R. M., *Punishment and Aversive Behavior* (New
York: Appleton-Century-Crofts, 1969), pp. 157–81.

28 What comes first . . . pounding hearts and twisting stomachs as anxiety: Brooks A. W., 'Get excited: Reappraising pre-performance
anxiety as excitement'. *Journal of Experimental Psychology: General*,
2014; 143(3):1144–58.

29 Sports psychology researchers . . . improve self-confidence when performing the task: Barker J., Jones M., Greenlees I., 'Assessing the
immediate and maintained effects of hypnosis on self-efficacy and
soccer wall-volley performance'. *Journal of Sport and Exercise Psychology*, 2010; 32(2):243–52.

29 On Thursday, 23 June 2016 . . . warnings from the Governor of the
Bank of England: Tapsfield J., 'Bank of England boss Mark Carney
warns No Deal could drive Britain into recession and cause inflation
spike in new Project Fear warning as the Pound tumbles AGAIN'.
Daily Mail, 1 August 2019.

30 While only 27 per cent of eighteen- to twenty-four-year-olds . . . over
the age of sixty-five did so: Becker S., Fetzer T., Novy D., 'Who voted
for Brexit?'. ifo DICE Report, 2017; 15(4):3–5.

30 Two years later . . . shrank to 18 per cent: Curtice J., 'How young
and old would vote on Brexit now'. *BBC News*, 2018. [Available
from: https://www.bbc.com/news/uk-politics-45098550] Accessed 5
November 2020.

31 It chalks up positive scores . . . *asymmetric updating*: Sharot T., Garrett
N., 'Forming beliefs: Why valence matters'. *Trends in Cognitive Sciences*, 2016; 20(1):25–33.

31 . . . most people think they're above-average drivers: McKenna F. P.,
Stanier R. A., Lewis C., 'Factors underlying illusory self-assessment
of driving skill in males and females'. *Accident Analysis and Prevention*, 1991; 23(1):45–52.

31 Surgeons and many other occupations . . . than the average person:
Pandey V., Wolfe J., Black S., Cairols M., Liapis C., Bergqvist D.,
'Self-assessment of technical skill in surgery: The need for expert

feedback'. *Annals of the Royal College of Surgeons of England*, 2008; 90(4):286–90.

31 **They also believe ... upon which a multi-trillion-dollar gambling industry is built:** Weinstein N. D., 'Unrealistic optimism about future life events'. *Journal of Personality and Social Psychology*, 1980; 39(5): 806–20.

31–2 **Good news – learning that your chances ... the right inferior frontal gyrus:** Mitchell D. G., Luo Q., Avny S. B., Kasprzycki T., Gupta K., Chen G., et al., 'Adapting to dynamic stimulus-response values: Differential contributions of inferior frontal, dorsomedial, and dorsolateral regions of prefrontal cortex to decision making'. *Journal of Neuroscience*, 2009; 29(35):10827–34.

32 **... positive thinking also inclines you ... shaping your memories more positively:** Devitt A. L., Schacter D. L., 'An optimistic outlook creates a rosy past: The impact of episodic simulation on subsequent memory'. *Psychological Science*, 2018; 29(6):936–46. *See also*: Schacter D. L., Addis D. R., 'The optimistic brain'. *Nature Neuroscience*, 2007; 10(11):1345–7.

32 **The brains of glass-half-empty people ... less of a bias in favour of good news:** Sharot T., Korn C. W., Dolan R. J., 'How unrealistic optimism is maintained in the face of reality'. *Nature Neuroscience*, 2011; 14(11):1475–9.

32 **The same is also true of mildly depressed individuals:** Garrett N., Sharot T., Faulkner P., Korn C. W., Roiser J. P., Dolan R. J., 'Losing the rose tinted glasses: Neural substrates of unbiased belief updating in depression'. *Frontiers in Human Neuroscience*, 2014; 8:639.

32 **Our brains react to negative news ... a level in eighty-year-olds far below that seen in children:** Sharot T., Garrett N., 'Forming beliefs: Why valence matters'. *Trends in Cognitive Sciences*, 2016; 20(1):25–33.

33 **Walt Disney's cartoon character Oswald the Lucky Rabbit ... *Confidence*:** *Oswald the Lucky Rabbit* [animated drawing]. Lantz W., dir. (USA, 1933). [Available from: https://www.youtube.com/watch?v=VjGTC chapOk] Accessed 5 November 2020.

33 **Those who endured ... the Great Recession ended:** Forbes M. K., Krueger R. F., 'The Great Recession and mental health in the United States'. *Clinical Psychological Science*, 2019; 7(5):900–13.

33 **Across Europe and North America . . . extra ten thousand people to commit suicide:** Reeves A., McKee M., Stuckler D., 'Economic suicides in the Great Recession in Europe and North America'. *British Journal of Psychiatry*, 2014; 205(3):246–7.

34 **If you lose your job . . . sending your mood low and your anxiety levels sky high:** Dunlop B. W., Nemeroff C. B., 'The role of dopamine in the pathophysiology of depression'. *Archives of General Psychiatry*, 2007; 64(3):327–37.

35 **. . . economic recessions that reduce your hope . . . lessen your self-confidence:** Schoon I., Mortimer J., 'Youth and the Great Recession: Are values, achievement orientation and outlook to the future affected?' *International Journal of Psychology*, 2017; 52(1):1–8.

35 **. . . the ups and downs of the English national football team . . . the closest of sisters:** Kaplanski G., Levy H., Veld C., Veld-Merkoulova Y., 'Do happy people make optimistic investors?' *Journal of Financial and Quantitative Analysis*, 2015; 50(1–2):145–68.

36 **Prince Harry . . . just had to try to hide it:** Sykes T., 'Prince Harry on his panic attacks: "We're all mental" '. *Daily Beast*, 21 June 2017. [Available from: https://www.thedailybeast.com/prince-harry-on-panic-attacks-were-all-mental] Accessed 5 November 2020.

36–7 **Similarly, the actor Hugh Grant . . . would often forget his lines:** Vilkomerson, S., 'Hugh Grant: *Florence Foster Jenkins* star discusses panic attacks while acting'. *Entertainment Weekly*, 11 August 2016. [Available from https://ew.com/article/2016/08/11/hugh-grant-panic-attacks-acting] Accessed 5 November 2020.

37 **'I have learned one thing . . . I've done both':** Braudy S., 'He's Woody Allen's not-so-silent partner'. *New York Times*, 21 August 1977.

38 **People like Jo . . . do less stuff in their lives:** Ireland M. E., Hepler J., Li H., Albarracín D., 'Neuroticism and attitudes toward action in 19 countries'. *Journal of Personality*, 2015; 83(3):243–50.

38 **. . . it is the *confidence* to do the thing you fear . . . you will overcome it:** Bandura A., Reese L., Adams N. E., 'Microanalysis of action and fear arousal as a function of differential levels of perceived self-efficacy'. *Journal of Personality and Social Psychology*, 1982; 43(1): 5–21.

39   **Confident people choose goals that stretch and improve them:** Zim-
      merman B. J., Bandura A., Martinez-Pons M., 'Self-motivation for
      academic attainment: The role of self-efficacy beliefs and personal
      goal setting'. *American Educational Research Journal*, 1992; 29(3):
      663–76.

39   **... end up more resilient emotionally:** Milioni M., Alessandri G.,
      Eisenberg N., Castellani V., Zuffianò A., Vecchione M., et al., 'Recip-
      rocal relations between emotional self-efficacy beliefs and
      ego-resiliency across time'. *Journal of Personality*, 2015; 83(5):552–63.

40   **... what happened to these test scores ... given different information
      about the test:** Haslam C., Morton T. A., Haslam S. A., Varnes L., Gra-
      ham R., Gamaz L., ' "When the age is in, the wit is out": Age-related
      self-categorization and deficit expectations reduce performance on
      clinical tests used in dementia assessment'. *Psychology and Aging*, 2012;
      27(3):778–84.

43–4 **... Claude Steele ... Self-doubt flared and poor performance fol-
      lowed:** Steele C. M., Aronson J., 'Stereotype threat and the intel-
      lectual test performance of African Americans'. *Journal of Personality
      and Social Psychology*, 1995; 69(5):797–811.

44   **... if female participants are 'primed' ... they perform just as well on this
      supposedly gender-sensitive task:** Moè A., 'Are males always better
      than females in mental rotation? Exploring a gender belief explan-
      ation'. *Learning and Individual Differences*, 2009; 19(1):21–7.

44   **... brain imaging to discover how these stereotypes change brain
      function:** Wraga M., Helt M., Jacobs E., Sullivan K., 'Neural basis of
      stereotype-induced shifts in women's mental rotation performance'.
      Social Cognitive and Affective Neuroscience, 2007; 2(1):12–9.

44   **Sometimes these can be positive, such as being physically attractive:**
      Mulford M., Orbell J., Shatto C., Stockard J., 'Physical attractiveness,
      opportunity, and success in everyday exchange'. *American Journal of
      Sociology*, 1998; 103(6):1565–92.

44   **Height also tends to increase confidence and hence success:** Judge
      T. A., Cable D. M., 'The effect of physical height on workplace suc-
      cess and income: Preliminary test of a theoretical model'. *Journal of
      Applied Psychology*, 2004; 89(3):428–41.

46   **Participants responded faster . . . rewarded for success than when being punished for failure:** Ballard T., Sewell D. K., Cosgrove D., Neal A., 'Information processing under reward versus under punishment'. *Psychological Science*, 2019; 30(5):757–64.

48   **Confidence . . . makes you an influencer and a salesman:** Pulford B. D., Colman A. M., Buabang E. K., Krockow E. M., 'The persuasive power of knowledge: Testing the confidence heuristic'. *Journal of Experimental Psychology: General*, 2018; 147(10):1431–44.

48–9 **When Cameron's memoirs . . . had had to make the decision:** Davies C., 'Five things we learned from David Cameron's memoir'. *Guardian*, 15 September 2019.

49–50 **Confidence in your thoughts binds them much more strongly to concrete action:** Briñol P., DeMarree K. G., Petty R. E., 'Processes by which confidence (vs. doubt) influences the self' in Arkin R., Oleson K., Carroll P. (editors), *Handbook of the Uncertain Self* (New York: Psychology Press, 2010), pp. 13–35.

53   **US Navy SEALS have a 40 per cent rule . . . 40 per cent of your capacity:** Itzler J., *Living with a SEAL: 31 days training with the toughest man on the planet* (London: Hachette, 2015).

53   **. . . there is good scientific evidence . . . can enable us to boost our strength and endurance:** Halper L. R., Vancouver J. B., 'Self-efficacy's influence on persistence on a physical task: Moderating effect of performance feedback ambiguity'. *Psychology of Sport and Exercise*, 2016; 22:170–7.

53   **. . . researchers made students . . . your hand grows tired and sore:** Hutchinson J. C., Sherman T., Martinovic N., Tenenbaum G., 'The effect of manipulated self-efficacy on perceived and sustained effort'. *Journal of Applied Sport Psychology*, 2008; 20(4):457–72.

54   **. . . used the same method with people aged between fifty-two and ninety-one:** Stephan Y., Chalabaev A., Kotter-Grühn D., Jaconelli A., ' "Feeling younger, being stronger": An experimental study of subjective age and physical functioning among older adults'. *Journals of Gerontology: Series B*, 2013; 68(1):1–7.

54–5 **One grim test of endurance is cycling . . . endurance time didn't change at all:** Blanchfield A. W., Hardy J., De Morree H. M., Staiano W., Marcora S. M., 'Talking yourself out of exhaustion: The effects of self-talk on endurance performance'. *Medicine & Science in Sports & Exercise*, 2014; 46(5):998–1007.

55 ... researchers applied painful but harmless heat ... the objective pain stimulus was the same: Salomons T. V., Johnstone T., Backonja M.-M., Davidson R. J., 'Perceived controllability modulates the neural response to pain'. *Journal of Neuroscience*, 2004; 24(32): 7199–203.

55 The more pain-sufferers feel helpless ... the higher their disability and distress: Samwel H. J., Evers A. W., Crul B. J., Kraaimaat F. W., 'The role of helplessness, fear of pain, and passive pain-coping in chronic pain patients'. *Clinical Journal of Pain*, 2006; 22(3):245–51.

56 The slowest walkers ... twice as likely to die in the next few years compared to the fastest: Liu B., Hu X., Zhang Q., Fan Y., Li J., Zou R., et al., 'Usual walking speed and all-cause mortality risk in older people: A systematic review and meta-analysis'. *Gait & Posture*, 2016; 44: 172–7.

56 ... when people slow down their walking ... their chances of dying in the next few years almost double: White D. K., Neogi T., Nevitt M. C., Peloquin C. E., Zhu Y., Boudreau R. M., et al., 'Trajectories of gait speed predict mortality in well-functioning older adults: The health, aging and body composition study'. *Journals of Gerontology: Series A*, 2013; 68(4):456–64.

57 The walking speed of those who felt least confident about growing old ... more than those who felt most confident: Robertson D. A., Savva G. M., King-Kallimanis B. L., Kenny R. A., 'Negative perceptions of aging and decline in walking speed: A self-fulfilling prophecy'. *PLoS ONE*, 2015; 10(4):e0123260.

57 ... the researchers found a similar link ... decline in their self-reported day-to-day memory: Robertson D. A., King-Kallimanis B. L., Kenny R. A., 'Negative perceptions of aging predict longitudinal decline in cognitive function'. *Psychology and Aging*, 2016; 31(1):71–81.

57 The research showed that subjective beliefs about memory appeared before changes in objective memory did: Snitz B. E., Small B. J., Wang T., Chang C.-C. H., Hughes T. F., Ganguli M., 'Do subjective memory complaints lead or follow objective cognitive change? A five-year

population study of temporal influence'. *Journal of the International Neuropsychological Society*, 2015; 21(9):732–42.

57–8   **Research on seventy thousand nurses in the US . . . more likely to reach eighty-five than the pessimists:** Lee L. O., James P., Zevon E. S., Kim E. S., Trudel-Fitzgerald C., Spiro A., et al., 'Optimism is associated with exceptional longevity in 2 epidemiologic cohorts of men and women'. *Proceedings of the National Academy of Sciences*, 2019; 116(37):18357–62.

60   **. . . a very narrow victory in the first set . . . likely that a player will win the whole match:** Page L., Coates J., 'Winner and loser effects in human competitions: Evidence from equally matched tennis players'. *Evolution and Human Behavior*, 2017; 38(4):530–5.

60   **The 'hot hand effect' . . . other sports, such as tennis:** Miller J., Sanjurjo A., 'A cold shower for the hot hand fallacy: Robust evidence that belief in the hot hand is justified'. *Open Science Framework*, 30 October 2018. [Available from: https://osf.io/pj79r/] Accessed 3 September 2020.

61   **. . . halfway through a tournament, players of almost identical skill . . . the bigger was this winner – or hot hand – effect:** Rosenqvist O., Skans O. N., 'Confidence enhanced performance? – The causal effects of success on future performance in professional golf tournaments'. *Journal of Economic Behavior & Organization*, 2015; 117:281–95.

61   **Let's say a child turns ten . . . younger team-mates:** Helsen W. F., van Winckel J., Williams A. M., 'The relative age effect in youth soccer across Europe'. *Journal of Sports Sciences*, 2005; 23(6):629–36.

61   **Similar effects have been seen in professional hockey:** Addona V., Yates P. A., 'A closer look at the relative age effect in the National Hockey League'. *Journal of Quantitative Analysis in Sports*, 2010; 6(4):1–9.

61–2   **. . . what children think about their abilities in school . . . consequences of these self-assessments are:** Filippin A., Paccagnella M., 'Family background, self-confidence and economic outcomes'. *Economics of Education Review*, 2012; 31(5):824–34.

63   **. . . social class is by far the most significant factor . . . no matter their underlying abilities:** Gregg P., Washbrook E., 'The role of attitudes and behaviours in explaining socio-economic differences in attainment at age 11'. *Longitudinal and Life Course Studies*, 2011; 2(1):41–58.

63   . . . artificially lifting someone's mood will boost their self-confidence:
      Kavanagh D. J., Bower G. H., 'Mood and self-efficacy: Impact of joy
      and sadness on perceived capabilities'. *Cognitive Therapy and Research*,
      1985; 9(5):507–25.

64   . . . it also makes people more confident in the decisions they make:
      Deldin P. J., Levin I. P., 'The effect of mood induction in a risky
      decision-making task'. *Bulletin of the Psychonomic Society*, 1986; 24(1):
      4–6.

64   **Poor people live unhappier, unhealthier and shorter lives . . . just above
      that of the US:** Sachs J. D., Layard R., Helliwell J. F., 'World Happi-
      ness Report', 14 March 2018. [Available from: https://worldhappiness
      .report/ed/2018/] Accessed 2 September 2020.

65   **These citizens are** *less* **happy on average . . . given their objective cir-
      cumstances:** Djankov S., Nikolova E., Zilinsky J., 'The happiness
      gap in Eastern Europe'. *Journal of Comparative Economics*, 2016;
      44(1):108–24. *See also*: Inglehart R., Foa R., Peterson C., Welzel C.,
      'Development, freedom, and rising happiness: A global perspective
      (1981–2007)'. *Perspectives on Psychological Science*, 2008; 3(4):264–85.

65   **Witold Szabłowski has tried to explain this phenomenon with a story
      about Bulgarian bears:** Szabłowski W., *Dancing Bears: True stories of
      people nostalgic for life under tyranny* (New York: Penguin Random
      House, 2014).

66–7 **That sensation arises deep in your brain . . . while looking at that photo-
      graph:** Berridge K. C., Kringelbach M. L., 'Affective neuroscience of
      pleasure: Reward in humans and animals'. *Psychopharmacology*, 2008;
      199(3):457–80.

67   **. . . the greater your wellbeing and happiness, the higher the level of dopa-
      mine activity in this circuit:** Volkow N. D., Tomasi D., Wang G.-J., Fowler
      J. S., Telang F., Goldstein R. Z., et al., 'Positive emotionality is associ-
      ated with baseline metabolism in orbitofrontal cortex and in regions of
      the default network'. *Molecular Psychiatry*, 2011; 16(8):818–25.

67   **This pleasure-related brain activity is a natural anti-depressant . . .
      depressed people have much lower levels of it:** Heller A. S., Johnstone
      T., Shackman A. J., Light S. N., Peterson M. J., Kolden G. G., et al.,
      'Reduced capacity to sustain positive emotion in major depression

reflects diminished maintenance of fronto-striatal brain activation'. *Proceedings of the National Academy of Sciences*, 2009; 106(52): 22445–50.

67 **... dopamine-driven pleasurable activity dramatically reduces the amount of the stress hormone cortisol that your body makes:** Heller A. S., van Reekum C. M., Schaefer S. M., Lapate R. C., Radler B. T., Ryff C. D., et al., 'Sustained striatal activity predicts eudaimonic well-being and cortisol output'. *Psychological Science*, 2013; 24(11): 2191–200.

67 **The effect cocaine has on people ... when you take the drug:** Greer A. M., Martin G., Joordens C., Macdonald S., 'Motivations for use of crack cocaine' in Preedy V. R. (editor), *Neuropathology of Drug Addictions and Substance Misuse: Vol. 2* (San Diego: Academic Press, 2016), pp. 229–36.

67 **... neurologists can create similar psychological states by electrically stimulating the reward network:** Synofzik M., Schlaepfer T. E., Fins J. J., 'How happy is too happy? Euphoria, neuroethics, and deep brain stimulation of the nucleus accumbens'. *AJOB Neuroscience*, 2012; 3(1): 30–6.

67 **Great national sporting victories ... increases in the hormone testosterone:** Bernhardt P. C., Dabbs Jr J. M., Fielden J. A., Lutter C. D., 'Testosterone changes during vicarious experiences of winning and losing among fans at sporting events'. *Physiology & Behavior*, 1998; 65(1):59–62.

68 **She found clear evidence ... the brain's pleasure centre:** Martinez D., Orlowska D., Narendran R., Slifstein M., Liu F., Kumar D., et al., 'Dopamine type 2/3 receptor availability in the striatum and social status in human volunteers'. *Biological Psychiatry*, 2010; 67(3):275–8.

69 **... confidence and happiness are interlinked in the brain ... more confident in social situations:** Cervenka S., Hedman E., Ikoma Y., Djurfeldt D. R., Rück C., Halldin C., et al., 'Changes in dopamine D2-receptor binding are associated to symptom reduction after psychotherapy in social anxiety disorder'. *Translational Psychiatry*, 2012; 2(5):e120.

69–70 **On 9 November 1989 ... twenty-five thousand people flooded through the wall into West Berlin:** 'The man who opened the Berlin

Wall', *The Local*, 7 November 2009. [Available from: https://www.the-local.de/20091107/23091] Accessed 5 November 2020.

71   **Some GDR schools also had meetings . . . training children to accurately self-assess – continually and publicly:** Oettingen G., Little T. D., Lindenberger U., Baltes P. B., 'Causality, agency, and control beliefs in East versus West Berlin children: A natural experiment on the role of context'. *Journal of Personality and Social Psychology*, 1994; 66(3):579–95.

71   **Not all children mentally succumbed . . . attempts to set up new lives:** Jerusalem M., Mittag W., 'Self-efficacy in stressful life transitions' in Bandura A. (editor), *Self-efficacy in Changing Societies* (New York: Cambridge University Press, 1995), pp. 177–201.

73   **. . . a sense of control buffers people against the stresses of life:** Lachman M. E., Weaver S. L., 'The sense of control as a moderator of social class differences in health and well-being'. *Journal of Personality and Social Psychology*, 1998; 74(3):763–73.

73   **Feeling in control means . . . there will be consequences of that action:** Von Stumm S., Gale C. R., Batty G. D., Deary I. J., 'Childhood intelligence, locus of control and behaviour disturbance as determinants of intergenerational social mobility: British Cohort Study, 1970'. *Intelligence*, 2009; 37(4):329–40.

74   **Separate reviews of scores of international studies have shown . . . are particularly useful at staving off some of the effects of economic disadvantage:** Burger K., 'How does early childhood care and education affect cognitive development? An international review of the effects of early interventions for children from different social backgrounds'. *Early Childhood Research Quarterly*, 2010; 25(2):140–65. *See also*: Barnett W. S., 'Effectiveness of early educational intervention'. *Science*, 2011; 333(6045):975–8.

74   **Increased confidence is one element of what such programmes provide:** Diamond A., Lee K., 'Interventions shown to aid executive function development in children 4 to 12 years old'. *Science*, 2011; 333(6045):959–64.

74   **. . . people would go for 'choose to choose' . . . the product or experience:** Bown N. J., Read D., Summers B., 'The lure of choice'. *Journal of Behavioral Decision Making*, 2003; 16(4):297–308.

74   The desire to make choices . . . as happiness does: Leotti L. A., Iyengar
     S. S., Ochsner K. N., 'Born to choose: The origins and value of the
     need for control'. *Trends in Cognitive Sciences*, 2010; 14(10):457–63.

74   *Are you satisfied or dissatisfied . . .* lower levels of negative emotions:
     Sachs J. D., Layard R., Helliwell J. F., 'World Happiness Report', 14
     March 2018. [Available from: https://worldhappiness.report/ed/2018/]
     Accessed 2 September 2020.

75   This triumvirate of psychological states also leads to economic growth:
     Kaplanski G., Levy H., Veld C., Veld-Merkoulova Y., 'Do happy
     people make optimistic investors?' *Journal of Financial and Quantita-
     tive Analysis*, 2015; 50(1–2):145–68.

75   Happy, confident people . . . independently of your socioeconomic sta-
     tus: Diener E., Seligman M. E., 'Beyond money: Toward an economy
     of well-being'. *Psychological Science in the Public Interest*, 2004;
     5(1):1–31.

75   This is true both within and between countries: Sachs J. D., Layard R.,
     Helliwell J. F., 'World Happiness Report', 14 March 2018. [Available
     from: https://worldhappiness.report/ed/2018/] Accessed 2 September
     2020.

75   Across the globe . . . wealth, marital status or religion: Verme P.,
     'Happiness, freedom and control'. *Journal of Economic Behavior &
     Organization*, 2009; 71(2):146–61.

75   . . . such confidence strongly predicts . . . will perform: Hitlin S.,
     Kirkpatrick Johnson M., 'Reconceptualizing agency within the life
     course: The power of looking ahead'. *American Journal of Sociology*,
     2015; 120(5):1429–72.

75   . . . my subjective sense of how rich or poor I am is as important . . .
     independently of how objectively wealthy or poor I am: Glei D. A.,
     Goldman N., Weinstein M., 'Perception has its own reality: Subject-
     ive versus objective measures of economic distress'. *Population and
     Development Review*, 2018; 44(4):695–722.

75   Something similar applies to my subjective versus objective physical
     health: Helmer C., Barberger-Gateau P., Letenneur L., Dartigues
     J.-F., 'Subjective health and mortality in French elderly women and
     men'. *Journals of Gerontology: Series B*, 1999; 54(2):S84–S92.

76 **Remarkably, among adult twins . . . pre-existing differences between the twins:** Rivenbark J., Arseneault L., Caspi A., Danese A., Fisher H. L., Moffitt T. E., et al., 'Adolescents' perceptions of family social status correlate with health and life chances: A twin difference longitudinal cohort study'. *Proceedings of the National Academy of Sciences*, 2020; 111(38):23323–8.

76 **. . . silver-medal winners are on average less happy . . . bronze-medal competitors they beat:** McGraw A. P., Mellers B. A., Tetlock P. E., 'Expectations and emotions of Olympic athletes'. *Journal of Experimental Social Psychology*, 2005; 41(4):438–46.

76–7 **Our reward system is switched on . . . what other people are getting:** Fliessbach K., Weber B., Trautner P., Dohmen T., Sunde U., Elger C. E., et al., 'Social comparison affects reward-related brain activity in the human ventral striatum'. *Science*, 23 November 2007; 318(5854): 1305–8.

78 **Police officers arriving at the scene found the driver lying unconscious on the street:** 'Tiger Woods injured in crash'. *ESPN*, 27 November 2009. [Available from: https://www.espn.co.uk/golf/news/story?id=4693657] Accessed 15 August 2020.

78 **Blood tests revealed five different drugs in his system:** 'Tiger Woods had 5 drugs in his system after arrest, police report says'. *New York Times*, 16 August 2017.

79 **Then, on 14 April 2019, something remarkable happened . . . sporting and personal failure:** Fordyce T., 'Tiger Woods comeback: A tale of implausible redemption it is hard to resist'. *BBC Sport*, 24 September 2018. [Available from: https://www.bbc.com/sport/golf/45625712] Accessed 15 August 2020.

79 **. . . super-elite performers . . . they were bullied and lonely:** Hardy, L., et al., 'Great British medalists: Psychosocial biographies of super-elite and elite athletes from Olympic sports'. *Progress in Brain Research*, 2017; 232:1–119.

79 **Woods wrote a letter . . . loneliness and bullying that come from having a stutter:** 'Tiger Woods: Golfer writes to teen being bullied for his stutter'. *BBC Sport*, 13 May 2015. [Available from: https://www.bbc.com/sport/golf/32717455] Accessed 1 September 2020.

80 **Plagued with anxiety . . . she wishes that someone had told her that it was 'OK to be anxious':** Pittman T., 'Mara Wilson's important message for teens living with mental illness.' *Huffington Post*, 5 May 2015; updated 7 December 2017. [Available from: https://www.huffingtonpost.co.uk/entry/mara-wilson-project-urok_n_7213598?ri18n=true] Accessed 23 September 2020.

81 **The feeling of having got through – mastered – painful or difficult experiences swells self-belief like little else:** Bandura A., Cervone D., 'Self-evaluative and self-efficacy mechanisms governing the motivational effects of goal systems'. *Journal of Personality and Social Psychology*, 1983; 45(5):1017–28.

81 **Until she was ten, Venus Williams lived in Compton – a poor, gang-ridden city south of Los Angeles:** Sullivan J. J., 'Venus and Serena against the world'. *New York Times Magazine*, 23 August 2012. [Available from: https://www.nytimes.com/2012/08/26/magazine/venus-and-serena-against-the-world.html] Accessed 15 August 2020. *See also*: 'Serena Williams sits down with Common to talk about race and identity'. *The Undefeated*, 19 December 2016. [Available from: https://theundefeated.com/features/serena-williams-sits-down-with-common-to-talk-about-race-and-identity/] Accessed 15 August 2020.

82 **Children who have a robust and secure attachment . . . with other people:** Coleman P. K., 'Perceptions of parent-child attachment, social self-efficacy, and peer relationships in middle childhood'. *Infant and Child Development*, 2003; 12(4):351–68.

82 **A parental focus on ranking . . . risks sapping a child's self-confidence:** Koivula N., Hassmén P., Fallby J., 'Self-esteem and perfectionism in elite athletes: Effects on competitive anxiety and self-confidence'. *Personality and Individual Differences*, 2002; 32(5):865–75.

84 **When you choose to do one thing over another . . . you experience from moment to moment:** Naqvi N., Shiv B., Bechara A., 'The role of emotion in decision making: A cognitive neuroscience perspective'. *Current Directions in Psychological Science*, 2006; 15(5):260–4.

88 **Your adrenal glands will produce more . . . physiological resilience:** Crum A. J., Akinola M., Martin A., Fath S., 'The role of stress mindset in shaping cognitive, emotional, and physiological responses to challenging and threatening stress'. *Anxiety, Stress & Coping*, 2017; 30(4):379–95.

88 **Stanford psychologist Carol Dweck . . . our bodies and our minds:**
Dweck C. S., 'Can personality be changed? The role of beliefs in
personality and change'. *Current Directions in Psychological Science*,
2008; 17(6):391–4.

89 **Adolescents who have a fixed theory . . . more isolated and unhappy:**
Yeager D. S., Miu A. S., Powers J., Dweck C. S., 'Implicit theories of
personality and attributions of hostile intent: A meta-analysis, an
experiment, and a longitudinal intervention'. *Child Development*,
2013; 84(5):1651–67.

89 *Can I change how anxious I am? . . .* **losing a job:** Schroder H. S., Yalch
M. M., Dawood S., Callahan C. P., Donnellan M. B., Moser J. S.,
'Growth mindset of anxiety buffers the link between stressful life
events and psychological distress and coping strategies'. *Personality
and Individual Differences*, 2017; 110:23–6.

89 **People who don't cripple themselves with a fixed mindset . . . those
with fixed views:** De Castella K., Goldin P., Jazaieri H., Heimberg
R. G., Dweck C. S., Gross J. J., 'Emotion beliefs and cognitive behavioural therapy for social anxiety disorder'. *Cognitive Behaviour
Therapy*, 2015; 44(2):128–41.

90–1 **Where did this mindset . . . risks to their confidence and performance
that this entails:** Haimovitz K., Dweck C. S., 'What predicts children's fixed and growth intelligence mind-sets? Not their parents'
views of intelligence but their parents' views of failure'. *Psychological
Science*, 2016; 27(6):859–69.

95 **When asked to describe . . . said that he wouldn't advise having your
wife earn more than you:** McDermott J., 'What it's like for guys whose
wives or girlfriends earn more than they do'. *Melmagazine.com*, 2018.
[Available from: https://melmagazine.com/en-us/story/what-its-like-
for-guys-whose-wives-or-girlfriends-earn-more-than-they-do]
Accessed 1 September 2020.

95 **The men's stress levels dropped . . . their wives were earning nothing at
all:** Syrda J., 'Spousal relative income and male psychological distress'. *Personality and Social Psychology Bulletin*, 2019; 46(6):976–92.

95–6 **The higher earning a woman is . . . more financially equal homes:** Ber-
trand M., Kamenica E., Pan J., 'Gender identity and relative income

within households'. *Quarterly Journal of Economics*, 2015; 130(2): 571–614.

96 **A 2012 study across twenty-seven countries showed that ... higher levels of sexism and female disempowerment:** Fischer R., Hanke K., Sibley C. G., 'Cultural and institutional determinants of social dominance orientation: A cross-cultural meta-analysis of 27 societies'. *Political Psychology*, 2012; 33(4):437–67.

96 **Evolutionary psychologists argue ... dominating the field in athletics:** Burke J., 'Caster Semenya ruling "tramples on dignity" of athletes, South Africa says'. *Guardian*, 3 May 2019.

96–7 **Higher levels of testosterone ... increase confidence:** Eisenegger C., Kumsta R., Naef M., Gromoll J., Heinrichs M., 'Testosterone and androgen receptor gene polymorphism are associated with confidence and competitiveness in men'. *Hormones and Behavior*, 2017; 92: 93–102.

97 **... women are more sexually competitive ... testosterone levels are higher:** Hahn A. C., Fisher C. I., Cobey K. D., DeBruine L. M., Jones B. C., 'A longitudinal analysis of women's salivary testosterone and intrasexual competitiveness'. *Psychoneuroendocrinology*, 2016; 64: 117–22.

97 **Parents of schoolchildren ... performed better than the men:** Cassar A., Wordofa F., Zhang Y. J., 'Competing for the benefit of offspring eliminates the gender gap in competitiveness'. *Proceedings of the National Academy of Sciences*, 2016; 113(19):5201–5.

97 **Women can be just as cut-throat competitive as men ... when they are provoked:** Bettencourt B. A., Kernahan C., 'A meta-analysis of aggression in the presence of violent cues: Effects of gender differences and aversive provocation'. *Aggressive Behavior*, 1997; 23(6):447–56.

97 **Taller men are, on average, esteemed more by others ... and earn more:** Judge T. A., Cable D. M., 'The effect of physical height on workplace success and income: Preliminary test of a theoretical model'. *Journal of Applied Psychology*, 2004; 89(3):428–41.

98 **... 681 five- to thirteen-year-old Swiss schoolboys and schoolgirls ... with 71 per cent accuracy:** Antonakis J., Dalgas O., 'Predicting elections: Child's play!' *Science*, 2009; 323(5918):1183.

99   In general, people tend to rate men as more competent . . . as guilty of this bias as men: Broverman I. K., Vogel S. R., Broverman D. M., Clarkson F. E., Rosenkrantz P. S., 'Sex-role stereotypes: A current appraisal'. *Journal of Social Issues*, 1972; 28(2):59–78. *See also*: Spence J. T., Helmreich R., Stapp J., 'Ratings of self and peers on sex role attributes and their relation to self-esteem and conceptions of masculinity and femininity'. *Journal of Personality and Social Psychology*, 1975; 32(1):29–39.

99   Those with a facial façade of competence end up as CEOs more often and are paid much more: Graham J. R., Harvey C. R., Puri M., 'A corporate beauty contest'. *Management Science*, 2017; 63(9):3044–56.

99   . . . they don't perform better than less competent-looking people: Stoker J. I., Garretsen H., Spreeuwers L. J., 'The facial appearance of CEOs: Faces signal selection but not performance'. *PLoS ONE*, 2016; 11(7):e0159950.

99   . . . something that also happens with politicians: Wyatt M., Silvester J., 'Do voters get it right? A test of the ascription-actuality trait theory of leadership with political elites'. *Leadership Quarterly*, 2018; 29(5):609–21.

99   Unfortunately, this man-favouring bias . . . across almost all cultures: Williams J. E., Best D. L., *Measuring Sex Stereotypes: A multination study*, revised edition (New York: Sage Publications, Inc., 1990).

99–100 Researchers at Princeton University . . . the competence ratings slumped: Oh D., Buck E. A., Todorov A., 'Revealing hidden gender biases in competence impressions of faces'. *Psychological Science*, 2019; 30(1):65–79.

101   . . . confident women who are seen as competent self-promote at the cost of being liked less: Phelan J. E., Moss-Racusin C. A., Rudman L. A., 'Competent yet out in the cold: Shifting criteria for hiring reflect backlash toward agentic women'. *Psychology of Women Quarterly*, 2008; 32(4):406–13.

101   Likewise, men in similar situations . . . because they are not behaving according to their gender stereotype: Rudman L. A., Phelan J. E., 'Backlash effects for disconfirming gender stereotypes in organizations'. *Research in Organizational Behavior*, 2008; 28:61–79.

101 Perhaps this is one reason that women inadvertently sabotage their promotion prospects . . . tend to be less selfishly individualistic and self-promoting than men: Babcock L., Recalde M. P., Vesterlund L., Weingart L., 'Gender differences in accepting and receiving requests for tasks with low promotability'. *American Economic Review*, 2017; 107(3):714–47.

101–2 It seems that something happens to girls at around age six . . . new game for really smart children: Bian L., Leslie S.-J., Cimpian A., 'Gender stereotypes about intellectual ability emerge early and influence children's interests'. *Science*, 2017; 355(6323):389–91.

102 On 2 March 2011, a newly elected member of the Irish parliament . . . male photographers who were watching: 'TD drives down Leinster House steps' [video]. *Irish Independent*, 3 March 2011. [Available from: https://www.independent.ie/irish-news/video-td-drives-down-leinster-house-steps-26710125.html] Accessed 1 September 2020.

102–4 One spatial thinking test shows a picture . . . an abstract spatial test: Tarampi M. R., Heydari N., Hegarty M., 'A tale of two types of perspective taking: Sex differences in spatial ability'. *Psychological Science*, 2016; 27(11):1507–16.

104 This is the stiff headwind of stereotype-threat that all women face . . . such as empathy: Rueckert L., Naybar N., 'Gender differences in empathy: The role of the right hemisphere'. *Brain and Cognition*, 2008; 67(2):162–7.

104 Women are much less inclined . . . spatial thinking is no exception to this: Phan M. H., Jardina J. R., Hoyle S., Chaparro B. S. (editors), 'Examining the role of gender in video game usage, preference, and behavior'. *Proceedings of the Human Factors and Ergonomics Society*, 2012; 56:1496–500.

104–5 . . . test women's spatial thinking . . . when they felt inclined to practise them: Feng J., Spence I., Pratt J., 'Playing an action video game reduces gender differences in spatial cognition'. *Psychological Science*, 2007; 18(10):850–5.

105–6 . . . Canadian researchers decided . . . plummet to an average of 6: Dar-Nimrod I., Heine S. J., 'Exposure to scientific theories affects women's math performance'. *Science*, 2006; 314(5798):435.

106   **In most countries, women are just as good . . . women are less math-confident**: Else-Quest N. M., Hyde J. S., Linn M. C., 'Cross-national patterns of gender differences in mathematics: A meta-analysis'. *Psychological Bulletin*, 2010; 136(1):103–107.

106   **. . . girls have lower self-confidence than boys . . . genetic theory of their abilities**: Diseth Å., Meland E., Breidablik H. J., 'Self-beliefs among students: Grade level and gender differences in self-esteem, self-efficacy and implicit theories of intelligence'. *Learning and Individual Differences*, 2014; 35:1–8.

107   **Girls and women are more prone to anxiety than boys and men**: Feingold A., 'Gender differences in personality: A meta-analysis'. *Psychological Bulletin*, 1994; 116(3):429–56.

107   **. . . Japanese and black South African women . . . no more anxious than men**: Costa Jr P. T., Terracciano A., McCrae R. R., 'Gender differences in personality traits across cultures: Robust and surprising findings'. *Journal of Personality and Social Psychology*, 2001; 81(2): 322–331.

107   **In November 2018, the Democratic Party . . . rose from 920 to 42,000**: Zhou L., '12 charts that explain the record-breaking year women have had in politics'. *Vox*, 6 November 2018. [Available from: https://www.vox.com/2018/11/6/18019234/women-record-breaking-midterms] Accessed 1 September 2020.

107   **This was a remarkable turnaround . . . less confident in competitive arenas**: Fox R. L., Lawless J. L., 'Uncovering the origins of the gender gap in political ambition'. *American Political Science Review*, 2014; 108(3):499–519.

108   **'. . . over the previous twelve months, young women were much more likely than young men . . . greater political engagement than their male peers'**: Galston W. A., 'Data point to a new wave of female political activism that could shift the course of US politics'. Brookings Institution, 10 January 2018. [Available from: https://www.brookings.edu/blog/fixgov/2018/01/10/a-new-wave-of-female-political-activism/] Accessed 15 August 2020.

109   **In 2014, researchers at the University of Cologne . . . surged to even higher levels**: Hügelschäfer S., Achtziger A., 'On confident men and

rational women: It's all on your mind (set)'. *Journal of Economic Psychology*, 2014; 41(C):31–44.

109   **As men and women tend to play by different rules . . . wins the game:** Niessen-Ruenzi A., Ruenzi S., 'Sex matters: Gender bias in the mutual fund industry'. *Management Science*, 2019; 65(7):3001–25.

111   **'It was a very, very small signal . . . because of impostor syndrome':** Sample I., 'British astrophysicist overlooked by Nobels wins $3m award for pulsar work'. *Guardian*, 6 September 2018. [Available from: https://www.theguardian.com/science/2018/sep/06/jocelyn-bell-burnell-british-astrophysicist-overlooked-by-nobels-3m-award-pulsars] Accessed 1 September 2020.

111–12 **Take a minute or two to think . . . your true abilities:** Clance P. R., Imes S. A., 'The imposter phenomenon in high achieving women: Dynamics and therapeutic intervention'. *Psychotherapy: Theory, Research & Practice*, 1978; 15(3):241–7.

112   **Students at Cornell University . . . women guessed 5.8 out of 10, on average, and the men 7.1 out of 10:** Ehrlinger J., Dunning D., 'How chronic self-views influence (and potentially mislead) estimates of performance'. *Journal of Personality and Social Psychology*, 2003; 84(1): 5–17.

113   **In negotiating with their bosses, they expect . . . than do men of the same status and ability:** Small D. A., Gelfand M., Babcock L., Gettman H., 'Who goes to the bargaining table? The influence of gender and framing on the initiation of negotiation'. *Journal of Personality and Social Psychology*, 2007; 93(4):600–13.

113   **A survey of almost 1,400 Americans . . . show no drop:** 'Teen girls are less confident than boys and it's affecting their futures'. *Ypulse*, 12 April 2018. [Available from: https://www.ypulse.com/article/2018/04/12/teen-girls-are-less-confident-than-boys-its-affecting-their-futures/] Accessed 1 September 2020.

113   **A remarkable study . . . lower level of self-esteem than men:** Bleidorn W., Arslan R. C., Denissen J. J., Rentfrow P. J., Gebauer J. E., Potter J., et al., 'Age and gender differences in self-esteem – A cross-cultural window'. *Journal of Personality and Social Psychology*, 2016; 111(3): 396–410.

114   'I'm a bit of a fighter . . . I'd know I had done my best': Sample I., 'British astrophysicist overlooked by Nobels wins $3m award for pulsar work'. *Guardian*, 6 September 2018. [Available from: https://www. theguardian.com/science/2018/sep/06/jocelyn-bell-burnell-british-astrophysicist-overlooked-by-nobels-3m-award-pulsars] Accessed 1 September 2020.

114–15 I like not to be the same as others . . . *interdependent* self-view – or *self-construal*: Singelis T. M., 'The measurement of independent and interdependent self-construals'. *Personality and Social Psychology Bulletin*, 1994; 20(5):580–91.

116   Individualists have a bigger superiority illusion . . . abilities, achievements and success: Kitayama S., Uskul A. K., 'Culture, mind, and the brain: Current evidence and future directions'. *Annual Review of Psychology*, 2011; 62:419–49.

117   Because their upbringing fosters a less individualistic frame of mind . . . less true of males: Cross S. E., Madson L., 'Models of the self: Self-construals and gender'. *Psychological Bulletin*, 1997; 122(1):5–37.

117   . . . the winner of the first set . . . see this only in men, not in women: Page L., Coates J., 'Winner and loser effects in human competitions: Evidence from equally matched tennis players'. *Evolution and Human Behavior*, 2017; 38(4):530–5.

117   And while individual confidence . . . in women it plays hardly any role at all: Woodman T., Hardy L., 'The relative impact of cognitive anxiety and self-confidence upon sport performance: A meta-analysis'. *Journal of Sports Sciences*, 2003; 21(6):443–57.

117–18 Boys are more likely to boast . . . self-congratulatory comments as the opposite sex: Maccoby E. E., Jacklin C. N., *The Psychology of Sex Differences* (California: Stanford University Press, 1974).

118   Girls are more inclined . . . than about themselves: ibid.

119   Each year, 3,400 eager candidates . . . making it through to the final cohort: Ors E., Palomino F., Peyrache E., 'Performance gender gap: Does competition matter?' *Journal of Labor Economics*, 2013; 31(3): 443–99.

120–1 In early June every year . . . women of a similar standard: Garratt R. J., Weinberger C., Johnson N., 'The state street mile: Age and gender differences in competition aversion in the field'. *Economic Inquiry*, 2013; 51(1):806–15.

121   This apparent lack of appetite for competition . . . just as good as the men's: Ehrlinger J., Dunning D., 'How chronic self-views influence (and potentially mislead) estimates of performance'. *Journal of Personality and Social Psychology*, 2003; 84(1):5–17.

121   So, women don't like competition? . . . the reason is *confidence*: Niederle M., Vesterlund L., 'Gender and competition'. *Annual Review of Economics*, 2011; 3(1):601–30.

123   Some nine- and ten-year-olds had to run a 40-metre race . . . when they compete against girls: Gneezy U., Rustichini A., 'Gender and competition at a young age'. *American Economic Review*, 2004; 94(2): 377–81.

124   When the women were up against other women . . . competition gender gap disappeared: Gneezy U., Niederle M., Rustichini A., 'Performance in competitive environments: Gender differences'. *Quarterly Journal of Economics*, 2003; 118(3):1049–74.

126–7   A 2014 University of Louisville study . . . pre-empt the risk of failure: Snyder K. E., Malin J. L., Dent A. L., Linnenbrink-Garcia L., 'The message matters: The role of implicit beliefs about giftedness and failure experiences in academic self-handicapping'. *Journal of Educational Psychology*, 2014; 106(1):230–41.

128   . . . talented students like Kim . . . undercut their true academic potential: Schwinger M., Wirthwein L., Lemmer G., Steinmayr R., 'Academic self-handicapping and achievement: A meta-analysis'. *Journal of Educational Psychology*, 2014; 106(3):744–61.

128–9   IQ embodies a fixed theory of ability . . . too low for them to compete: Chorley M., Groves J., 'Some people are just too stupid to get on in life, Boris Johnson claims sparking row about his "unpleasant, careless elitism" '. *Daily Mail*, 27 November 2013.

129   . . . giving financial incentives to perform well on an IQ test . . . in the lower IQ range: Duckworth A. L., Quinn P. D., Lynam D. R., Loeber R., Stouthamer-Loeber M., 'Role of test motivation in intelligence testing'. *Proceedings of the National Academy of Sciences*, 2011; 108(19): 7716–20.

129   **Researchers from leading universities . . . an advanced mathematics course the following year:** Yeager D. S., Hanselman P., Walton G. M., Murray J. S., Crosnoe R., Muller C., et al., 'A national experiment reveals where a growth mindset improves achievement'. *Nature*, 2019; 573(7774):364–9.

130   **. . . the more generally anxious people are, the less they tend to do in life:** Ireland M. E., Hepler J., Li H., Albarracín D., 'Neuroticism and attitudes toward action in 19 countries'. *Journal of Personality*, 2015; 83(3):243–50.

130   **Former Facebook COO Sheryl Sandberg . . . you strengthen the muscle, she claimed:** Walravens S., '5 exercises Sheryl Sandberg, Silicon Valley women do to build confidence'. *Forbes*, 6 September 2016.

131   **'The self is not something ready-made . . . choice of action':** Dewey J., *Democracy and Education: An introduction to the philosophy of education* (New York: Macmillan, 1923).

132   **A 2014 University of Vienna study . . . to plan how they were going to do it:** Büttner O. B., Wieber F., Schulz A. M., Bayer U. C., Florack A., Gollwitzer P. M., 'Visual attention and goal pursuit: Deliberative and implemental mindsets affect breadth of attention'. *Personality and Social Psychology Bulletin*, 2014; 40(10):1248–59.

134   **Research shows that, at best . . . deprived of the confidence-building benefits of taking action:** Gollwitzer P. M., 'Setting one's mind on action: Planning out goal striving in advance' in Scott, R., Kosslyn, S. (editors), *Emerging Trends in the Social and Behavioral Sciences* (New York: Wiley, 2015), pp. 1–14.

135   **. . . planning out the detail . . . taking physical exercise:** Bélanger-Gravel A., Godin G., Amireault S., 'A meta-analytic review of the effect of implementation intentions on physical activity'. *Health Psychology Review*, 2013; 7(1):23–54.

135   **. . . planning out the detail . . . stopping smoking:** Mutter E. R., Oettingen G., Gollwitzer P. M., 'An online randomised controlled trial of mental contrasting with implementation intentions as a smoking behaviour change intervention'. *Psychology & Health*, 2020; 35(3): 318–45.

135   . . . planning out the detail . . . eating more healthily: O'Toole S., New-
ton T., Moazzez R., Hasan A., Bartlett D., 'Randomised controlled
clinical trial investigating the impact of implementation planning on
behaviour related to the diet'. *Scientific Reports*, 2018; 8(1):1–6.

135   . . . planning out the detail . . . many other mental health problems: Toli
A., Webb T. L., Hardy G. E., 'Does forming implementation intentions help people with mental health problems to achieve goals? A
meta-analysis of experimental studies with clinical and analogue sam-
ples'. *British Journal of Clinical Psychology*, 2016; 55(1):69–90.

136   The trouble with daydreams like this . . . *mental contrasting*: Oettingen
G., 'Future thought and behaviour change'. *European Review of Social
Psychology*, 2012; 23(1):1–63.

138   Fantasies on their own sap energy . . . trick the brain into thinking that
the goals have been achieved: Kappes A., Singmann H., Oettingen G.,
'Mental contrasting instigates goal pursuit by linking obstacles of
reality with instrumental behavior'. *Journal of Experimental Social
Psychology*, 2012; 48(4):811–8. *See also*: Gollwitzer P. M., Oettingen G.,
'Planning promotes goal striving' in Vohs K. D., Baumeister R. F.
(editors), *Handbook of Self-regulation: Research, theory, and applications*
(New York: Guilford Press, 2011), pp. 162–85.

142   Brain imaging . . . distinct pattern of activity during self-affirmation:
Cascio C. N., O'Donnell M. B., Tinney F. J., Lieberman M. D., Tay-
lor S. E., Strecher V. J., et al., 'Self-affirmation activates brain systems
associated with self-related processing and reward and is reinforced
by future orientation'. *Social Cognitive and Affective Neuroscience*, 2016;
11(4):621–9.

142   This combined activity of thinking about yourself . . . make you feel
more self-confident: Cohen G. L., Sherman D. K., 'The psychology
of change: Self-affirmation and social psychological intervention'.
Annual Review of Psychology, 2014; 65:333–71.

143   But if people self-affirm . . . They then go on to exercise more: Falk
E. B., O'Donnell M. B., Cascio C. N., Tinney F. J., Kang Y., Lieberman M. D., et al., 'Self-affirmation alters the brain's response to
health messages and subsequent behavior change'. *Proceedings of the
National Academy of Sciences*, 2015; 112(7):1977–82.

143   **Self-affirmation greatly eases ... hormone cortisol in the blood:**
        Creswell J. D., Welch W. T., Taylor S. E., Sherman D. K., Gruenewald
        T. L., Mann T., 'Affirmation of personal values buffers neuroendo-
        crine and psychological stress responses'. *Psychological Science*, 2005;
        16(11):846–51.

143   **... chronically stressed students who self-affirm ... solve difficult
        problems better:** Creswell J. D., Dutcher J. M., Klein W. M., Harris
        P. R., Levine J. M., 'Self-affirmation improves problem-solving under
        stress'. *PLoS ONE*, 2013; 8(5):e62593.

144   **Our brains respond to mistakes ... ego-threatening 'WRONG!'
        message on the screen:** Legault L., Al-Khindi T., Inzlicht M., 'Pre-
        serving integrity in the face of performance threat: Self-affirmation
        enhances neurophysiological responsiveness to errors'. *Psychological
        Science*, 2012; 23(12):1455–60.

144   **... defensiveness is one of the most significant predictors of discord in
        a marriage – and eventual divorce:** Gottman J. M., Murray J. D.,
        Swanson C. C., Tyson R., Swanson K. R., *The Mathematics of Mar-
        riage: Dynamic nonlinear models* (Cambridge, MA: MIT Press, 2005).

145   **A 2010 study ... during a fifteen-week physics course:** Miyake A.,
        Kost-Smith L. E., Finkelstein N. D., Pollock S. J., Cohen G. L., Ito
        T. A., 'Reducing the gender achievement gap in college science: A
        classroom study of values affirmation'. *Science*, 2010; 330(6008):
        1234–7.

145   **Elizabeth Warren, senior state senator ... like the centreboard
        of a dinghy:** Warren E., 'Senator Elizabeth Warren speaks at Suffolk
        University Commencements, 2016'. [Available from: https://www.
        graduationwisdom.com/speeches/0207-Elizabeth-Warren-
        Commencement-Address.htm] Accessed 1 September 2020.

145   **... young American teenagers who affirmed ... improvements in their
        school performance:** Borman G. D., Rozek C. S., Pyne J., Hanselman P.,
        'Reappraising academic and social adversity improves middle school
        students' academic achievement, behavior, and well-being'. *Proceedings
        of the National Academy of Sciences*, 2019; 116(33):16286–91.

145   **Affirming your values buffers you against that stress and makes you
        smarter:** Harris P. S., Harris P. R., Miles E., 'Self-affirmation improves

performance on tasks related to executive functioning'. *Journal of Experimental Social Psychology*, 2017; 70:281–5.

146 **Marissa Mayer, former CEO of Yahoo! . . . good things sometimes followed**: Hoare R., 'Marissa Mayer: Six life lessons from Yahoo CEO'. *CNN*, 19 July 2012. [Available from: https://edition.cnn.com/2012/07/17/tech/mayer-yahoo-career-advice/index.html] Accessed 1 September 2020.

146 **Research shows that those who have sailed through their young lives . . . cope with some moderately negative experiences**: Seery M. D., Leo R. J., Lupien S. P., Kondrak C. L., Almonte J. L., 'An upside to adversity? Moderate cumulative lifetime adversity is associated with resilient responses in the face of controlled stressors'. *Psychological Science*, 2013; 24(7):1181–9.

147 **Those who feel that sense of control . . . memory centres in their brains**: Pruessner J. C., Baldwin M. W., Dedovic K., Renwick R., Mahani N. K., Lord C., et al., 'Self-esteem, locus of control, hippocampal volume, and cortisol regulation in young and old adulthood'. *Neuro-Image*, 2005; 28(4):815–826.

147 **Worry is a gruelling mental addiction . . . illusion of control**: Grol M., Schwenzfeier A. K., Stricker J., Booth C., Temple-McCune A., Derakshan N., et al., 'The worrying mind in control: An investigation of adaptive working memory training and cognitive bias modification in worry-prone individuals'. *Behaviour Research and Therapy*, 2018; 103: 1–11.

149 **The first group would learn from their errors . . . the second group would not**: Lee W., Kim S., 'Effects of achievement goals on challenge seeking and feedback processing: Behavioral and fMRI evidence'. *PLoS ONE*, 2014; 9(9):e107254.

149 **'Just believe in yourself . . . at some point, you will'**: Poppy N., 'Venus Williams courts success in fashion, fun . . . and tennis'. *ABC News*, 25 April 2013. [Available from: https://abcnews.go.com/blogs/headlines/2013/04/venus-williams-courts-success-in-fashion-fun-and-tennis/] Accessed 1 September 2020.

150 **. . . an expansive, confident-looking power pose . . . weren't replicated in further studies**: Ranehill E., Dreber A., Johannesson M., Leiberg

S., Sul S., Weber R. A., 'Assessing the robustness of power posing: No effect on hormones and risk tolerance in a large sample of men and women'. *Psychological Science*, 2015; 26(5):653–6.

150 **On his first day in his new post . . . and was largely ridiculed for it:** Belam M., 'Sajid Javid and the return of the Tory power stance'. *Guardian*, 30 April 2018. [Available from: https://www.theguardian.com/politics/2018/apr/30/sajid-javid-tory-power-stance] Accessed 1 September 2020.

150 **A 2020 review of all the studies on posture showed . . . diminished people's confidence quite significantly:** Elkjær E., Mikkelsen M. B., Michalak J., Mennin D. S., O'Toole M. S., 'Expansive and contractive postures and movement: A systematic review and meta-analysis of the effect of motor displays on affective and behavioral responses'. *Perspectives on Psychological Science*, 2020; 1745691620919358.

150 **In addition, people tend to think more abstractly . . . wearing it makes them feel more powerful:** Slepian M. L., Ferber S. N., Gold J. M., Rutchick A. M., 'The cognitive consequences of formal clothing'. *Social Psychological and Personality Science*, 2015; 6(6):661–8.

150 **Just putting on a white lab coat improves your ability to focus your attention and concentrate:** Adam H., Galinsky A. D., 'Enclothed cognition'. *Journal of Experimental Social Psychology*, 2012; 48(4): 918–25.

151 **Reassurance-seeking reduces anxiety in the short term but worsens it in the long run:** Rector N. A., Kamkar K., Cassin S. E., Ayearst L. E., Laposa J. M., 'Assessing excessive reassurance seeking in the anxiety disorders'. *Journal of Anxiety Disorders*, 2011; 25(7):911–7.

155 **Ally MacLeod was . . . generated its own academic research:** Jerrim J., Parker P., Shure D., 'Bullshitters: Who are they and what do we know about their lives?' (Bonn: Institute of Labor Economics, 2019). Contract No.: IZA DP No. 12282.

156 **. . . the lower your ability, the more you tend to overestimate your skill:** Kruger J., Dunning D., 'Unskilled and unaware of it: How difficulties in recognizing one's own incompetence lead to inflated self-assessments'. *Journal of Personality and Social Psychology*, 1999; 77:1121–34.

156   ... 74 per cent of fund managers ... above-average investment per-
       formers: Montier, J., 'Behaving Badly'. *SSRN*, 2 February 2006.
       [Available from: http://dx.doi.org/10.2139/ssrn.890563] Accessed 1
       September 2020.

156   Mildly depressed people ... than those who aren't depressed: Strunk
       D. R., Lopez H., DeRubeis R. J., 'Depressive symptoms are associ-
       ated with unrealistic negative predictions of future life events'.
       Behaviour Research and Therapy, 2006; 44(6):861–82.

157   But a 2016 study concluded that medical error is the third leading
       cause of death in the US, after heart disease and cancer: Makary M. A.,
       Daniel M., 'Medical error – the third leading cause of death in the
       US'. *British Medical Journal*, 2016; 353:i2139.

157   Mistakes include one Rhode Island hospital ... three times in one year:
       Childs D., 'Medical errors, past and present'. *ABC News*, 19 February
       2009. [Available from: https://abcnews.go.com/Health/story?id=
       3789868&page=2] Accessed 1 September 2020.

157   Of course, doctors make mistakes ... one of the main reasons for this
       is overconfidence: Croskerry P., Norman G., 'Overconfidence in clin-
       ical decision making'. *American Journal of Medicine*, 2008; 121(5):
       S24–S9.

157-8 ... in 1980, Saddam Hussein led Iraq ... with millions more
       maimed: Johnson D. D., *Overconfidence and War: The havoc and glory
       of positive illusions* (Cambridge, MA: Harvard University Press,
       2004).

158   But overconfident political leaders ... an illusion of superiority: Winter
       D. G., 'Power, affiliation, and war: Three tests of a motivational model'.
       Journal of Personality and Social Psychology, 1993; 65(3):532–45.

158   On 16 November 1532 ... bluffs underpin success in many battles:
       Johnson D. D., *Overconfidence and War: The havoc and glory of positive
       illusions* (Cambridge, MA: Harvard University Press, 2004).

158   Johnson uncovered numerous examples of military leaders defying the
       odds ... overestimating their opponent's real strength: Johnson
       D. D., Wrangham R. W., Rosen S. P., 'Is military incompetence adap-
       tive?: An empirical test with risk-taking behaviour in modern
       warfare'. *Evolution and Human Behavior*, 2002; 23(4):245–64.

159   A 2007 University of Toronto study asked 527 petroleum geolo-
       gists . . . abandoned the fruitless and expensive search much earlier:
       Whyte G., Saks A. M., 'The effects of self-efficacy on behavior in
       escalation situations'. *Human Performance*, 2007; 20(1):23–42.

159   Such radicals are even overconfident . . . grains of sand there are in a
       glass: van Prooijen J.-W., Krouwel A. P. M., 'Psychological features of
       extreme political ideologies'. *Current Directions in Psychological Sci-
       ence*, 2019; 28(2):159–63.

160   . . . he needed the largest possible valuation . . . *elevate the world's con-
       sciousness*: Weideman R., 'The I in we: How did WeWork's Adam
       Neumann turn office space with "community" into a $47 billion
       company? Not by sharing'. *New York Magazine*, 10 June 2019.

160   In the space of nine years he had grown his start-up . . . with locations
       in over twenty-three countries: Gjonbalaj, G., 'WeWork becomes big-
       gest private office tenant in Manhattan'. WeWork Newsroom, 17
       September 2018. [Available from: https://www.wework.com/ideas/
       newsroom-landing-page/newsroom/posts/wework-becomes-biggest-
       private-office-tenant-in-manhattan] Accessed 19 November 2020.

160   Neumann called executives . . . or otherwise ignored them: Brooker
       K., 'WeFail: How the doomed Masa Son-Adam Neumann relation-
       ship set WeWork on the road to disaster'. *Fast Company*, 15 November
       2019.

160–1 The winner's curse . . . paid more than the eventual real value of the
       fields: Thaler R. H., 'Anomalies: The winner's curse'. *Journal of Eco-
       nomic Perspectives*, 1988; 2(1):191–202.

161   . . . for all his visionary idealism . . . investors' doubts over the com-
       pany's annual losses and inflated valuation: Neate, R., 'Hubris of a
       high-flyer: How investors brought WeWork founder down to earth'.
       Guardian, 28 September 2019. [Available from: https://www.the-
       guardian.com/business/2019/sep/28/hubris-of-a-high-flyer-how-
       investors-brought-wework-founder-down-to-earth] Accessed 19 No-
       vember 2020.

161   If 74 per cent of the fund managers . . . that fact should give us pause:
       Montier, J., 'Behaving Badly'. SSRN, 2 February 2006. [Available from:
       http://dx.doi.org/10.2139/ssrn.890563] Accessed 1 September 2020.

161–2 **In 2008, a University of Haifa study subtly 'primed' . . . risk-prone attitudes than the economics students:** Gilad D., Kliger D., 'Priming the risk attitudes of professionals in financial decision making'. *Review of Finance*, 2008; 12(3):567–86.

162 **Cognitively speaking, they relied on hunch . . . overconfidence in their hunches:** Abbink K., Rockenbach B., 'Option pricing by students and professional traders: A behavioural investigation'. *Managerial and Decision Economics*, 2006; 27(6):497–510.

162 **In 1999, the *Wall Street Journal* . . . caused its share price to surge:** Emshwiller J. R., 'Follow the dotted line: First up – then down'. *Wall Street Journal*, 3 March 1999. [Available from: https://www.wsj.com/articles/SB920421525958599000] Accessed 1 September 2020.

162 **. . . as global financial markets expand . . . they tend to follow the lead of bigger investors:** Calvo G. A., Mendoza E. G., 'Rational contagion and the globalization of securities markets'. *Journal of International Economics*, 2000; 51(1):79–113.

162–3 **. . . the amount of morning sunshine was found to strongly correlate with a city's stock exchange returns that day:** Hirshleifer D., Shumway T., 'Good day sunshine: Stock returns and the weather'. *Journal of Finance*, 2003; 58(3):1009–32.

163 **They were able to study citizens' trades . . . the Finnish state records showed:** Grinblatt M., Keloharju M., 'Sensation seeking, overconfidence, and trading activity'. *Journal of Finance*, 2009; 64(2):549–78.

163 **Using data from thirty-five thousand US households . . . annual losses were 50 per cent greater:** Barber B. M., Odean T., 'Boys will be boys: Gender, overconfidence, and common stock investment'. *Quarterly Journal of Economics*, 2001; 116(1):261–92.

163 **Economists have discovered that for 75 per cent of entrepreneurial start-ups . . . going out on one's own:** Koellinger P., Minniti M., Schade C., ' "I think I can, I think I can": Overconfidence and entrepreneurial behavior'. *Journal of Economic Psychology*, 2007; 28(4): 502–27.

163 **The poet T. S. Eliot famously noted that humankind cannot bear very much reality:** Eliot T. S., *Four Quartets*, IV, 239–242 (New York: Harcourt Brace, 1943).

164 **In 1957, the Danish architect Jørn Utzon . . . $65 million at today's value:** Irvine J., 'Why Sydney's Opera House was the world's biggest planning disaster'. *Courier Mail*, 22 October 2013. [Available from: https://www.couriermail.com.au/news/why-sydneys-opera-house-was-the-worlds-biggest-planning-disaster/news-story/9a596cab579a 3b96bba516f425b3f1a6] Accessed 1 September 2020.

164 **According to Danish economist Bent Flyvbjerg . . . history of world megaprojects:** Flyvbjerg B., Bruzelius N., Rothengatter W., *Megaprojects and Risk: An anatomy of ambition* (Cambridge: Cambridge University Press, 2003).

164 **. . . the brains of overconfident people suffer less 'loss aversion' . . . preference for avoiding losses more than acquiring gains:** Inesi M. E., 'Power and loss aversion'. *Organizational Behavior and Human Decision Processes*, 2010; 112(1):58–69.

165 **The employees in these pairs . . . and were unable to make suggestions and give opinions:** Locke C. C., Anderson C., 'The downside of looking like a leader: Power, nonverbal confidence, and participative decision-making'. *Journal of Experimental Social Psychology*, 2015; 58:42–7.

165 **Smart teams have their own group intelligence . . . reading other people's emotions:** Woolley A. W., Chabris C. F., Pentland A., Hashmi N., Malone T. W., 'Evidence for a collective intelligence factor in the performance of human groups'. *Science*, 2010; 330(6004):686–8.

166 **In 2012, Virginia Tech researchers . . . they also deplete our brain function:** Kishida K. T., Yang D., Quartz K. H., Quartz S. R., Montague P. R., 'Implicit signals in small group settings and their impact on the expression of cognitive capacity and associated brain responses'. *Philosophical Transactions of the Royal Society B: Biological Sciences*, 2012; 367(1589):704–16.

166 **'People are really surprised I understand this stuff . . . Maybe I have a natural ability':** Nakamura D., ' "Maybe I have a natural ability": Trump plays medical expert on coronavirus by second-guessing the professionals'. *Washington Post*, 7 March 2020.

166–7 **'I'm great looking and smart, a true Stable Genius':** Cummings W., 'Trump says he's "so great looking and smart, a true Stable Genius" in tweet bashing 2020 Dems'. *USA Today*, 11 July 2019.

167 ... **University of Minnesota researchers ... than was statistically possible**: Burks S. V., Carpenter J. P., Goette L., Rustichini A., 'Overconfidence and social signalling'. *Review of Economic Studies*, 2013; 80(3):949–83.

167 **Personality played a big part ... in the top 20 per cent in smarts**: Tellegen A., Waller N. G., 'Exploring personality through test construction: Development of the multidimensional personality questionnaire' in Boyle G. J., Matthews G., Saklofske D. H. (editors), *The SAGE Handbook of Personality Theory and Assessment: Vol. 2* (New York, Sage Publications, Inc., 2008), pp. 261–92.

167 **Identical twins are more alike in overconfidence ... life experience also makes a significant contribution**: Cesarini D., Lichtenstein P., Johannesson M., Wallace B., 'Heritability of overconfidence'. *Journal of the European Economic Association*, 2009; 7(2–3):617–27.

169 **One persuasive reason emerged in an experiment ... buying into their overconfidence**: Anderson C., Brion S., Moore D. A., Kennedy J. A., 'A status-enhancement account of overconfidence'. *Journal of Personality and Social Psychology*, 2012; 103(4):718–35.

170–1 **But what if they were to reveal the true performance scores ... remained respected as high-status influencers**: Kennedy J. A., Anderson C., Moore D. A., 'When overconfidence is revealed to others: Testing the status-enhancement theory of overconfidence'. *Organizational Behavior and Human Decision Processes*, 2013; 122(2): 266–79.

173 **'I don't think we're ever going to lose money again ... Something will *always* happen, Reed asserted**: Reed D., 'Airlines won't ever lose money again? Boasts by American's CEO dismiss history'. *Forbes*, 4 October 2017.

173–4 **Power is one of the most potent brain-changing agents in the world ... focus on goals and rewards, neglect – risk**: Robertson I., *The Winner Effect: How power affects your brain* (London: Bloomsbury, 2012).

175 **But a pandemic had been widely predicted ... three years before Covid-19 hit**: Gates B., 'Bill Gates has a warning about deadly epidemics'. *Business Insider*, 22 January 2017. [Available from https://www.youtube.com/watch?v=jDxb21qIilM] Accessed 2 September 2020.

176　　Atop a plinth on London's Highgate Hill . . . suddenly sensed a mouse: Lederer, H., 'Dick Whittington's Cat'. [Available from: http://www.talk-ingstatueslondon.co.uk/statues/whittington/] Accessed 2 September 2020.

177　　The bigger a city . . . the benefits mushrooming disproportionately with size: Bettencourt L. M., Lobo J., Strumsky D., West G. B., 'Urban scaling and its deviations: Revealing the structure of wealth, innovation and crime across cities'. *PLoS ONE*, 2010; 5(11):e13541.

177　　Today, 55 per cent of the world's population lives in cities . . . will live in a metropolis: Ritchie H., Roser, M., 'Urbanization'. *Our World in Data*, 2018; updated November 2019. [Available from: https://ourworldindata.org/urbanization] Accessed 23 September 2020.

177　　Yet the majority – 56 per cent – of forty-year-old Americans . . . that figure is 40 per cent: De la Roca J., Ottaviano G. I., Puga D., 'City of dreams'. London School of Economics, Centre for Economic Performance, 2014. Report No.: 2042–2695.

177–8　Youth and education . . . more mobile than those without: McCormick B., Wahba J., 'Why do the young and educated in LDCs concentrate in large cities? Evidence from migration data'. *Economica*, 2005; 72(285):39–67.

178　　Intellect predicts so many things in our lives . . . more successful than those who stayed home: De la Roca J., Ottaviano G. I., Puga D., 'City of dreams'. London School of Economics, Centre for Economic Performance, 2014. Report No.: 2042–2695.

179　　Between 2000 and 2014 . . . a two-way causal relationship with confidence, each shaping the other: Demirel S. K., Artan S., 'The causality relationships between economic confidence and fundamental macroeconomic indicators: Empirical evidence from selected European Union countries'. *International Journal of Economics and Financial Issues*, 2017; 7(5):417–24.

179　　We know that more confident people are more likely to start businesses: Chen C. C., Greene P. G., Crick A., 'Does entrepreneurial self-efficacy distinguish entrepreneurs from managers?' *Journal of Business Venturing*, 1998; 13(4):295–316.

180　**Inventors with patents . . . if they are more confident:** Markman G. D., Balkin D. B., Baron R. A., 'Inventors and new venture formation: The effects of general self-efficacy and regretful thinking'. *Entrepreneurship Theory and Practice*, 2002; 27(2):149–65.

180　**And, as Arizona State University researchers showed . . . boost their productivity:** Peterson S. J., Luthans F., Avolio B. J., Walumbwa F. O., Zhang Z., 'Psychological capital and employee performance: A latent growth modeling approach'. *Personnel Psychology*, 2011; 64(2): 427–50.

180　**Imagine a ladder . . . based on the so-called Cantril Scale:** Cantril H., *The Pattern of Human Concerns* (New Brunswick, NJ: Rutgers University Press, 1965).

180　**. . . used by the Gallup organization to monitor human happiness . . . in over 160 countries across the world:** Harter J. K., Gurley V. F., 'Measuring well-being in the United States'. *Association for Psychological Science Observer*, 1 September 2008; 21(8):23–6.

180–1　**If you are** *thriving* **. . . chronically sick and depressed:** Ortiz-Ospina E., Roser M., 'Happiness and life satisfaction'. *Our World in Data*, 2013. [Available from: https://ourworldindata.org/happiness-and-life-satisfaction] Accessed 2 September 2020.

181　**It had captured the mood of the British people . . . the thriving–struggling–suffering graph:** Clifton J., 'Is your country ready for change?' *Gallup*, 20 October 2017. [Available from: https://news.gallup.com/opinion/gallup/220712/country-ready-change.aspx] Accessed 2 September 2020.

182　**That was the** *austerity* **public spending of the UK's Conservative government . . . people's confidence collapsed:** Fetzer T., Becker S. O., Novy D., 'Austerity, immigration or globalisation: Was Brexit predictable?' Social Market Foundation, November 2018. [Available from: http://www.smf.co.uk/wp-content/uploads/2018/11/SMF-paper-austerity-immigration-or-globalisation-1.pdf] Accessed 2 September 2020.

182　**In the smaller cities and towns . . . a 15 per cent fall:** Schraer R., 'Have police numbers dropped?' *BBC News*, 26 July 2019. [Available from: https://www.bbc.com/news/uk-47225797] Accessed 2 September 2020.

183 **Across the Atlantic . . . 50 per cent in 2016**: 'What happiness today tells us about the world tomorrow'. Gallup, 2017. [Available from: https://news.gallup.com/reports/220601/what-happiness-today-tells-us-about-the-world-tomorrow.aspx] Accessed 2 September 2020.

183 **What's more, the most significant shift towards voting for Donald Trump . . . in the preceding four years**: Herrin J., Witters D., Roy B., Riley C., Liu D., Krumholz H. M., 'Population well-being and electoral shifts'. *PLoS ONE*, 2018; 13(3):e0193401.

183 **. . . the US saw life expectancy fall . . . in recent history**: Sachs J. D., Layard R., Helliwell J. F., 'World Happiness Report', 14 March 2018. [Available from: https://worldhappiness.report/ed/2018/] Accessed 2 September 2020.

183 **He noted that there were countries in which wealth and happiness were disconnected . . . average happiness dropped slightly**: Sachs J. D., Layard R., Helliwell J. F., 'World Happiness Report', 14 March 2018. [Available from: https://worldhappiness.report/ed/2018/] Accessed 2 September 2020.

184 **'Tuberculosis . . . is coming from Southern and Eastern Europe'**: Wintour P., 'Nigel Farage defends plan to bar immigrants with HIV from NHS care'. *Guardian*, 10 October 2014.

184 **People who voted for Brexit . . . more than they loved the idea of being English**: Van de Vyver J., Leite A. C., Abrams D., Palmer S. B., 'Brexit or Bremain? A person and social analysis of voting decisions in the EU referendum'. *Journal of Community & Applied Social Psychology*, 2018; 28(2):65–79.

184 **One remarkable feature of the US collapse . . . die younger than expected**: Case A., Deaton A., 'Rising morbidity and mortality in midlife among white non-Hispanic Americans in the 21st century'. *Proceedings of the National Academy of Sciences*, 2015; 112(49): 15078–83.

185 **Hispanic and Black Americans . . . swelling life expectancy**: Marquine M. J., Maldonado Y., Zlatar Z., Moore R. C., Martin A. S., Palmer B. W., et al., 'Differences in life satisfaction among older community-dwelling Hispanics and non-Hispanic Whites'. *Aging & Mental Health*, 2015; 19(11):978–88.

185 **A parallel set of circumstances played out . . . for the Brexit vote:** Blanchflower D. G., Oswald A. J., 'Well-being over time in Britain and the USA'. *Journal of Public Economics*, 2004; 88(7–8):1359–86.

186 **. . . it was more often the less educated who defied the pollsters by voting against the establishment when given the opportunity:** Goodwin M. J., Heath O., 'The 2016 Referendum, Brexit and the left behind: An aggregate-level analysis of the result'. *Political Quarterly*, 2016; 87(3):323–32.

186 **A racial narrative also played out . . . status of white people in society:** Bhambra G. K., 'Brexit, Trump, and "methodological whiteness": On the misrecognition of race and class'. *British Journal of Sociology*, 2017; 68(3):S214–S32.

186 **A globalized world means that we are all smaller fish . . . affecting the Western world:** Calling S., Midlöv P., Johansson S.-E., Sundquist K., Sundquist J., 'Longitudinal trends in self-reported anxiety: Effects of age and birth cohort during 25 years'. *BMC Psychiatry*, 2017; 17(1):119. *See also*: Duffy M. E., Twenge J. M., Joiner T. E., 'Trends in mood and anxiety symptoms and suicide-related outcomes among US undergraduates, 2007–2018: Evidence from two national surveys'. *Journal of Adolescent Health*, 2019; 65(5):590–8.

186 **Researchers from the University of Tübingen discovered:** Göllner R., Damian R. I., Nagengast B., Roberts B. W., Trautwein U., 'It's not only who you are but who you are with: High school composition and individuals' attainment over the life course'. *Psychological Science*, 2018; 29(11):1785–96.

190 **They updated to the positive and negative feedback equally . . . in line with the feedback:** Mobius M. M., Niederle M., Niehaus P., Rosenblat T. S., 'Managing self-confidence: Theory and experimental evidence'. National Bureau of Economic Research, 2011. Report No.: 0898-2937.

191 **The world is changing very fast . . . accelerating exponentially:** Friedman T. L., *Thank You for Being Late: An optimist's guide to thriving in the age of accelerations*, second edition (New York: Picador, 2016).

191 **Using a method known as game theory mathematical modelling . . . equilibrium in an economic system:** Dessi R., Zhao X., 'Overconfidence, stability and investments'. *Journal of Economic Behavior & Organization*, 2018; 145:474–94.

193 'So, I want to speak to you first tonight . . . the days of our children would be better than our own': Carter J., 'President Jimmy Carter's "Crisis of Confidence" Speech', 15 July 1979. [Available from: https://www.youtube.com/watch?v=PYWqveU1Tdk] Accessed 25 July 2020.

194 These advisers blamed this collective feeling . . . mile after featureless mile: Shirley C., *Rendezvous with Destiny: Ronald Reagan and the campaign that changed America* (New York: ISI Books, 2011).

194 . . . a gloomy slowdown that matched the sepulchral tone of Carter's address: ibid.

194–5 In the election year 1980 . . . still resonate today: ibid.

195 The thirty-seven-year-old Soviet officer nervously eyed the angry crowd . . . other offices of the Stasi state to ransack: Walker S., 'The humiliation that pushed Putin to try and recapture Russian glory'. *History*, 26 March 2019. [Available from: https://www.history.com/news/vladimir-putin-russia-power] Accessed 20 July 2020.

195 'I had the feeling . . . It had disappeared': Putin V., Gevorkyan N., Timakova N., Kolesnikov A., *First Person: An astonishingly frank self-portrait by Russia's President Vladimir Putin* (New York: PublicAffairs, 2000).

195 'Above all, we should acknowledge . . . outside Russian territory': Putin, V., 'Annual Address to the Federal Assembly of the Russian Federation', 25 April 2005. [Available from: http://en.kremlin.ru/events/president/transcripts/22931] Accessed 2 September 2020.

195 Putin's major preoccupation . . . the case for millions of Russians: Walker S., 'The humiliation that pushed Putin to try and recapture Russian glory'. *History*, 26 March 2019. [Available from: https://www.history.com/news/vladimir-putin-russia-power] Accessed 2 September 2020.

195 Russians have the lowest level of trust in their public institutions in the world: Shlapentokh V., 'Trust in public institutions in Russia: The lowest in the world'. *Communist and Post-Communist Studies*, 2006; 39(2):153–74.

195 The quality of life of the average citizen has declined to a level below that experienced in China: Rapoza K., 'Russia quality of life indicators worse than China's'. *Forbes*, 19 March 2017.

196   'For the first time in the past 200–300 years' . . . a *first-tier* nation: Walker S., 'The humiliation that pushed Putin to try and recapture Russian glory'. *History*, 26 March 2019. [Available from: https://www. history.com/news/vladimir-putin-russia-power] Accessed 2 September 2020.

196   The US government continued the Vietnam War for many years . . . the self-esteem of a government and nation: McMaster H. R., *Dereliction of Duty: Lyndon Johnson, Robert McNamara, the Joint Chiefs of Staff, and the lies that led to Vietnam* (New York: HarperCollins, 2018).

196–7 Any football, hockey, rugby or team player . . . persist more despite failure: Bruton A. M., Mellalieu S. D., Shearer D. A., 'Validation of a single-item stem for collective efficacy measurement in sports teams'. *International Journal of Sport and Exercise Psychology*, 2016; 14(4): 383–401.

197   . . . teams with this collective confidence achieve better results in competitions: Bruton A. M., Mellalieu S. D., Shearer D. A., 'Observation as a method to enhance collective efficacy: An integrative review'. *Psychology of Sport and Exercise*, 2016; 24:1–8.

197   Leaders can transmit their level of confidence to the team's collective *can do* spirit: Fransen K., Haslam S. A., Steffens N. K., Vanbeselaere N., De Cuyper B., Boen F., 'Believing in "us": Exploring leaders' capacity to enhance team confidence and performance by building a sense of shared social identity'. *Journal of Experimental Psychology: Applied*, 2015; 21(1):89–100.

197–8 . . . a hundred Belgian basketball players . . . netting 30 per cent more of their shots than the others: ibid.

198   CEOs who convey confidence in their organizations end up with better company performance: Resick C. J., Whitman D. S., Weingarden S. M., Hiller N. J., 'The bright-side and the dark-side of CEO personality: Examining core self-evaluations, narcissism, transformational leadership, and strategic influence'. *Journal of Applied Psychology*, 2009; 94(6):1365–81.

198   Deprived areas of big cities . . . informal controls over their communities: Sampson R. J., Raudenbush S. W., Earls F., 'Neighborhoods and violent crime: A multilevel study of collective efficacy'. *Science*, 1997; 277(5328):918–24.

199   **Research from Chile and the US in 2017 . . . taking further political action:** Halpern D., Valenzuela S., Katz J. E., 'We face, I tweet: How different social media influence political participation through collective and internal efficacy'. *Journal of Computer-Mediated Communication*, 2017; 22(6):320–36.

199   **So, confidence is contagious, spreading vertically downwards from leaders and horizontally across groups:** Kramer T., Block L. G., 'Like Mike: Ability contagion through touched objects increases confidence and improves performance'. *Organizational Behavior and Human Decision Processes*, 2014; 124(2):215–28.

199   **And the more cohesive a group, the higher the contagion of confidence:** Heuzé J.-P., Raimbault N., Fontayne P., 'Relationships between cohesion, collective efficacy and performance in professional basketball teams: An examination of mediating effects'. *Journal of Sports Sciences*, 2006; 24(1):59–68.

199   **Confidence evolved in human beings . . . helping people to work together effectively:** Shea N., Boldt A., Bang D., Yeung N., Heyes C., Frith C. D., 'Supra-personal cognitive control and metacognition'. *Trends in Cognitive Sciences*, 2014; 18(4):186–93.

200–1 **'I think it is a reality that the bomb is a currency of self-esteem . . . treated as inferiors or being patronized':** Ghosh A., 'Explosion of self-esteem: Interview with Chandan Mitra'. *Outlook India*, 11 May 2002. [Available from: https://www.outlookindia.com/website/story/explosion-of-self-esteem/215504] Accessed 5 November 2020.

201–2 **Nations with a history of being colonizers . . . in relation to these:** Robertson I., *The Winner Effect: How power affects your brain* (London: Bloomsbury, 2012).

202–3 **These are called 'minimal groups' . . . favour that ingroup at the expense of an outgroup:** Tajfel H., Billig M. G., Bundy R. P., Flament C., 'Social categorization and intergroup behaviour'. *European Journal of Social Psychology*, 1971; 1(2):149–78.

203–4 **A clue comes from a 2003 German study . . . the ingroup offered some protection:** Petersen L. E., Blank H., 'Ingroup bias in the minimal group paradigm shown by three-person groups with high or low state self-esteem'. *European Journal of Social Psychology*, 2003; 33(2):149–62.

204   **Research from 2008 shows that simply being made to feel part of an arbitrary ingroup . . . brain's reward network:** Rilling J. K., Dagenais J. E., Goldsmith D. R., Glenn A. L., Pagnoni G., 'Social cognitive neural networks during in-group and out-group interactions'. *Neuro-Image*, 2008; 41(4):1447–61.

204–5 **Supporters of extreme right or left ideologies . . . solutions dangled in front of them by extremists:** van Prooijen J.-W., Krouwel A. P. M., 'Psychological features of extreme political ideologies'. *Current Directions in Psychological Science*, 2019; 28(2):159–63.

205   **On 11 April 2020 . . . black people not being allowed to enter the restaurant:** Fifield A., 'Africans in China allege racism as fear of new virus cases unleashes xenophobia'. *Washington Post*, 13 April 2020.

205   **A few weeks earlier, on 24 February in London's Oxford Street . . . before smashing his fist into Mok's nose:** Coates M., 'Covid-19 and the rise of racism'. *British Medical Journal*, 2020; 369:m1384.

205–6 **In 2014, rates of another highly infectious disease, Ebola, mushroomed in West Africa . . . and West Africans in particular:** Kim H. S., Sherman D. K., Updegraff J. A., 'Fear of Ebola: The influence of collectivism on xenophobic threat responses'. *Psychological Science*, 2016; 27(7):935–44.

207–8 **According to terror management theory . . . you are mortal:** Greenberg J., Solomon S., Pyszczynski T., Rosenblatt A., Burling J., Lyon D., et al., 'Why do people need self-esteem? Converging evidence that self-esteem serves an anxiety-buffering function'. *Journal of Personality and Social Psychology*, 1992; 63(6):913–22.

208   **. . . being reminded of death leads us to think, feel, and behave in very particular ways:** Burke B. L., Martens A., Faucher E. H., 'Two decades of terror management theory: A meta-analysis of mortality salience research'. *Personality and Social Psychology Review*, 2010; 14(2):155–95.

208   **Above all, it makes us rush to shore up our self-esteem . . . the void of eternity:** Pyszczynski T., Greenberg J., Solomon S., 'A dual-process model of defense against conscious and unconscious death-related thoughts: An extension of terror management theory'. *Psychological Review*, 1999; 106(4):835–45.

208–10 **A group were selected for their strong pro-Canadian views . . . ward off existential anxiety:** Schimel J., Hayes J., Williams T., Jahrig J., 'Is death really the worm at the core? Converging evidence that worldview threat increases death-thought accessibility'. *Journal of Personality and Social Psychology*, 2007; 92(5):789–803.

210 **Such inklings of death at the fringes of consciousness . . . that could kill thousands of citizens:** Pyszczynski T., Abdollahi A., Solomon S., Greenberg J., Cohen F., Weise D., 'Mortality salience, martyrdom, and military might: The great Satan versus the axis of evil'. *Personality and Social Psychology Bulletin*, 2006; 32(4):525–37.

210 **We have all seen distressing images . . . support military aggression or terrorism against the other:** Vail K., Motyl M., Abdollahi A., Pyszczynski T., 'Dying to live: Terrorism, war, and defending one's way of life' in Antonius D., Brown A. D., Walters T. K., Ramirez J. M., Sinclair S. J. (editors), *Interdisciplinary Analyses of Terrorism and Political Aggression* (Newcastle upon Tyne: Cambridge Scholars Publishing, 2011), pp. 49–70.

210–11 **It's a sobering and vicious cycle . . . personal and communal humiliation:** Stern J. (editor), *Terror in the Name of God: Why religious militants kill* (New York: Ecco, 2003).

212 **The problem with these self-esteem-enhancing drugs . . . when Narendra Modi became prime minister:** Lall J., 'Indians' life satisfaction goes bust as economy booms'. *Gallup News*, 1 July 2018. [Available from: https://news.gallup.com/opinion/gallup/236357/indians-life-satisfaction-goes-bust-economy-booms.aspx] Accessed 2 September 2020.

213 **In the wintry afternoon gloom of 29 December 2019 . . . in his home city of Beirut, Lebanon:** 'Carlos Ghosn: How did the Nissan ex-boss flee from Japan?' *BBC News*, 8 January 2020. [Available from: https://www.bbc.com/news/world-50964040] Accessed 2 September 2020.

214–15 **Carlos Ghosn's oblivion to . . . 'He never saw it coming':** Campbell M., Inoue K., Ma J., Nussbaum A., 'Inside the takedown that put Carlos Ghosn in jail: He never saw it coming'. *Bloomberg Businessweek*, 31 January 2019.

215 **'No, I don't want to think about it . . . I might not like what I see':** Barbaro M., 'What drives Donald Trump? Fear of losing status, tapes show'. *New York Times*, 25 October 2016.

215   **They proposed that people routinely deceive themselves . . . diverge from their beliefs:** Mijović-Prelec D., Prelec D., 'Self-deception as self-signalling: A model and experimental evidence'. *Philosophical Transactions of the Royal Society B: Biological Sciences*, 2010; 365(1538): 227–40.

215   **'nobody knows more than I do' . . . ISIS to environmental impact:** 'Hilarious: Watch Trump claim expertise at nearly everything'. *The Kyle Kulinski Show*, 2018. [Available from: https://www.youtube.com/watch?v=cEcNMir6aSs] Accessed 20 July 2020.

216   **Characterized by hyper-certainty . . . helps to quell underlying anxieties:** McGregor I., Marigold D. C., 'Defensive zeal and the uncertain self: What makes you so sure?' *Journal of Personality and Social Psychology*, 2003; 85(5):838–52.

216   **Overconfidence is a critical ingredient in the narcissistic personality . . . every potential leader should be scrutinized:** Raskin R., Terry H., 'A principal-components analysis of the Narcissistic Personality Inventory and further evidence of its construct validity'. *Journal of Personality and Social Psychology*, 1988; 54(5):890–902.

217   **Research from 2015 on narcissism among leaders . . . Narcissism got him the boss's job but didn't make him good at it:** Grijalva E., Harms P. D., Newman D. A., Gaddis B. H., Fraley R. C., 'Narcissism and leadership: A meta-analytic review of linear and nonlinear relationships'. *Personnel Psychology*, 2015; 68(1):1–47.

217   **'the leader himself need love no one else . . . self-confident and independent':** Freud S., 'On narcissism: An introduction' in Sandler J., Person E. S., Fonagy P. (editors), *Freud's 'On Narcissism: An Introduction'* (New Haven, CT: Yale University Press, 1991), pp. 123–4.

217–18 **. . . a 1997 study extracted personality descriptions of US presidents . . . during the Great Depression and the Second World War:** Deluga R. J., 'Relationship among American presidential charismatic leadership, narcissism, and rated performance'. *Leadership Quarterly*, 1997; 8(1):49–65.

219–20 **Former UK prime minister Margaret Thatcher . . . former UK foreign secretary David Owen:** Owen D., Davidson J., 'Hubris syndrome: An acquired personality disorder? A study of US Presidents and UK

Prime Ministers over the last 100 years'. *Brain*, 2009; 132(5): 1396–406.

220 . . . women are less vulnerable to the addictive and personality-distorting effects that power can have on the brain: Robertson I., *The Winner Effect*: *How power affects your brain* (London: Bloomsbury, 2012).

220 Another feature of the hormonal surges . . . interferes with perform-ance: Mobbs D., Hassabis D., Seymour B., Marchant J. L., Weiskopf N., Dolan R. J., et al., 'Choking on the money: Reward-based per-formance decrements are associated with midbrain activity'. *Psychological Science*, 2009; 20(8):955–62.

220 . . . in high-stake professional tennis games . . . compared to lower-stake games: Cohen-Zada D., Krumer A., Rosenboim M., Shapir O. M., 'Choking under pressure and gender: Evidence from profes-sional tennis'. *Journal of Economic Psychology*, 2017; 61(C):176–90.

220 Disliking losing more than you enjoy gaining . . . a healthier appreci-ation of risk than men do: Hermann D., 'Determinants of financial loss aversion: The influence of prenatal androgen exposure (2D:4D)'. *Personality and Individual Differences*, 2017; 117:273–9.

220 This cautious approach paid off among amateur financial traders . . . 50 per cent greater losses: Barber B. M., Odean T., 'Boys will be boys: Gender, overconfidence, and common stock investment'. *Quarterly Journal of Economics*, 2001; 116(1):261–92.

221 'I'm shaking hands continually . . . I shook hands with *everybody*': ' "I shook hands with everybody," says Boris Johnson weeks before coro-navirus diagnosis' [video]. *Guardian*, 27 March 2020. [Available from: https://www.theguardian.com/world/video/2020/mar/27/i-shook-hands-with-everybody-says-boris-johnson-weeks-before-coronavirus-diagnosis-video] Accessed 3 September 2020.

221 A month later . . . 'fighting for his life': Ferguson E., 'Boris Johnson in intensive care: PM "struggling to breathe" as coronavirus symptoms worsen'. *Daily Express*, 7 April 2020.

221 Had Johnson been more willing to consider risk . . . a UK government scientific adviser stated: Stewart H., Sample I., 'Coronavirus: enforc-ing UK lockdown one week earlier "could have saved 20,000 lives" '. *Guardian*, 11 June 2020.

222   ... women's more social self-concept ... surge in response to exercising power: Schultheiss O. C., Wirth M. M., Torges C. M., Pang J. S., Villacorta M. A., Welsh K. M., 'Effects of implicit power motivation on men's and women's implicit learning and testosterone changes after social victory or defeat'. *Journal of Personality and Social Psychology*, 2005; 88(1):174–88.

222   **Women make just as good leaders as men ... studies of leadership effectiveness have concluded:** Eagly A. H., Karau S. J., Makhijani M. G., 'Gender and the effectiveness of leaders: A meta-analysis'. *Psychological Bulletin*, 1995; 117(1):125–45. *See also*: Paustian-Underdahl S. C., Walker L. S., Woehr D. J., 'Gender and perceptions of leadership effectiveness: A meta-analysis of contextual moderators'. *Journal of Applied Psychology*, 2014; 99(6):1129–45.

223   **'If we were to rethink ourselves as social creatures ... conception of self would not be defined by individual self-interest':** Gessen M., 'Judith Butler wants us to reshape our rage'. *New Yorker*, 9 February 2020.

225   **Rice farming is exceptionally labour intensive ... part of the culture, transmitted parent to child:** Talhelm T., Zhang X., Oishi S., Shimin C., Duan D., Lan X., et al., 'Large-scale psychological differences within China explained by rice versus wheat agriculture'. *Science*, 2014; 344(6184):603–8.

226   **Analytical thinkers are more prone to experiencing emotions that are focused on them ... the feelings of social harmony, in other words:** Kitayama S., Park H., Sevincer A. T., Karasawa M., Uskul A. K., 'A cultural task analysis of implicit independence: Comparing North America, Western Europe, and East Asia'. *Journal of Personality and Social Psychology*, 2009; 97(2):236–55.

226–7   **Western liberals tend to show more WEIRD thinking than moderates or conservatives, wherever they live:** Talhelm T., Haidt J., Oishi S., Zhang X., Miao F. F., Chen S., 'Liberals think more analytically (more "WEIRD") than conservatives'. *Personality and Social Psychology Bulletin*, 2015; 41(2):250–67.

227   **In contrast, conservatives espouse a set of values ... core beliefs that bind people together:** Haidt J., *The Righteous Mind: Why good people are divided by politics and religion* (London: Vintage, 2012).

228   But we know it's not racial factors explaining these national differences ... *more* individually self-confident: Heine S. J., Lehman D. R.,
'Move the body, change the self: Acculturative effects on the self-
concept' in Schaller M., Crandall C. S. (editors), *The Psychological
Foundations of Culture* (New York, Psychology Press: 2004), pp.
305–31.

228   Having an individually focused versus a collectively focused ego biases
your memory ... not the case for Americans: Heine S. J. Lehman
D. R., 'Culture, dissonance, and self-affirmation'. *Personality and
Social Psychology Bulletin*, 1997; 23(4):389–400.

228   We know that one way in which confidence works is by the distorting
lens ... domains such as driving ability: Kruger J., Dunning D.,
'Unskilled and unaware of it: How difficulties in recognizing one's
own incompetence lead to inflated self-assessments'. *Journal of Personality and Social Psychology*, 1999; 77(6):1121–34.

228–9 This self-enhancement effect is much higher in individualistic cultures ... more realistic about their abilities: Heine S. J., Lehman
D. R., Markus H. R., Kitayama S., 'Is there a universal need for positive self-regard?' *Psychological Review*, 1999; 106(4):766–94.

229   These variations in ego lead to quite different responses to success
and failure ... where they think they have done badly: Heine S. J.,
Kitayama S., Lehman D. R., Takata T., Ide E., Leung C., et al.,
'Divergent consequences of success and failure in Japan and North
America: An investigation of self-improving motivations and malle-
able selves'. *Journal of Personality and Social Psychology*, 2001; 81(4):
599–615.

230   According to media reports ... houses in Paris, Tokyo, Amsterdam,
Beirut and Rio de Janeiro: Furukawa, Y., 'Ghosn got six houses from
Nissan, including in Tokyo and New York'. *Bloomberg*, 22 November
2018. [Available from: https://www.bloomberg.com/news/articles/
2018-11-22/ghosn-got-six-houses-from-nissan-including-in-tokyo-
new-york] Accessed 19 November 2020.

230   A 2018 comment piece in *The Japan Times* ... Nissan's Japanese
employees': Mikyake K., 'The Protestant ethic and Carlos Ghosn'.
The Japan Times, 26 November 2018.

230 **Ghosn has denied all allegations of wrongdoing . . . :** 'Ghosn: Decision to flee was hardest of my life'. *BBC News*, 8 January 2020. [Available from: https://www.bbc.co.uk/news/business-51035206] Accessed 19 November 2020.

231 **On social media, teenage girls follow men more than women celebrities:** 'The Female Lead' and Terri Apter, 'Our 2019 Research: Disrupting the feed'. *The Female Lead*, 2020. [Available from: https://www.thefemalelead.com/research] Accessed 3 September 2020.

231 **When teenage girls were encouraged by 'The Female Lead' . . . a greater sense of collective confidence in achievement:** ibid.

231–2 **The researchers at the Centre for Economic Policy Research . . . significant changes in their behaviour six months later:** Bernard T., Dercon S., Orkin K., Taffesse A., 'The future in mind: Aspirations and forward-looking behaviour in rural Ethiopia'. CSAE Working Paper Series 2014–16, Centre for the Study of African Economies, University of Oxford, 2014.

233–4 **Merely using abstract language . . . and how long you live:** Smith P. K., Wigboldus D. H. J., Dijksterhuis A., 'Abstract thinking increases one's sense of power'. *Journal of Experimental Social Psychology*, 2008; 44(2):378–85.

234 **In one experiment, a group of people were asked to plan a new organization . . . roles in the organizations they were planning:** ibid.

235 **Company CEOs with a robust moral and ethical code make better bosses . . . optimistic about their company's future:** De Hoogh A. H., Den Hartog D. N., 'Ethical and despotic leadership, relationships with leader's social responsibility, top management team effectiveness and subordinates' optimism: A multi-method study'. *Leadership Quarterly*, 2008; 19(3):297–311.

235 **Wealthy people have more power and confidence . . . dominate their values:** Piff P. K., 'Wealth and the inflated self: Class, entitlement, and narcissism'. *Personality and Social Psychology Bulletin*, 2014; 40(1): 34–43.

235–6 **People across 132 countries were asked this question . . . Belgium and Hong Kong:** Oishi S., Diener E., 'Residents of poor nations have a greater sense of meaning in life than residents of wealthy nations'. *Psychological Science*, 2014; 25(2):422–30.

236 **Values are the *raison d'être* of most religions . . . without a sense of meaning:** Hill P. L., Turiano N. A., 'Purpose in life as a predictor of mortality across adulthood'. *Psychological Science*, 2014; 25(7): 1482–6.

Acknowledgements

Without the love, support and teaching of my wife, Dr Fiona O'Doherty, who is the best clinical psychologist I know, I would have never written this book. Over decades, she has told me repeatedly that almost all human behaviour is shaped by confidence, or the lack of it. Almost all of the 'case studies' in this book are disguised composites of real people, and my job has been to unpack the science around her observations and insights.

Nor would the book have been written without the inspiration of my three children – Deirdre, Ruairi and Niall. Thank you, dear chums, for your comments, corrections and insights.

Gratitude to Donagh, my dear grandchild, for his thoughtful gnaws of my notebooks and to his dad, Brian, for the companionship of our lockdown swims in the icy Irish Sea. Thanks to Aedeen for walking the confidence walk during lockdown and to Jim for being a great big brother.

Thanks to Lise-Anne McLaughlin for her first-rate comments on the gender chapters and to my good friend Bobby McDonagh for his insights and encouragement.

Andrea Henry, from Transworld, has been a brilliant editor and a joy to work with. I'm grateful for her thoughtful engagement with the book and careful editing.

A huge thanks and tribute to my fantastic agent, Sally Holloway, without whom I would not have written this, nor my previous two books. Thank you, Sally, for your ideas, responsiveness, judgement, incisive reading of proposals and manuscripts – and for your warm encouragement over many years.

Finally, a sad and loving farewell to Felicity Bryan – dear friend and colleague to me and Sally – who died on 21 June 2020. Felicity was my first agent, and a remarkable person whose vivaciousness, intelligence and confidence lit up very many lives.

Index

About the Author

Ian Robertson is Co-Director of the Global Brain Health Institute (Trinity College Dublin and University of California at San Francisco) and T. Boone Pickens Distinguished Scientist at the Center for BrainHealth at University of Texas at Dallas. A trained clinical psychologist as well as a neuroscientist, he is internationally renowned for his research on neuropsychology. He has written five books and numerous newspaper and magazine articles and comment pieces, including in the *Guardian*, *Times*, *Telegraph*, *Irish Times*, *Time* magazine and *New York* magazine. He has appeared on BBC Radio and featured in several major television documentaries. He is a regular speaker at major futurology and business conferences in Europe, the USA and Asia.